TOYS OF OTHER DAYS

G. Morland pinxt   G. Graham sculpt

THE YOUNG NURSE & QUIET CHILD.

Hodson & Kennier Ltd.   London Pubd. April 17 1791 by T. Simpson St. Pauls Church Yard.

Toys of Other Days

by Mrs F. Nevill Jackson

WHITE LION PUBLISHERS LIMITED
London, New York, Sydney and Toronto

Copyright © Mrs. F. Nevill Jackson 1948, 1975

First published in Great Britain
by Country Life Ltd in association with
George Newnes Ltd, 1908

White Lion Edition, 1975

ISBN 85617 179 4

Made and printed in Great Britain
for White Lion Publishers Limited,
138 Park Lane, London W1Y 3DD
by Hendington Limited,
Deadbrook Lane, Aldershot, Hampshire.

TO

THE CHILDREN OF TO-DAY

WE DEDICATE THIS STORY

OF

THE TOYS OF YESTERDAY

PREFACE

IN preparing our notes for a history of toys, we desire to
give an account, however imperfect, of the early companions of the youth of the world.

The importance of suitably chosen toys is fully understood by those who realise that children's minds and
tastes are run into the mould which their environment
forms for them. The starting-point of every man and
woman's character is the nursery, and from its contents
the mind of the child takes form and colour.

In our research we have been assisted by the valuable
works of which a list is given on page xxi. We are
indebted also to Messrs. Murray and Methuen, through
whose courtesy we are able to reproduce respectively the
interesting illustrations of Egyptian toys from Sir J.
Gardiner Wilkinson's *Manners and Customs of Ancient
Egypt*, and early English toys from Strutt's *Sports and
Pastimes*.

Amongst the many who have facilitated our study of
specimens in public and private collections we would
specially mention Viscountess Hayashi, wife of the
Japanese Ambassador at the Court of St. James, who so
kindly invited our examination of the old toys of Japan ;

Preface. Hon. Sir Schomberg McDonnell, K.C.B., Secretary of Works and Public Buildings ; Professor Uhde-Bernays of Nuremberg ; the late Monsieur Maury, to whose fine collection of old dolls, marionettes, and toys of the First Empire we constantly refer ; Herr Ehrenbacher, British Consul at Nuremberg ; the late Mr. Cripps, whose delightful correspondence on the subject of old silver playthings is one of the pleasantest episodes in the course of our work ; Mr. FitzHenry, Dr. Williamson, the Director of the Bibliotheque National, and many others who have assisted our study, or who, owning interesting specimens of old toys, have courteously placed them at our disposal for examination.

E. J.

CONTENTS

Contents.

CHAPTER IX

RATTLES, BELLS, BAUBLES, MUSICAL INSTRUMENTS,
TOYS OF PERCUSSION

CHAPTER X

BALLS, BALL-PLAY, SWINGING, AND OTHER GAMES

CHAPTER XI

MARIONETTES, PUNCH AND JUDY, DANCING DOLLS

CHAPTER XII

SPECIAL TOYS FOR SPECIAL OCCASIONS AND THOSE SUGGESTED
BY SACRED HISTORY

Contents.

LIST OF ILLUSTRATIONS

xiii

xiv

xv

xvii

Illustra-
tions.

xix

AUTHORITIES CONSULTED

Manners and Customs of Ancient Egypt.
Joséphine de Beauharnais Impératrice et Reine.
Life on a Chinese Farm.
Les Jeux des Anciens.
The Atlas of Greek Life.

Manual of Ethnology.
The Evolution of the Aryan.
Wild Races of South-Eastern India.
The Past and Future of the Kaffir Races.
Native Races of the Pacific States.
Le Folklore de l'Ile Mauria.
The Pre- and Proto-historic Times.
A Diplomatist's Wife in Japan.
Popular Antiquities.
The Ruling Races of Prehistoric Times.
The Law of Kosmic Order.
Histoire des Marionnettes.
Modern Egypt.
Parents and Children.
Behar Peasant Life.

Picturesque Burma.
The Parsees.
The Complete Art of making Fireworks.
Hindu Manners, Customs, and Ceremonies.
Indian Life, Religious and Social.
Punch and Judy.
Bengal Peasant Life.
Untrodden Peaks.
Cycling.
Pompeii.
Émile.
Don Quixote.
Egypt.

Sir J. G. Wilkinson.
M. Masson.
Mrs. Archibald Little.
Becq. de Fouquières.
A. C. F. Anderson
Schreiber.
Chas. L. Brace.
Rudolph von Iherny.
Captain T. H. Lewin.
R. W. C. Holden.
Bancroft.
C. Baissan.
John Abercromby.
Mrs. H. Fraser.
Brand.
J. F. Hewett.
Robert Brown, F.S.A.
Charles Magnin.
E. W. Lacie.
C. M. Mason.
G. Grierson, M.A.S.,
B.M.R.A.S.
Mrs. Ernest Hart.
Dasabhoy Framjee.
Thomas Kentish.
Dubois and Keauchamp.
John Campbell Oman.
Payne Collier.
The Rev. Lal Behâre Dag.
A. B. Edwards.
H. H. Griffin.
T. H. Dyer.
J. J. Rousseau.
Cervantes.
Professor Roselini.

Authorities.

Die Kulturgeschichte des Kinderlebens.	Hans Boesch.
Weihnachten in Kirchekunst und Volksleben.	Professor Georg Keetschel.
Emblems for the Entertainment and Improvement of Youth.	
Toys and Toy-making.	Lukin.
Electric Toy-making.	Sloane.
Town of Toys.	S. Wood.
Pottery and Porcelain.	F. Telchfield.
Hall Marks on Gold and Silver Plate.	W. Chaffers.
Les Jouets.	Léo. Claretie.
Histoire des Jouets.	Almeigne.
Gold and Silver.	Hungerford Pollen.
Old English Plate.	W. J.Cripps,C.B., F.S.A.
Der Goldschmiede Werbezeichen.	Dr. Marc. Rosenberg.
Top-spinning.	E. Falkener.
Child Life in Japan.	C. Ayrton.
Korean Games.	Stewart Culen.
The Child : A Study in Evolution.	A. F. Chamberlain, M.A., Ph.D.
Child Life in Colonial Days.	A. M. Earle.
Old English Customs.	P. H. Ditchfield, M.A., F.S.A.
A History of Domestic Manners and Sentiments in England during the Middle Ages.	F. Wright, M.A., F.S.A.
Social England.	H. D. Traill, D.C.L.
Sports and Pastimes.	Strutt.
Early History of Mankind and the Development of Civilisation.	Edward Tylor.
The History of Java.	Thomas Slawford Raffles.
Playing and other Cards.	W. H. Willshire, M.D.
Rural Employments.	M. Belson Elliot.
Games.	M. Gomme.
Le Vieux Neuf.	E. Fournier.
Kindergarten Toys.	H. Hoffman,
The Juvenile Spectator.	Arabella Argus.
History of Playing Cards.	E. S. Taylor.
Playing Cards.	C. E. Guest.
Punch and Judy.	T. E. Weatherley.
History of the Horn Book.	Andrew Tuer.
Domestic Pleasures.	F. B. Vaux.
The Twentieth-Century Child.	H. J. Cooper.
Sunny Sicily.	Mrs. Alec. Tweedie.
The Catacombs of Rome.	W. T. Wilkrow, M.A.

INTRODUCTION.

GLANCING at the toy world of the past is like looking at history through a diminishing glass ; we can see things exactly reproduced in miniature. There is no important event which has not left its mark in a plaything, even to the guillotine of the French Revolution, and the Emigrette, the toy of the aristocratic emigrant.

The simplest forms of play are based on mimicry ; the type of the majority of toys is thus determined. The baby of two years, who is petted and caressed, must have her doll to caress in turn ; the boy watches horses and carts, and drives chairs and tables or little sisters, unless the wooden horse and cart is provided. The desire of the little ones to imitate the occupations of their environment is a natural instinct, so that we find the forms of playthings invariably modified by the customs of the times. Two thousand years before Christ there were toys in the shape of water-carriers and kneaders of bread. Toy wine-carts of primitive construction are dug up in Cyprus, miniature bows and arrows were in the hands of the boys of the Middle Ages in Europe and also in the East, while guns and steam-engines are the playthings of the youngsters of the present day.

1

According to the temperament of the player, the toy
needs to be simple or elaborate ; the plaything which
makes no demand on the imagination, the skill, or the
ingenuity of the player, is the lowest in the scale of
desirability, and for this reason the mechanical toy is the
most suitable for dull children and adults.

" I want a toy to play with, not one that plays with me,"
was the cry of the wise child who watched the antics of
a mechanical toy for twenty minutes, and then played
with the paper and string it had been wrapped in, for
the rest of the afternoon. The child richly gifted with
fancy will weave the most elaborate situations out of two
or three simple figures ; an artist in make-believe can
almost entirely discard material form ; but the game of
" let's pretend " is not an easy one to play in its higher
grades, some have not the imagination to play it at all.
This heaven-sent gift to the little ones is, in some rare
instances, retained throughout life ; happy the man or
woman who has the heart and fancy of a little child :
there is a delicate fascination in " let's pretend " unknown
in any form of materialism.

Self-absorption is necessary for such a game ; this is
happily a universally shared trait of childhood, and is one
of its chief charms. Many children live with a few
favourite toys in a little world of their own ; the concrete
figures of parents and attendants, and the real environment, either grouping entirely separate from the imagined
figures of the story world, or being made to figure in
it, in subservience and masquerade. An imaginative
boy, engrossed in a cabman game, dismounted from his
box to obey some small command of his nurse, and resumed the reins, explaining to his make-believe fare

2

that he had to attend to a private affair connected with his home ; the real and imaginary world thus held their course in his mind, side by side, without infringing each other's rights, for in the delicious irrelevance of the child mind, realism and romance are not necessarily at war.

It is only the dull child, like the dull adult, who needs an elaborate toy to amuse him, for he himself cannot supply details which are lacking. Everything must be seen and touched, or it is not there, nor can he understand that beauties unattainable, are in the land of make-believe, for they must exist in the mind of the player. Cinderella makes her triumphant progress in a gilded coach dressed in silks and satins, even though the old doll that represents her might be called a battered specimen, and her coach bears visible marks of its original use as a soap box, while the splendid charger that is bearing the Black Prince so nobly into action, in the mind of its owner, has only three legs to stand upon, and his royal master is unable to sit upright.

But if the joys of imagination with regard to toys are great, so the terrors are equally vivid—the tin lizard becomes a dragon belching forth flames, yawning chasms must be bridged and mountains climbed before the soldiers can storm the fort. The savage who peoples the forest and rocky places with terrible gods is closely in line with the child of facile imagination, whose brain has been modified by a thousand generations of progress, for in the child mind, as in the mind of primitive man, there is a divine irrelevancy which leaves no room for logic, in the peopling of the world.

No apology is needed for introducing the old playthings of the world as a subject for study ; we see side-

lights on the life of ancient Egypt, Greece, and Rome, in
looking at their toys ; the linen doll stuffed with papyrus
grown on the banks of old Nile, or the ball of twisted
rushes, may have been playthings of Moses himself.

When fathers and brothers rode chariot races and
fought quails, we may be sure the boys and girls played
chariot games in ancient Athens and Rome ; their knuckle-
bones, chessmen, and spotted cows with movable jaws may
be handled now, and the classic drapery of the Roman toga
is humanised, as it were, if we believe that sometimes its
voluminous folds may have hidden a surprise parcel for
the nursery.   In the toys of the Middle Ages of Europe
and of the days of the Renaissance, we find the same
fine workmanship which characterises all the handicraft
of the period ; the reason is not far to seek.   There were
no special toy-makers in those days, toy-making had no
separate guild ; the workmen, whether in gold, silver,
leather, or wood, who made articles for adult use, would
sometimes make a miniature replica for a child's toy, so
that we find toys amongst the other objects in the cabinets
of connoisseurs all over Europe, and it is possible that
Cellini may have carved silver toy soldiers, and that
Chippendale may have furnished a doll's house.   According
to the late Mr. Cripps, the first English teaspoon known
with its correct date mark is a toy teaspoon dated 1689.
In 1671 Merlin, silversmith to Louis XIV., made an
army of silver, " tout de cavalerie, infanterie et les machines
de guerre, le tout en argent," from the models of Chassel
de Nancy for Monseigneur le Dauphin.

Each step in science is shown in contemporary toy-
making.   When the Montgolfier brothers were making
their experiments with balloons, air-balls and parachutes

amused the children. It is give and take between science
and the little ones, for if the tea-kettle of Stephenson's
boyhood has given us locomotives, bicycles were in
embryo in the nursery long before they achieved their
present popularity as aids to adult locomotion.

There is hardly any great discovery in the working
of nature's laws, which has not been utilised by the toy-
maker to charm our boys and girls. Gravitation, centri-
fugal force, magnetism, hydraulics, balancing compensation,
all give us delightful toys.

Baby is mystified when the monkey nimbly climbs
up a palm-tree, and detaching a cocoa-nut, descends with
it on his head, only baby's big brother knows that the
balance of weights carries the monkey up the tree and
brings him down again inevitably.

In the waddling elephant slowly descending the
inclined board, each weight, roughly formed like the joint
of an animal's leg, knocks on the connecting link so that
progress is made. Baby will patiently pump water on
to his pinafore during an entire afternoon, nor is nurse
consoled by knowing that he is studying hydraulics.

The ductility of metals and the elasticity of india-
rubber are the means of working many toys, and the
mechanical toy at popular price dates from the introduction of india-rubber. The slow unwinding of a spring makes
the toy circus horse go round, while little figures wheel
barrows, dance, or box, because elastic stretched to its
utmost limit, by winding up, relaxes in the way nature
dictates. The charm of the plaything casts a glamour
over the most serious subject. Dry-as-dust geography,
history, heraldry, have formed the bases of many a game ;
and though we doubt if the sugar-coated pill will ever be

5

Introduction. a really popular form of sweetmeat in the nursery, there has always been a supply of educational toys from the days of the Dauphin until now. The sentimental side of our subject is too obvious to need comment, but there is a note of pathos in the fact that the little army of silver soldiers made for that same Dauphin, joined the splendid gold and silver plate in the smelting pots of Paris, in order that the expenses of the army of flesh and blood should be paid. There is undoubtedly a pathetic interest in old toys. They have inspired the games of men and women long since passed away. They are the instruments of play which is the life-work of childhood. To what degree they have biassed the taste, imagination, and character of their little owners we can only guess.

Early Egyptian Dolls, now at the British Museum. The wooden bodies are painted in colour, the hair thread, with beads of clay. Natural size.

CHAPTER I

DOLLS AND DOLL-DRESSING.

IT is probable that the baby girl of Paleolithic ages **Dolls and** treasured her chip of stone or bone, wrapping it in a **Doll-** scrap of hide, and "mothering" it with as much care as **dressing.** is now bestowed on the latest *bébé* from Paris.

Leaving the realms of supposition, we find that a doll of ancient Thebes has many of the characteristics seen in our toys of to-day. She has a well-shaped head from which hair, made of beads of Nile mud strung upon thread, is still depending in graceful ringlets.

We forbear to say that this doll is 3000 years old, knowing the dislike of ladies to acknowledge their age, but certain it is that she was made 3000 years ago.

Early Egyptian dolls, as will be seen from our illustration, have life-like heads, but the bodies and lower limbs are in many cases practically non-existent. Occasionally the wooden doll is gaily coloured. Such specimens are less elaborately carved, and we can safely conjecture that these were the "knock-about" dollies of the younger members of the family, who loved bright colouring and solidity rather than refinements of ex-

Dolls and Doll-dressing. pression and feature, just as in our own day the dolls for younger children are made more solidly and in more brilliant colour than those for children whose critical faculties have already been awakened.

In few instances have the wigs of the Egyptian dolls survived the thousands of years since their construction,

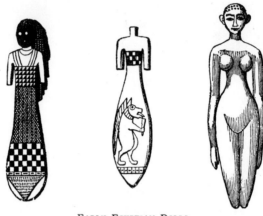

EARLY EGYPTIAN DOLLS.
Painted in colour.   The pig symbolises good luck.

but often the small round holes where the hair was rooted or embedded are to be seen.

Small pictures of gods in the guise of animals were sometimes painted on the flat, handle-shaped bodies. Other more or less elaborate decoration, largely symbolical, is traced on these Egyptian dolls.

The dolls of ancient Greece have well-modelled heads with hair arranged in true Grecian style ; the bodies are made with great care, following exactly the proportions of the human figure, so that when clothed with the flowing draperies of the period the result must have been extremely good.

10

The arms and legs of these dolls were made separately, **Greek** and were far less elaborate in shape than the head and **Dolls with** trunk, which are cut in one piece. These limbs were not **Movable** much more than plain slips attached to the body with **Joints.** pins of wire running through holes and turned down for security. Such dolls were, of course, intended for dressing, so that, like those of the present day, the elaborate head and well-modelled neck would be in full view, but the more simply made arms and legs would be hidden by drapery.

The resemblance of these early Greek specimens to the doll of to-day is clearly shown in an antique example

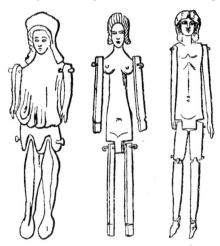

GREEK AND ROMAN DOLLS.

6½ inches long. Arms, legs, and, in one, knees are jointed.

to which we have had access, whose head, neck, hands, and feet are well formed, and the body in due proportion, but roughly finished, like many of our cheap modern dolls. This doll has boots on of the same substance as

11

the legs ; she has pins for the suspension of the limbs at the knees as well as at the shoulders and hips.

Occasionally dolls *de luxe* of archaic age have been found, of ivory, with modelling of the muscles attempted. Such dolls are also found, made of walrus ivory, by the primitive Esquimaux. Dolls with elaborately articulated limbs, belonging to the fourth century before Christ, have been found at Cyrenaica, at Athens, Cameiras, and many other places.

These are usually made with head and bust in one piece, the arms and legs being attached separately, by means of wire pins run through a hole in the limb and body. There is a pathetic saucerful of arms and legs, severed from the bodies, in the British Museum, proto-types of such scattered members as one finds in every nursery of the present day, when the toy cupboard is cleared out. Occasionally one may see a doll amongst these archaic relics whose legs are also articulated at the knee, and we have twice met with a doll made in the seated position, the arms only being articulated.

The hair of Roman dolls is elaborately dressed ; generally the headgear is all in the same block with the head and body. There is a specimen of a doll's knitted cap at South Kensington Museum. It measures one and a half inches in diameter, and is the only article of doll's clothing, except a woven red band round the waist of a linen doll, dating from archaic times, that we can discover.

Dolls of wax are spoken of, but on account of their fragility none have survived : they were evidently of higher price than those of wood or pottery.

That the Greeks were well acquainted with moving

12

Early Egyptian Dolls of carved wood covered with compo. The largest measures 8 in. At the British Museum.

Egypto-Roman Rag Doll stuffed with papyrus
Found at Behnesch during the excavations in
1896. As this toy dates from the IIIrd Century
before Christ we may accept the red woollen
band as the earliest known example of doll
dressing. At South Kensington Museum. 3½ in.

dolls or puppets, is proved by the fact that Plato compares man to a doll, and his passions to the cords which cause his movements and actions; the simile is also used by Horace. Such puppets were made of wood, and Aristotle gives a description of their movements. A string is pulled, he says, and the member to which the cord is attached makes a movement; the head nods, the eyes turn, the hands make the corresponding movement, and the figure appears to have life. Such dancing dolls are described fully in our chapter on Marionettes.

The virgins of Greece and Rome, on arriving at years of discretion, took their discarded dolls, miniature furniture, and household plenishings, to the temple of Venus or Diana for consecration to the goddess. It was the custom also to bury the toys of a dead child with the body; and it is owing to this custom, carried on in unbroken succession from the remotest times in Egyptian history, that we are now able to see, touch, and handle the identical playthings of the children of archaic times.

It is interesting to know that this custom, originating in the pagan belief of the Egyptians, that the dead would require the toys for use in the other world, and continued by the pagans of Greece and Rome, was in a few instances practised by early Christians,—so difficult is it to throw off the old customs, even when their meaning is no longer an article of belief. Possibly the fact that toys were placed in the sarcophagi of Christian children was due to the sentiment of the mother, who desired that the toys, which had given her little one so much pleasure in life, should not be used by others.

In *The Catacombs of Rome*, by W. I. Wilkrow, M.A., we read :—" Affecting memorials of domestic affection

15

Dolls and Doll-dressing. are found in the toys and trinkets of little children enclosed in their graves, or affixed to the plastic without. The dolls strikingly resemble those with which children amuse themselves to-day. They are made of ivory, and some are furnished with wires by which the joints can be worked after the manner of modern Marionettes."

There is a legend dating from the time of Vitruvius, attributing the classic shape of the Corinthian column to the custom of burying the toys, or of placing them in a receptacle close to the tomb. It is related that a young girl of Corinth fell ill and died ; she was buried, and her nurse gathering all her toys together, placed them in a basket, which she covered with a large tile to preserve them from the destroying effects of sun and rain. This basket she placed upon the ground of the burying-place. As it happened, the seed of an acanthus was just beneath, and as the plant grew, it lifted the toys in its twisted stems until they assumed the shape of a lovely column, supporting and following the lines of the basket, and spreading over the outstanding edges of the tile, suggested the form of the capital. The sculptor Callenacus, happening to pass close to the tomb, remarked the basket and graceful disposition of the branches, and adopted the new form as a model for the columns in his work, in the architecture of Corinth.

There is a quaint representation of a man of the Middle Ages engaged in doll-making ; whether these puppets were to be used as saints or angels in the elaborate Church ceremonials of the day, or as children's toys, we are not able to decide. Materials for doll history are indeed meagre at this period. At the time of the Renaissance, however, links in the chain of

16

evidence are again available, and a few rare specimens of the sixteenth century have survived, in which the elaboration of the dressing is very marked.
When the house of Valois was reigning in France an example was made which was recently to be seen in Paris. White silk, elaborately embroidered, was the material used for the dress. This is quilted finely in lozenges in such a manner that the tiny bouquet of the conventionally designed blossoms forms the centre of each lozenge. Guipure and passementerie of the period are used in lavish quantities round the skirt, in horizontal trimming of the bodice, and in ornamenting the over-sleeve, which partly conceals the richly embroidered under-sleeve. A ruffle, edged with lace, is worn at the neck ; a high cap of satin, embroidered and trimmed with galloon, is worn on the head. A miniature doll, dressed with much elaboration, is supported on the left arm. This tiny figure, the doll's doll, has flowing skirts of blue, long sleeves reaching almost to the hem of the skirt, and under-sleeves trimmed with bands of silver galloon.

Another sixteenth-century doll, in the possession of a private collector, has a richly embroidered dress of green satin. Crowns form the design, which is carried out with infinite minuteness in gold and silver thread ; the falling ruffle is edged with the guipure of Gothic design characteristic of the period. This doll, which is of wood, measures more than twenty-seven inches in height, an unusually large size.

We examined three specimens recently, measuring nine inches, eight and a half, and eight inches respectively. In each case the head, shoulders, and bust, besides the hands, were of beautifully modelled composition ; wax had

17

been used for securing the hair, of which little remained on the head ; in one case wax had also been used to support the rolls of hair. The dresses were very elaborate, but the underclothes practically non-existent,—a single cambric petticoat to set out the skirt being all that was provided or that had survived. The largest doll had a very beautifully embroidered white silk skirt ; a blue silk cloak flowed from the shoulders ; it was trimmed with hand - made thread lace, the "purling" of the sixteenth century ; this mantle was richly embroidered with gold thread ; the little pointed shoes were also embroidered, the heels were red.

The fitting of the pointed yellow silk bodice of the second doll was as neat as a Paquin or a Redfern could desire ; it was laced across the front with silver cords, and showed a vest of cloth of silver ; a large ruffle of fine Valenciennes lace was worn round the neck ; a muslin apron, lace-edged, and lace-trimmed turned-back cuffs, enable us to date the fashion of this dress to the period when for a short time neck-ruffles were worn with flat cuffs, in the transition period before the flat collars of King Charles had been universally adopted with the flat cuffs.

An interesting feature in our third doll was that she had no feet or legs, the body being fixed upon a wicker stand like the skirt stand of a dressmaker's model. Though we have seen several prints of children playing with such dolls, this is the only specimen we have ever handled.

Early dolls when elaborately dressed were frequently placed upon such stands ; that these were dolls, and not costume puppets, is proved from the representation in

French Dolls of the period of Louis XV. They are elaborately dressed in the Court costume of the day. From the Musée Carnavalet. 9 in. in height.

XVIIth Century Doll, German
3½ in.   The dress is trimmed
with lace of the period.

English Doll, XVIIIth Century, with
quilted cap and petticoat.

Ecclesiastical Doll, XVIIIth Century.
From the South Kensington Collection.
14 in. in height.

Early Wax Doll, with human hair.   In
the possession of the author.   18 in. in
height.

contemporary portraits of children playing with such dolls.
Sometimes the stand was fixed with wires clasping the
doll at the waist, sometimes a wooden peg was fixed up
the doll's back. Such a stand not only maintained the
doll in the upright position, but also set out the skirts, and
gave the proper wide look, essential for the fashion of
the day, and greatly enhanced the long pointed waist.

Old dolls dressed in ecclesiastical costume, accurate
to the minutest detail, are sometimes to be met with,
and were undoubtedly used as toys. There is a very
charming engraving, by Chardin, of a child nursing such
a doll. Other details with regard to ecclesiastical dolls
are given under ecclesiastical toys, where we also describe
the splendid Biblical groups so much used in the seventeenth and eighteenth centuries as assistants in the teaching of sacred history by the Church of Rome.

When the luxury of the seventeenth century was affecting all articles in domestic use, it is little wonder that the
spirit of extravagance should enter the nurseries. The
cost of the toys was enormous. We may mention what
we hope was an extreme case, the doll presented to Mademoiselle de Bourbon by Louis d'Eperon ; the bed, the
bedroom furniture and doll's clothes, including the
déshabillé of the doll, cost 2000 écus.

Costliness in toys, though much to be deprecated, is
no new thing, witness as one instance only, the doll given
by the Duchess of Orleans in 1722 to the Infanta of
Spain ; the cost was 22,000 fcs.

A notable doll-dressing incident occurred in 1497,
when Anne of Bretagne had a doll dressed for presentation
to Isabella, Queen of Spain. When completed the clothes
were not considered sufficiently fine, and grander ones

Dolls and Doll-dressing. had to be provided. All this is set forth, together with the cost of the two sets of dresses, in the royal accounts The elaboration of doll-dressing in the sixteenth and seventeenth centuries would astonish some of those who provide the few garments for the cheap dolls of the present day.

Elaborate doll-dressing is, however, still occasionally done, and the outfit of the doll prepared for the little Grand-Duchess Olga, eldest daughter of the Czar and Czarina during their visit to Paris, would compare favourably with any in past centuries.

Wealthy women occasionally make extensive doll-dressing their hobby.

The Queen of Roumania has an extremely fine collection of modern dolls dressed to represent historical personages and to show the native dresses of many countries. The distinctive type of nearly every country in the world is represented ; sometimes a large group shows the dolls taking part in a marriage, a native dance, or some special festival ; some historical scenes are shown, the dolls being in the correct dress of the period with background and elaborate accessories necessary to complete the picture.

Another such collection on a smaller scale belongs to Madame Gerard Peogey. In this very choice selection even more attention has been paid to historical accuracy, so that the sixteen dolls which compose it form a really accurate record of the dress of the period to which each puppet belongs. A long period of inquiry and research was necessary before every detail of costume, jewels, hair-dressing, and mode of adjusting the accessories of each toilette, was achieved.

22

Early Wax Head with glass
eyes. About 1810. 4½ in.

Doll's head of composition, the hair
moulded with the head. Early
XIXth Century. 6½ in.

Detail of Quilted Cap of XVIIIth
Century doll. (See opposite, page 15.)
The frilled edging and tucker are
laces of the period.'

Fragment of Linen Doll, stuffed with
papyrus. IIIrd Century before Christ.
Egypto-Roman.

French Toys, from an illustrated catalogue of Napoleonic period. The Baby Doll with the ribbon and order represents the little King of Rome, the lower figures, Mamelukes.

Many substances have been used in making dolls— wood, papier-mâché, composition, porcelain, terra cotta, wax, cloth, calico, rag, india-rubber, gourds, and many other materials. The size also shows a very large scale of variations. A late eighteenth-century doll is to be seen in a print, which is almost as large as the child. This size is exceptional ; as a rule old dolls run from seven to fourteen inches ; the jointed wooden dolls of Northern Europe, and the carved Italian dolls whose clothes are also of the carving roughly coloured, were generally about seven and a half inches long.

Dolls of india-rubber or gutta-percha were not known till the beginning of the nineteenth century, when the commercial value of the gum was discovered. Heads of china and wax, made in England, were imported into France as late as the middle half of the nineteenth century. A wax head of Napoleonic times is before us, the hair is painted, the eyes are of glass, the head and neck measure four and a half inches in height.

Superior rag dolls, whose heads of wax were covered with muslin, thus rendering them practically unbreakable, are first mentioned in the report of the exhibits in the 1855 Exhibition in Paris, but rag dolls were known in ancient Egypt.

A finely illustrated book of the designs of a toy-maker in Paris at the time of the first Empire shows dolls dressed and undressed, some have china heads and kid bodies and limbs ; the preference of children for baby dolls had evidently begun. A few of the dressed dolls are ladies, fashionably attired in the high-waisted bodices of the time, and men figure occasionally. The picturesque Mameluke costume is shown, and the wave of orientalism

25

which set Indian gods on the armoires, Nankin china in the boudoirs, and even necessitated pagodas and Indian chiefs in the lace of an earlier period, showed itself in the turbans of the lady dolls and the waving paradise plumes of their bonnets.

In this trade pattern book, little boy dolls appear in the dress of the Directoire period, and there is a pattern of a baby doll decorated with a star and order, which was brought out as the King of Rome, and was doubtless vastly popular in consequence.

That dolls should ever be put to utilitarian uses seems unlikely, but all students of the customs of the seventeenth and eighteenth centuries are aware that fashion puppets or dolls, elaborately dressed, were the forerunners of our pictorial fashion papers of to-day.

Soon after the time when Padua and Milan, Venice and Siena had ceased to set the fashions for Europe, when Catherine de Medici, that famous dresser and wearer of costly and beautiful fabrics, had married the French King, and Colbert had declared that France should one day be "the wardrobe of the world," thereby swelling her revenues, a custom arose of dressing two dolls in the newest fashion, one *en grande tenue*, the other in *déshabille*.

These dolls, which were about half life-size, were exposed to view at the Hotel Rambouillet. They were called the Grande Pandore and the Petite Pandore. Gradually the convenience of the plan caused its expansion; replicas of the dolls were made for sending to Vienna, Madrid, and other great cities, so that those who were prevented from visiting the French capital should be able to shape their farthingales and petticoats, ruffles

26

and wigs, according to the latest dictates of Parisian **Fashion**
modes. **Dolls.**

As early as 1321 there appears amongst the royal
expenses a fashion doll for the Queen of England. After
a time fashion puppets were sent at regular intervals,
about four times a year, at the commencement of the
spring, summer, autumn, and winter seasons, so that
the frills and puffs invented in the Rue Saint Honoré
were successfully imitated in London or St. Petersburg,
and the style of lace ruffle and manches was equally well
worn in Rome, Lisbon, and Berlin.

Strangely enough these fashion puppets were the
subject of special regulations in times of war, being
allowed to pass when nearly all articles were considered
contraband. The Grande Poupée had her special pass-
port, though war was declared, for court dames must
arrange their hair *à la* Fantange, or according to any
other mode, though the nations were at war ; all ships
were bombarded that did not contain her precious person.
This courtesy ceased at the end of the First Empire.

In the inventory of the belongings of Catherine de
Medici, made after the death of her husband, eight of
these fashion dolls were dressed in elaborate mourning
garb ; their cost appears as an entry in her account book.

We can well imagine that many a fashion puppet,
when it had served its purpose in showing the mode,
gradually drifted to the nursery, and was loved and
cherished by some little girl as her plaything.

A very beautiful doll, probably one of the fashion
puppets of the period of Louis XVI., until recently formed
one of the valuable exhibits in a private collection. She
is perfectly proportioned, standing about fifteen inches

in height ; the face, neck, hands, and arms are of wax, and quite perfect except for the loss of one finger ; the hair, white in imitation of the powdering effect of the day, is dressed with soft curls high on the head *à la* Pompadour, a bunch of tufted feathers and a velvet ribbon form the raised head-dress on one side. The dress, which is *décolleté*, shows the well-modelled neck ; round the throat is worn a black velvet ribbon, tied in front. The rich brocade saque is trimmed with bullion cords, which form a kind of glittering stomacher ; the bodice is deeply pointed in front and ornamented with ribbons caught down with bright buttons. The bullion cords are used to unite the edges of the over-dress, and are finished at the sides with rosettes of the hand-made silver lace of the period. Hand-made lace flounces ornament the under petticoat, and form ruffles in the three-quarter bell-shaped sleeves.

Dolls made in the Netherlands were much imported into England in the eighteenth century ; they were sometimes called Flanders' babies, so that the old rhyme came to be repeated :

What the children of Holland take pleasure in making,
The children of England take pleasure in breaking.

A writer in 1695 warns a farmer to choose a wife "not trickt up with ribbons and knots like a Bartholomew baby." ·This alludes to the fact that dolls were much sold like all other toys at the great Bartholomew and other fairs, and were specially gaily dressed. "Drums, hobby-horses, rattles, babies, and Jew trumps," are mentioned amongst the toys sold at such places.

The early German dolls were frequently made without

28

Poupard or indestructible
Doll for a young child.
German carved wood,
15 in. in height.

Figures of Country People bringing produce to market. Such puppets of the early
XIXth Century show elaborate dressing and attention to every detail. Hats, baskets,
and vegetables are home made, and the faces and hands of cambric stuffed and
embroidered. Belonging to the Secretan family.

Doll's Sunshade in the **Germanische Museum**, Nuremburg.   6 in.

Doll of the XVIIIth Century.   Wax hands
and face, wooden feet.   14 in.   In the
collection of Monsieur Maury.   The human
hair is supported on wool pads.

Doll of Louis XV. period.   Wax face a
hands.   Court dress of brocade and silver la
9½ in.   Sold recently for £14.

legs, the body terminating in a kind of cone or handle **Solid** which made the toy convenient for holding. Such dolls **Dolls for** are called *poupards* in France, and still exist as cheap **Young** toys. **Children.**

Some figures of early nineteenth-century make, standing ten inches in height, are rather costume models like the famous Neapolitan specimens, than dolls in the sense of the loved and fondled playthings of little girls, but we describe them as illustrating to perfection the painstaking methods of the old doll-dressing of that period.

The figures are those of a country man and woman belonging to the class of small farmers or cottage folk, who occasionally act as itinerant vendors of the produce of their farm or garden. They are made of stuffed calico, the limbs carefully modelled with a due regard to size and proportion. The face is painted on the calico, every article worn is of home manufacture, even the neatly made straw bonnet of the woman, the hat of the man, and probably the dainty baskets carried by the pair, each of the four being a different shape. The woman wears a dress of print, the serviceable apron reaching to the ankles, a little cross-over shawl with pretty border is worn on the shoulders. The man's striped trousers and neatly made coat and vest are triumphs of home sartorial skill, the large stock is neatly twisted and tied in the fashion of the day. In the basket are fowls and vegetables for sale, made in the most realistic manner in stuffed calico or print, duly coloured.

An interesting doll of about this period is spoken of in *Child Life in Colonial Days* as " The White House Doll," who spent the days of her youth in the White House at Washington, with the children of President John

Quincy Adams, and is still cherished by his descendants. She is of the stolid type so delightfully described amongst the dolls of Queen Victoria as " Mrs. Martha House-keeper,"—" a big and substantial doll . . . with a fat, round, good-humoured face, a broad nose, and an air of prosperous complacency which send your thoughts back to oak chests, lavender-pressed sheets, and the attractive family housekeeper of a certain type of domestic novel." The Quincy Adams doll has a full skirt, large, wide sleeves, and a buttoned-up jacket bodice which, in fit and shape, does credit to the Jenny Wren who fashioned it.

It was at an Industrial Exhibition in Paris that the first "talking doll" was shown, according to a child's journal, *Le bon Genie*; the patent for a doll which could say " Papa " and " Mamma " was taken out in 1824 by a Parisian mechanician. The mechanism was worked by lifting one arm for one word, the other arm for the other word, when a kind of bellows was worked, so that a syllable was repeated, which by courtesy could be recognised as a word.

The opening and shutting of eyes by counter balance also appeared first at the beginning of the nineteenth century, when the development of doll-making and doll-dressing was very marked, the prices becoming more popular. At this time the faces were usually of composition pressed into moulds, the arms and legs of wood. Paris began to take the lead, which she still holds, in this branch of toy-making ; Germany and Austria continued to supply the world with cheap toys, especially those of roughly carved wood. Bodies of kid stuffed with sawdust were also in vogue ; they were generally furnished with porcelain or composition heads.   These were replaced by **Modern** the composition dolls with ball and socket joints fixed **Types.** inside with wires and strings, so as to make them movable, which, together with many of the older types, obtain in the present day.

CHAPTER II

DOLL PLAY. ORIENTAL DOLLS.

Doll Play.
Oriental
Dolls.
BESIDES the more elaborately made dolls of wood or composition, there are many simpler ones, such as the paper dolls which are beloved of neat-fingered little girls who like to "cut out," and who are entrusted with gum to stick the backs and fronts of the dolls together. Sheets of such coloured representations of dolls were much in vogue in the early nineteenth century ; sometimes they were mounted on card, which was cut out also to fit the picture ; this card was then slipped into a block of wood so that the doll would "stand." Other toys besides dolls were represented on sheets, and a whole garden, a farm-yard, or group of animals, could be mounted and used as the home and familiar surroundings of the doll. To a child who really takes interest in her dolls such surroundings are most important and add much to the reality of the toy world.

The wise mother will not look upon her child's doll as a worthless trifle ; to the little one it is not a toy nor a thing inanimate and soulless ; the imaginative child endues her doll with life, with reason, strangest of all, with temperament; in the subtle simplicity of a child's **Import-** mind it is her child, with like reasoning powers and **ance of** imagination. Who has not heard a child talking to **Doll Play.** her doll, living through the imaginary life of the puppet: the successes, the amusements, the sadness, the sickness, too, and the laughter, to say nothing of the naughtiness and the scrapes which have come within the experience of the child?

Let a mother watch the pretended joys and sorrows which are the foundations of the games with the doll, and she will see the development of her little girl's mind more clearly than by much questioning, however confidential the relationship may be between herself and her little one. The child lends the doll her soul, the mind that is being born will be reflected accurately in the dollie's games.

DOLL FOR CUTTING OUT.
French, eighteenth century.

An almost prophetic foreshadowing of character can be traced in Jane Welsh Carlyle's account of her doll. She had always loved it, but when she had got into the first book of Virgil, she thought it a shame to care for it any longer, and, having judged the victim, decided she must die, and die as became the doll of a young lady who read

35

Doll Play.
Oriental
Dolls.
Virgil. With some lead pencils, her four-post bed, her dresses, which were many, a few sticks of cinnamon and a nutmeg to provide the spices for the funeral pile, she poured

DOLL PLAY.

A domestic scene in the child life of the eighteenth century. French.

over it some perfume, then seating the doll on the four-post-bed, she recited the last speech of Dido on behalf of the doll, stabbed it with a penknife, and thus made it perish nobly.

The sequel to this story partakes of the nature of an anti-climax, for the grave student of Virgil had over-rated her callousness, and when the hungry flames licked up the bran stuffing of the second Dido, she would have

rescued her doll, and, being unable to do so, screamed **Jane**
and danced with anguish of mind, and was presently **Carlyle's**
carried forcibly into the house lest she should disturb the **Doll.**
neighbours. A strangely prophetic scene when we
remember the life of sacrifice she was to lead, as wife of
the great writer and thinker, Thomas Carlyle, sacrifices
which would sometimes have been better left unmade.
This woman seemed destined to try and act the Stoic,

GROUP OF OLD DOLLS' FURNITURE.
French.   From the collection of M. Bernard.

a character for which she was by no means suitably
equipped.

Professor Stanly Hall, from statistics gathered in
America, places the climax of the doll passion in girls at
the age of eight to nine. " It will," he says, " sometimes
linger a few years longer, and occasionally after it has died

away or remained quiescent for a long while, flare up again, when the girl is brought in contact with doll-love in another child, so that often an elder sister renews her pleasure in dolls with her younger sister."

We must specialise in describing this doll-love, for there are many varieties ; the child who delights to fondle and mother her doll will have little love for the grand ladies, the courtiers, or freaks which inhabit the doll-world as well as the babies and little girls ; probably the love of gay colours and dress, inherent in most children, has much to do with the pleasure taken in " grand " dolls, while the pure doll-love which prompts another child to cherish her rough-hewn, shapeless " baby," and neglect the finely

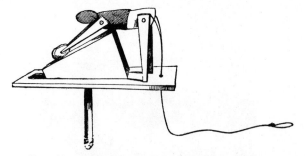

EARLY EGYPTIAN JOINTED TOY FOR DOMESTIC PLAY.
Bread-kneading, from Leyden Museum.

dressed lady doll, is a separate and distinct variety of dollatry.

The pleasure in black dolls, Punch dolls, monster dolls, animals used as dolls, soldier dolls, and sailor dolls, seems to be the kind of doll-love most shared by boys, and we should put it down as rather an enjoyment of the close association and feeling of power over grotesque and unusual forms, than the love of fondling and mothering,

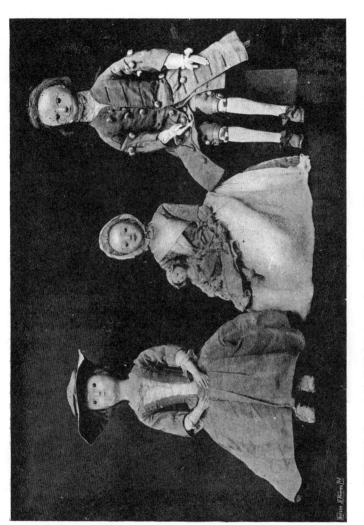

Group of XVIIIth Century Dolls, with compo faces and hands and human hair. The lady has drab dress and white vest laced across ; the nurse a pink and white dimity dress. The man wears a fawn silk coat, with buttons to match, and high stock of the per od. These interesting figures measure 15 in. in height. From South Kensington Museum.

Baby Doll in wooden chair, for a child learning to walk. Early XVIIIth Century. German.

Doll's Bed of wood, hung with brocade and thread lace. Small wax Doll. From the Musée Carnavalet.

Doll of Louis XV., in Court dress of silk painted with miniature pattern and trimmed with gold fringe. 9¼ in.

which is the root of pure dollatry.   This love of power is **Imitation**
undoubtedly common to all kinds of doll-lovers.   **inspires**
    Doll play seems clearly enough to be fostered by the **Doll Play.**

GROUP OF DOLL AND DOLLS' FURNITURE.
Shown at the Paris Exhibition, 1900.

craze for imitation of older people's ways, which runs
through the whole of children's play : it is certainly largely
induced by a child's natural desire to get away from
subjection, and to try her hand at the sweets of authority.
Perhaps the delight obtained through the exchange of
functions may, through some mysterious process of child
thought, be keener when the doll child to be instructed and
scolded looks like herself, that is to say, like a little girl ;
if so, this would explain the rarity of boy dolls.

41

**Doll Play.
Oriental
Dolls.**

Is not the child's love of power clearly shown in her delight in washing, brushing the hair, and endless dressings and undressings which form so large a portion of doll rites? We do not believe it is due to the superlative love of cleanliness and neatness, but rather to a delight in inflicting on others the bothers which nurse has so often inflicted on herself; unfortunately, with the old-fashioned English dolls the two separate pleasures of washing and hair-doing could seldom be combined in the person of the same doll, as the dolls were either made of wax which could not be washed except with butter, a poor substitute, and for obvious reasons seldom allowed by the authorities, or were of china, when the hair was uncombable. We well remember the joy of receiving a china doll with "real" hair from Paris; "Frenchy" she was always called, and the pleasure with which we realised that here at last was a doll which could be washed and combed as well, is still one of the clearest cut recollections of childhood.

Delightful to contemplate, not only as a record of our late Queen Victoria's industry and persevering accuracy, but also as an example of the pleasure and amusement which can be obtained from simple and inexpensive materials, is the now historical collection of dolls found amongst the half-forgotten treasures of her childhood. Sir Henry Ponsonby says :—

"Her Majesty was very much devoted to dolls, and indeed played with them till she was nearly fourteen years old. Her favourites were small dolls — small wooden dolls, which she could occupy herself with dressing, and who had a house in which they could be placed."

This house with its furnishings and accommodation will be found fully described in our chapter on Dolls' Houses

42

and Furnishing; it was, like the dolls, of the simplest **Queen** make, but made interesting by the individuality displayed **Victoria's** in the arrangement of its Liliputian fittings. **Dolls.**

"Miss Victoria Conroy," continues Sir Henry Ponsonby, "afterwards Mrs. Hanmer, came to see her once a week, and occasionally others played with her, but with these exceptions she was left alone with the companionship of her dolls. . . . The Queen usually dressed the dolls from some costumes she saw either in the theatre or private life," and it is most interesting to note, in showing the extraordinarily accurate memory that nearly fifty or sixty years after the doll-dressing had taken place, almost at the end of the Queen's long life, so full of important incidents and events, she remembered perfectly the details of the costumes, correcting inaccuracies in the description of them written by Miss Frances Low when it was submitted to her. For instance, in a description of "a doll representing Taglioni in 'La Sylphide' dressed by Baroness Letzen in a very much abbreviated muslin dress, which is, however, of less consequence when we perceive she has charming little gossamer wings painted in white and gold. A silver wreath is pinned on her hair. She again appears dressed by the Baroness as a peasant." The Queen corrects this with the words "Dancing girl."

Again an interesting correction occurs :—"A whole group of dolls represent characters in the ballet of 'Kenilworth,'" which was performed in 1831 at the famous King's Theatre. It would be interesting to know whether Her Majesty was herself taken to the opera (Note by the Queen, "she went to the opera and saw the ballet, of which she was very fond, several times"); or whether the costumes were described to her, or whether the knowledge was

43

obtained from prints. (Note by the Queen,—"None existed.") "To this set the Princess Victoria contributed two characters, Robert Dudley Earl of Leicester, and Amy Robsart in riding costume." (Note by the Queen, "Not riding costume.")

There are 132 of these dolls, the Queen herself having dressed no fewer than thirty-two, a remarkable example of painstaking industry for any girl of twelve years old. That they were of immense importance to her, is shown by the fact that records of the dolls were found with them in an old copy book, on the inside cover of which is written "List of my dolls," and an accurate description was given in the childish handwriting, the doll's name, by whom the doll was dressed, the date and name of the ballet, if the dress of a popular actress was given, the name of the court ladies and their children, and the names of the men, only seven or eight of which are amongst the collection.

As examples of doll-dressing these twopenny wooden puppets are unique ; no detail was considered too small or unimportant ; historical accuracy, daintiness of execution, and exquisite neatness are the leading characteristics in this remarkable assemblage. We quote from the *Strand Magazine* :—" The workmanship in the frocks is simply exquisite ; tiny ruffles are sewn with fairy stitches, wee pockets on aprons (it must be borne in mind for dolls of five or six inches) are delicately finished off with minute bows ; little handkerchiefs, not more than half an inch square, are embroidered with red silk initials and have drawn borders ; and there are chatelaines of white and gold beads so small that they almost slip out of one's hands in handling. . . . The Earl of Leicester, who presents a distinctly masculine physiognomy owing to the

44

"'TIS MY DOLL."
By C. Knight, after Singleton.

Old Doll, with wax face and hands, human hair. 7 in.

Doll from Korea. Linen face with embroidered features, rush arms and legs. Elaborate head-dress. 8 in. in height.

Old Doll of carved wood, finely painted, glass and human hair. Dress of brocade with gold Measures 17 in.

addition of painted black moustaches and whiskers, and the absence of a back comb, is attired in pink satin hose with pink satin slashings, and a white lace ruffle. On his breast he wears the blue ribbon of the Garter, and though he has no hat, probably a broad-brimmed velvet hat, with curling white plumes, found loose in the doll box, is his property."

Again, the description of the peasant's cap worn by Mlle. Rosalie Taglioni shows minute work and attention to detail, which is so necessary in the making of really shapely and successful dolls' clothes ; the cap is " fashioned of violet velvet trimmed with narrow gold braid, and has projecting out on either side two Liliputian gold pins with real round golden knobs. The headgear is especially interesting. " Philippa Countess of Jedburgh," wears an opera hat of exactly the same kind as was worn by court ladies at the theatre in the early part of this century. It is made of black velvet with an immense brim which is bound with pink cord, and is trimmed with pink marabout feathers both outside and inside the brim.

A delightful evidence of the Queen's sense of humour and feeling for the fitness of things is shown in the stately court lady, Lady Rothesay, in white satin and white boa, who holds on each arm an infant in long clothes. The twins are attired one in white satin, the other in cambric, doubtless to indicate in the quality of the material of their dresses, which was the heir.

In such human touches did Queen Victoria show her keen interest and sympathy, so that her dolls, though of the humblest make, have the distinction which only individual thought, delicate work, and accuracy in historical detail can give.

Doll Play. Oriental Dolls. Distinctly characteristic are the dolls of primitive and oriental races; their features always show a curious resemblance to those of the people or tribe by whom they are made. Though for obvious reasons we can only describe a few, it may be taken as a general rule that something in the semblance of a doll is in use wherever there are children, all over the world.

The native Sioux dolls are of leather, the flat face and staring bead eyes are curiously like the native type in feature. Such dolls are dressed entirely in leather, the long, coat-like garment reaching the feet; it is ornamented with a fringe made by the simple process of cutting the edge of the leather into strips; such strips are also sewn on to the dress in rows by means of bright-coloured stitching; the hair is most abundant, and hangs down the back in long smooth flat plaits; occasionally strings of beads are used instead of hair.

The Indian dolls from far Yarkand are rather similar; the faces are of linen with the features embroidered on it, the colour on the cheeks being decidedly pronounced, in red patches; the hair is real, and, in the female doll, is in long plaits which reach far below the waist; the headgear of this race is always the most elaborate item of attire, and that of the dolls does not fall short in this particular, elaborately embroidered in silks, gold thread, and bullion; the caps, which are twice the height of the head, are edged with fur. There is fur trimming also on the outer garment, shaped like an embroidered dressing-gown; silk and brocade sashes are used for suspending weapons, pockets, and pouches; a jade button was used on one of the eight-inch specimens that we examined.

The numerous models made in India must not be

48

considered as dolls. These show the Indian native of **Doll** every caste, from the native princes and rajahs to the **Models.** street-sellers and sweepers. Very pretty and instructive are some of the groups selling vegetables, vending their wares in the market, doing their washing, cooking their food, or attending the native court of justice. They illustrate all the varied scenes in Indian life, but the dolls, the playthings of the children, have little in common with these immobile plaster models. Indian dolls are of linen with painted or embroidered features. In imitation of European dolls they have cotton hair, moustaches or beard, and dresses glittering with pearls and tinsel, or of the simplest linen or cambric according to the station of the person represented by the doll. We have seen dancing girls, landholders, weavers, natives of Bengal, of Rangoon, of Madras, and many other native states.

The limbs are carefully proportioned to the size of the doll; about ten inches is the most usual size, the fingers and toes are sewn so as to give a separated effect, and round the tip of each, red ribbon is wound to suggest the coveted henna stain beloved of Orientals. The satin coats, embroidered garments, bullion-trimmed scarves are beautifully made; the women wear nose-rings and jewelled head-dresses, the men ear-rings and sometimes embroidered velvet slippers.

We have before us a picture of what is called an old Mexican doll. It is in the form of a seated figure of grotesque proportions; the head, which is one-third as large as the whole body, is decidedly primitive in make, the eyes are closed, the enormous mouth wide open, strange projections at the side of the head take the place of ears; at the top of the head is a similar pointed

knob like the upstanding hair usually worn by our old
friend Pantaloon. On the knees of this image, which is
of baked clay, is a pot or vase clasped in both hands ;
we are inclined to think this is rather a god, a fetish, or
votive image, than a doll in the true sense ; as with the
forms in clay of Egypt, Greece, and Rome, great care is
necessary in distinguishing such objects connected with
burial or religious rites, from toys.

Amongst the native toys of Khurdistan there is an
elaborate figure of a mother doll seated at the side of a
rude, but elaborately ornamental cradle, on which a baby
is lying covered over with a blanket of native workmanship ; this is tightly strapped on. The dolls are of roughly
carved wood and are painted in bright colours ; the
extremities are also of carved wood. A man doll drives
an astonishingly shaped camel, loaded with merchandise ;
his expression is one of patient imbecility combined with
mirth ; he is dressed in a coat strapped in at the waist
and wears enormously baggy trousers ; on his head is a
kind of tufted nightcap ; he holds an enormous stick in
his hand. Altogether the father doll of Khurdistan is
a pleasing-looking object.

A Japanese doll of the eighteenth century has a much
more dwarfed appearance than the Yum-Yums or Pitti
Sings of the present day ; the head is one-third as large
as the whole body, but in other respects she is similar in
construction to the dolls which now come from Japan.
Her dress is a loosely fitted coat of embroidered satin tied
in at the waist with a ribbon ; her shaven head has hair
hanging from the temples only, so that she must be a
very little girl ; in her hand she holds a stick on which is
mounted bauble-fashion the figure of a Japanese lady with

50

fan and elaborately dressed hair. This is a charming example of a doll's doll.

Some very rare and costly dolls are owned by the Japanese of good family, many of these puppets dating back several centuries. These dolls are displayed only once a year on the third day of the third month ; the festival is called Hina Matsuri, or the feast of girls, or "The Feast of Dolls."

For days before the festival, the shops are full of specially made dolls, which can be purchased only at this time of year. They are not very large—from four inches to twelve in height, and are superbly dressed in the richest silks and printed crapes and brocades. When a daughter has been born during the previous year, two of these dolls are bought, and so they accumulate from generation to generation. When the girl is married, her pair of dolls is taken with her to her new home, and she gives them to her children, adding to the stock as her girl babies are born. These images, which are made of wood or enamelled clay, are usually made to represent the Mikado and his wife, his courtiers and their wives and daughters, or favourite personages well known in Japanese mythology and history.

Besides these specially made dolls, all kinds of toys pertaining to doll life are to be bought at this girls' festival, and are played with on that day, and afterwards put away with the dolls until the following year. Some of the dolls' cooking utensils and miniature household furniture are made in the most costly and elaborate manner.

Offerings of saké and dried rice are made by the girls to the images of the Emperor and Empress before they are carefully wrapped up and put away, until the annual festival comes round again.

Owing to the courtesy of the Viscountess Hayashi, wife of the Japanese ambassador to the court of St. James, we have examined such dolls; very beautiful they are as works of art, and very beautiful too are their surroundings.

Miniature six-fold screens, nine and a half inches in height, formed a background; the Emperor and Empress dolls, six and a half to seven inches in height, were seated on low platforms of lacquer; the richness of their dress was very marked, the blending of the colours in the brocades and soft silks as lovely as only Japanese taste could make them; here and there a fleck of vivid orange or bright red showed up amongst the more subdued folds of indigo blue, green, or grey. Tiny lacquer pots, an inch high, ornamented the audience chamber; these were planted with flowers; palm-like plants stood also in miniature jars of porcelain; half-a-dozen courtiers stood about in a semicircle.

The elaboration of the Japanese dolls struck us very forcibly, and the preponderance of grown-up dolls was also most noticeable; the hairdressing of the ladies was an exact replica of that of the native lady of Japan, and the high rolled cushion much extended, very like the fashion obtaining to-day *à la* Pompadour; tortoiseshell combs in miniature, gaily decorated pins, and a few flowers were used in ornamenting the elaborate *coiffures*. Each lady doll had her inch-long fan stuck into her sash, and the tiny lacquer or ivory sticks were in themselves works of art.

Then there were baby Jap dolls, dear chubby things,

52

whose wide sashes slipped up under their chins as one **Japanese** cuddled them, just as a real baby's sash always gets **Dolls.** tucked up. The crowd of dolls of every size showed what Kipling has described—" children in every stage of spankable chubbiness." Dolls we saw, too, for the very young ; these were made about three and a half inches in height of some practically unbreakable and uneatable substance, with no sharp corners to hurt the tiny owner, no paint which could be licked or sucked off with disastrous results, and no flowing drapery, easy of destruction and indigestible.

Of the Japanese dolls' house and the lovely miniature fittings we speak elsewhere ; suffice it to say here, that Madame Chrysanthemum has the most charmingly furnished house in all doll-land, and her equipment is complete, even to a two-inch lacquer box with dollie's writing-brush, Indian ink tablet, palette, and water-bottle, lest she should wish to write a letter.

The humble, home-made dolls of Korea deserve special mention, for they are frequently made by the little girls themselves. A bamboo stem about five inches long is cut ; into the top of this a bunch of grass is inserted, which has previously been soaked in salt and water to pickle it and make it pliable. This is to form the hair of the doll ; a little paste with white powder makes the face, clothes are pinned on to the stick, and the inevitable hairpin, characteristic also of Japanese and Chinese hairdressing, is placed in the tangled bunch of hair.

The irreversible or tilting doll is known in many parts of the world—in China, Japan, India, Spain, Germany, Sweden, the United States, France, and England. We believe it to have originated in China, where it is called

" rising up little priest," and is made to represent Buddha
or a Buddhist priest.   In Korea, and also in India, it is
" the erect standing one," and is usually an image made
of paper with a rounded bottom made of clay, so that it
always stands erect.   Sometimes in India the doll is in
the form of a woman, who is riding on a tiger.   In France
the toy is made like a Chinese mandarin, and is called Le
Poussah, a corruption of the Chinese form of the Sanscrit
word for Buddha.   In Spain the tilting doll takes the
shape of a monk or a nun.   In Germany it is called
Putzelmann, and is alway of grotesque shape.   The
principle of the tilting doll is shown in a large ceremonial
pottery vase, found in a grave in south-eastern Missouri,
which is now in the Museum of Archæology at the
University of Pennsylvania.   Such objects in stone, always
with the tilting propensity, are found widely distributed
among the Indian tribes of the United States, by whom
they were used as objects connected with worship ; the
use of the tilting image in teaching baby the natural law,
that the heaviest part of an object is bound to be under-
most, is a curious development.   Baby has probably
learnt that a blow from a fat hand usually knocks a doll
down, and down he stops till, restored to baby's favour,
he is picked up again ; but this tilting dollie is evidently
very brave, for he gets up again, or, delightful thought,
he is very naughty, and on being put to bed he won't
lie down.   What fun to have a real naughty doll, who
hates going to bed as much as baby does !

CHAPTER III

TOYS OF POTTERY AND PORCELAIN.

THOUGH there are a few wooden relics, some rare bronze **Toys of** toys, and a relic or two of leather, it is to the toys of **Pottery** baked clay that we chiefly owe our knowledge of the **and** nursery treasures of lower Egypt, Greece, and Rome. **Porcelain.**

BALLS.

Made before the Christian era, of blue and grey glazed porcelain,
and of leather stitched and stuffed with papyrus.

The resistant nature of terra-cotta and of glazed ware, combined with the mode of air-tight packing in burial, has resulted in the extraordinary state of preservation, which is remarkable in objects so fragile. Bright-coloured clay balls of small size are as shining as when first used by boys of ancient Egypt ; the striped blue and grey

55

ones especially show no signs of decay. A clay doll of
Thebes, B.C. 2000, shows us what the girls loved to
play with, and a draughtboard of the Ptolemaic period,
made of coarse pottery, reveals the plaything of the
elder boys and girls and the adults of Egypt.

The primitive method of giving life-like movements to
an inanimate object is also preserved to us in various
pottery toys : a crocodile has a lower jaw hinged to the
upper, so that the mouth can be made to snap in a
manner terrible enough to delight any boy ; a spotted
cow also has a movable jaw ; while figures rolling a ball
on a sloping board, kneading dough or washing clothes,
have been found.

Amongst the terra-cotta toys found in tombs, are
many models in miniature of articles of domestic use,
little baskets of almonds and dates, rattles in the shape
of animals, masks, grotesque and otherwise, animals
with loads upon their backs, or ridden by male and
female figures, and in some cases yoked together ; it is
sometimes exceedingly difficult to decide which are the
toys of children and which are votive offerings.

Greek toys of coarse clay were made in great
quantities to be given away during the last two days
of the Saturnalia. Quantities of these are to be found
in museums, some being of the simplest form, and others
of more elaborate make. In gathering data from pictures,
however, conjecture no longer takes a part in forming an
opinion as to the use of the object, and not only are the
toys of Greece and Rome most frequently to be found
in terra-cotta, but the records of how the games were
played, and what toys were used at special seasons, are to
be found on the pottery of the day, thanks to the skilled

Toy Pig, from the Temple Collection.
Terra Cotta with glass ornaments. 2 in. high.

Greek Oil Vase, showing girl playing
at ball.   From the British Museum.

Miniature Cradle in Staffordshire Ware, probably made for a christening gift.
From the British Museum.

Terra Cotta Group, Greek Girls playing at Knuckle Bones.
From the British Museum.

draughtsmanship of the painters and decorators of the **Play** vases, oil-jars, and other domestic utensils. For this **depicted** reason alone, we should place pottery at the head of **on** those materials which have been the means of preserving **Pottery.** for us the knowledge of antique toys and the modes of using them.

The dolls of Cyrenaica, about a century before Christ, were made of baked clay, the arms, legs, trunk, and head being in separate pieces, and joined by wires running through holes made for the purpose; some limbs of terra-cotta show that they were attached to bodies of rag, long since crumbled to decay, exactly as are those of the present day, the hollow limb of pottery reaching only to the knee or elbow joint. A little clay chariot gives us the first wheeled toy that we have been able to find, dating a few centuries before the Christian era. Horsemen of pottery come from Cyprus, modelled and baked five centuries before Christ; specimens of the same date have been found at Rhodes and in Sardinia.

Moulds used in making toy masks, miniature fish-heads and animals, have been found on the site of Halicarnassus, just as they were found in the eighteenth century on the site of the pottery works at Bow, in the days which we call old, but which are young indeed, when we compare them with the archaic periods of which we have such extraordinarily complete records.

Nearly all the toys spoken of above are of roughly baked clay, or, in the case of essentially Greek specimens, of fine red terra-cotta. We know of a few samples of prehistoric toys in highly glazed ware; such a one is the model of a seat of Roman glazed ware, belonging to the " Temple " collection. A toy chariot in the same

Toys of Pottery and Porcelain.

ware, and a pig, five and a half inches long, which, though modelled in red terra-cotta, has fragments of glass ware stuck into the soft clay before baking—this belongs to the Sloane collection, and both are probably unique specimens.

A glass-like substance was also used for the astragals or knuckle-bones. So popular was this game that men, women, and children took part in it, and the "bones" have been found in pottery, glass, ivory, bronze, silver, and brass.

At the British Museum there is a beautiful little terra-cotta statuette of two girls playing at knuckle-bones, seated, and, in an attitude at once graceful and intent, the player is in the act of throwing the toys into the air. At the time of Pliny a sculptured group of children playing with these knuckle-bones was described as being in the apartments of the Emperor Titus; it was looked upon as one of the finest works of art in existence. There is no representation, that we know of, where the second part of the game is being played, when the bones which the player has failed to catch are being picked up between the outstretched fingers, those caught on the back of the hand remaining still in their position.

Many forms of the antique toys of Greece and Rome have been preserved to us owing to the custom of placing a chain round the neck of a child, from which hung diminutive toys in the form of amulets or charms; it is said that such chaplets were used as means of identification after the exposure of the young children according to the law, in order to test the health and strength of the infant. The picture of a child wearing

60·

such a chain may be seen in *Les Jeux des Anciens* by Fouquières. The tiny charms being wrought of ivory, cornelian pottery, or some such durable substance, stand, untouched by time, as records, whose accuracy there is no disputing ; amongst such objects have been found, a tiny metal crescent, a two-edged axe, a diminutive sword, a child's dagger, a tiny pig. This animal, owing to its connection with the rites of the infant Bacchus, is frequently found as a toy, or is used in ornamenting one ; the lucky pig charm remains with us still ; a basket, doubtless representing the mystic toy basket of the same god, and a hand, another amulet which is still supposed to avert the evil eye amongst semi-civilised races.

Toys in Chinese porcelain are of very early date ; there are miniature vases on an altar in a painted Kakanomo of the fourteenth or fifteenth century. Two toy saucers of lovely blue and white porcelain have the mark of Kang, the period which lasted from 1661 to 1722 ; these saucers, which measure one and a half inches in diameter, are painted in blue on the inside, with a four-clawed dragon on the outside, and two phœnixes amongst clouds.

Very interesting are the specimens of toys in the Schreiber collection ; some whistles are of clouded tortoiseshell ware, which was made in imitation of agate and marble. Thomas Whieldon of Little Fenton is the best known maker of this ware, as well as the green glazed and cauliflower ware. Between 1725 and 1775 this pottery was produced at other places, the demand for mottled and clouded ware being very large. Toy tea-services in Whieldon ware are sometimes to be found, and those of Lowestoft are rare.

Two whistles are evidently made for a pair; they are in the shape of birds, and are three and a half inches high; the colouring is brown, blue, and other less definite mottled combinations of tints.

Toy whistles of earthenware and porcelain are found in nearly every country. There are several interesting ones in the Schreiber collection; one the figure of a chimera, a somewhat alarming form to a child, is coloured brown and blue; it is three and a half inches in height. We have one of these whistles before us now which is made of the rough clay used in Spain; its form is that of a jug, of the kind used in Seville, with a small handle at the side and one also at the top; the whistle is blown through the side handle. Such toys are made in Sicily; we have seen them of grotesque shape from Palermo.

Some interesting toys were made at the close of the seventeenth century in the process introduced by the Dutch potter, John Philip Elers, who brought with him into Staffordshire the process of glazing with salt.

This salt-glazed Staffordshire ware, as it is called, is not very difficult to recognise, as it is unlike any other kind of white stone ware; it scarcely ever bears the maker's mark, however, though occasionally the initials of the modeller are found.

A very beautiful little toy tea-set is to be seen in the British Museum. This is not one of the earliest specimens of the Staffordshire salt-glazed ware, as the raised ornament is moulded probably in the brass or plaster moulds which were used at Burslem. The earlier specimens had applied ornaments only, which were placed on the vessels by means of impressed pieces. The texture of this in-

Toy Whistle, in the form of a
Chimera, in Whielden Ware.

Sauceboat, belonging to Toy Dinner
Service. The name of the owner is
painted on it "Miss de Vaux, 1774."
Height 2 in.

Toy Tea Service of Lowestoft China.   Teapot 3½ in. in height.

Toy Tea Service, in salt glaze, made at Burslem, Staffordshire.
From the British Museum.

Part of a Dinner Service belonging to the Thomas family.   Blue transfer pattern.
Height of tureen 4 in.   This Service is complete for 4 covers.

teresting toy tea-set is thin and delicate; occasionally pieces are to be seen which are almost translucent.

Two other examples of toys in this ware are the figures of cats seated; the eyes are enamelled in black, giving them a truly fearsome appearance, warranted to alarm the infant lover of the feline race; the bodies are marbled brown and grey in a most realistic manner. These cats measure five and a half inches in height.

A very beautiful toy is of the much sought for Rockingham ware. It must have been made early in the nineteenth century, as the factory was not established at Swinton near Rotherham in Yorkshire till 1820, and the name "Rockingham" was first applied to the Swinton productions in 1826. This most interesting piece, which is a toy teapot, stands two and a half inches in height; it is decorated with flowers in full relief, and painted in the finest and most brilliant colours; the edge is gilt. The mark, a griffin, is the crest of the Fitzwilliam family. Beneath this crest are the words: "Rockingham Works, Brameld, Manufacturer to the King," written in a rich crimson colour.

There is a personal charm about some specimens of Leeds ware, though knowledge of the owner of long ago is lost in the dim mist of a past century. On a pair of sauce-boats belonging to a toy service in Leeds ware, which we find enumerated amongst "pieces for domestic use," are the words: "Miss de Vaux. 1774." Who, we wonder, was the dainty Miss de Vaux who must have her name inscribed by the workers at a royal factory, on her toys? Where, alas, are the other pieces—the plates and dishes, soup-tureen and junket-bowls? Was Miss de Vaux a careless missy in handling her dollie's service, or have the descendants of Miss de Vaux broken or separated the other pieces belonging to the service ? There are panels ornamenting these pretty sauce-boats; the framework of the panels is in low relief. Inside there are narrow borders in black, and the delightfully suggestive inscription and date; outside a slightly indicated landscape and flowers under the lip.

These sauce-boats must have been made while " Dr. John Wall and Mr. William Davis, apothecary," the original inventors and founders, were still managing the factory. It was Dr. Wall who was chiefly concerned in the artistic part of the business, and Davis who was manager of the works.

A toy sauce-boat of Bow porcelain, Swanton, is three and an eighth by two inches; the ornament is of blossom in relief, such as has been identified as made at Bow, by the moulds disinterred on the site of the old works; this specimen is painted in roses in colours.

Another variety of the toy sauce-boats made at Bow justifies the old name of the works as New Canton, its powder-blue decoration having the fine blue tint of the Chinese porcelain; it is three and an eighth inches by two. Like so many of the Bow pieces this sauce-boat is unmarked ; possibly it belonged to a service of which only the most important item was marked. Those pieces painted in blue usually bear the mark of Thomas Frye, who was manager of the works till 1759.

Such fragments of services are interesting as specimens, but they are delightful, because so extremely rare to find a complete dinner-service. Tea-services in miniature we have found in fair number, but antique dinner-services are few and far between. Doubtless they were much

66

less frequently made. The dinner-service which belongs to a member of the author's family is in Leeds—cream ware ornamented with the wheat-ear pattern in black; there are fifty pieces; the soup-tureen measures two and a half inches in height; the vegetable dishes, salad and junket bowls, and salt-cellars are of the characteristic oval form.

We must describe with admiration a toy mug of the very rare Menecy porcelain, Villeroy, in the Department of Seine et Oise. The mug is one inch in height, and measures rather less in diameter; the handle, large in proportion to its size, is unornamented. This is probably one of the early specimens made while the factory was under the directorship of Messrs. Jacques and Julien, who continued the works till 1773. Chaffers tells us "the manufactory was founded by François Barbin in 1735, under the protection and on the estate of the Duc de Villeroy.

The earlier specimens are remarkable for the beauty of the soft paste; the decoration is generally floral and very simple. The general characteristics are similar to those of the productions of the St. Cloud factory. Of these works also we have been lucky in unearthing a toy specimen in the fine collection of Mr. Fitz Henry; but, alas! the specimen is incomplete, being the lid only, silver-mounted, of a little soup-tureen; the fine cream paste ornamented in relief is not decorated with colour. This tiny lid is round and measures one inch in diameter; it is slightly convex, and has a silver knob for a handle as well as a silver outside rim.

A similar covered bowl or soup-tureen of Chantilly porcelain is a perfect specimen, measuring one inch in diameter and an inch in height. It is of the Louis XV. period and decorated in colour in the "Chinese taste"; it has a silver rim and flat pierced handles, with a silver knob on the lid. Chantilly was one of the group of minor factories which sprang up in France, founded by unfaithful artisans from the St. Cloud manufactory. One named Seroux is said to have carried the secret of the paste to Chantilly in 1735, and under the patronage and support of Louis Henri, Prince of Conde, it flourished for a time, being conducted by the brothers Dubois till 1740. Productions were chiefly imitations of Corean porcelain, the paste being soft like that of Menecy, and the decoration very simple and often in blue. The factory ceased to exist at the commencement of the French Revolution.

A toy box, also in Menecy ware, is shaped like a miniature chest of drawers. It is decorated with rosebuds in colour, and is but half an inch high and one inch wide. It is mounted in silver, rims and hinge being of that metal.

Some pretty Dresden china toys and gifts were given by the King and Queen of Saxony to Princess Mary Adelaide, Duchess of Teck, when a little child of ten. She describes them in a letter written at the time, 1844, to the chaplain of the British Embassy at Rome:—" From Hanover we went by railroad to Dresden. It was the first time I had tried it, and I liked it very much. We arrived safely at Dresden after two days' journey. The King and Queen of Saxony live there: they were very kind to mama and me. . . . At Dresden I spent my tenth birthday. The King and Queen heard of it, and gave a party the day before in honour of it. I had a

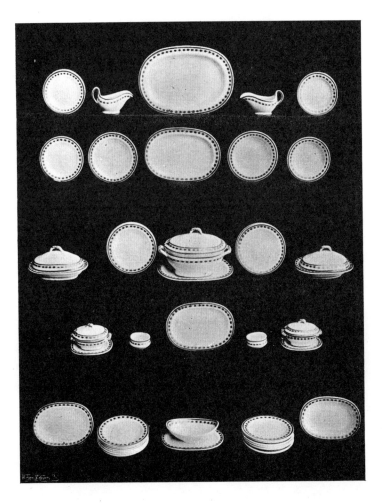

Complete Dinner Service of old Leeds china, with wheatear pattern. There are 50 pieces. The soup tureen measures 3½ in.

Miniature Plate, "A Prize for Sewing Well,"
in brown transfer.   2 in. in diameter.

Doll's Tea Service of white china, decorated with three different pictures of a mother and child.
This service, which is now at Kensington Palace, was used by Queen Victoria.

holiday and enjoyed it much, dined at the Austrian minister's, and drank tea at Prince John's. I received many very pretty presents. The King and Queen also invited us to their grand Christmas, which is kept with lighted trees and presents. To mama they gave two beautiful Dresden figures, and a china inkstand and candlestick, with views of the different places we had seen ; to me they gave a handsome china soup-basin, saucer, and ladle, also a complete band of monkeys in china, besides a doll, an antique necklace, and ear-rings. After we had looked at our presents we plundered the tree, and then played till bed-time."

It is interesting to note that " monkey musicians," painted in colours with gilding, were made at Chelsea also. A specimen of these with the mark, an anchor in red, stands five and a quarter inches in height.

In the Chelsea sale catalogue for 1756 we frequently meet with " Musical figures representing monkeys in different attitudes," or " Monkeys playing on music."

Two tiny tea-services of white china are preserved amongst the toys which belonged to the late Queen Victoria. One is of Lowestoft china in cream colour, ornamented with blue lines and pictures in red ; the subject is always that of a mother and children ; there are four different groups which are repeated. On the saucers one only is used : the cups are two inches in height ; each piece is perfect, with no crack or damage.

There is a smaller service in white china, ornamented with gold lines and landscapes painted in several colours. The coffee-pot and milk-jug are extremely pretty, and stand two and a half inches in height.

Some plates in Leeds ware with blue border stand on

71

a dresser of the Queen's dolls' house. These are two and a half inches in diameter.

One must briefly mention the porcelain playthings, toys rather of adults than of children, which are sometimes to be found in collections. These are the frog mugs which were made at Leeds, Sunderland, Nottingham, and other places, a frog, toad, or lizard being placed at the bottom of the mug ; the reptile, of porcelain like the mug, was usually coloured in a realistic manner. Occasionally a frog mug is to be found with a band or border ornament of pink lustre colour. This indicates that it was made at one of the potteries in the neighbourhood of Newcastle-on-Tyne between 1775 to 1825.

At the beginning of the nineteenth century, glass tumblers apparently full of wine or ale were made, the coloured fluid being placed between two pieces of glass which were sealed with the rim ; the tumbler was filled with water and offered to the victim of the joke. Such rough humour was much appreciated at that time.

The bowls or cups of tantalus nature are of much more ancient date, and we find very early specimens amongst collections of oriental porcelain. A figure in the centre of the bowl conceals the perforations into which the fluid recedes as the bowl is tilted towards the lips of the drinker. A good specimen was recently described in the *Connoisseur*. The cup holds water as though it were the ordinary teacup of commerce, until the surface of the liquid just touches the outstretched hand of the central figure, usually a goddess. Then—and here comes the puzzle—the water slowly subsides till the cup is entirely empty. No, it does not pass through the figure, for the hand has no sooner touched the surface than it subsides to a lower level, leaving no apparent connection between the water and the outstretched arm. The Chinese tell a pretty little story about the goddess who guards against storms and floods, and causes the latter to subside at a touch.

Amongst the ethnographical types in baked clay there is rough pottery from Mexico, which is most elaborately ornamented with painting. Miniature tumblers stand only half an inch high. Some of these are of black painted with yellow and red lines, red painted with blue and black, or green ornamented with red and white. Toy jugs, basins, and other utensils measure but a few inches in height, while the number and variety of animals is endless : pigs, ducks, tortoises—each are painted in one of the bright colours beloved of children, and ornamented with fine lines and geometric designs on the solid colour.

There are many grotesque figures belonging to primitive peoples, some of them in coarse baked clay, but in no case do we consider these the legitimate toys and playthings of children. They are either votive offerings, or fetishes or gods, and though we have frequently seen them classed amongst toys, we cannot find a single indication in support of this classification. On the Gold Coast, W. Africa, in North Africa, on the Niger Coast, near the Gaboon River, in Polynesia, in Queen Charlotte's Island, in Paraguay and Ecuador, such figures occur, but the fact that they are devils, deities, or votive offerings is in our mind undisputed.

CHAPTER IV

DOLLS' HOUSES AND SHOPS.

**Dolls'
Houses
and
Shops.**
THE architecture of dolls' houses always corresponds with great nicety to the prevailing taste of the day in which they were made. In early times single rooms were made, and though there were a few instances when a nobleman or wealthy burgher ordered a complete house, the one-room toys were most frequently produced.

In the seventeenth century one reads of gifts of miniature reception-rooms "the size of a table." These rooms were fitted up with every article of furniture and accessory in use at the time, and generally contained three or more doll occupants dressed in the height of the fashion. They were partly of wax, partly of rag and wool; the hands and feet would probably be of carved wood, and infinite pains were expended in the modelling. Not infrequently the faces resembled some important personage, for the popularity of the little girl and baby doll was not yet, and nearly all of the old dolls which have survived the wear and tear of little fingers are "grown up" dolls.

A historical specimen of a room of this kind was

Nuremburg Kitchen, of the type used as instructive toy for children in Germany in the last century. It contains 148 pieces of wood, porcelain, brass, copper and pewter, and measures 26 in. in width. Belonging to the Author.

Bazaar Stall made by Queen Victoria. The tiny purses, bead bags, shoes, etc., are each perfect in detail.   14 in. long.

Kitchen Dresser, containing china, baskets, copper cake moulds, pewter coffee pots and other useful articles.   From the Germanische Museum, Nuremburg.
12 in. in height.

presented to the Duc de Maine in 1675, and was called the *chambre du sublime.* The room was richly decorated with gilt ornamentation, and contained a bed, a grand sofa, on which was seated a wax model of M. le Duc himself; close to him stood M. de La Rochefoucauld, in whose hand are some verses ; other celebrated men of the day stood round.

There is an interesting specimen of these toys with portrait models in the house of Madame de Sevigne in Paris. Voltaire, represented by a figure nine inches high, is seated at a table on which are all the implements for writing ; the face is well modelled in wax, the hands and feet are of the same material, his cloth clothes fit with great nicety ; the meagre stand, table and chair, however, do not attain to the dignity of a furnished room.

In the seventeenth century Cardinal La Vallette presented to Mlle. de Bourbon, afterwards Duchesse de Longueville, then a child, a doll and a room which was furnished with a bed, chairs, tables, and accessories for the toilet ; different dresses for the doll, including specimens of the elaborate *déshabillés* of the period without which the wardrobe of miladi would have been incomplete, were included in the gift. This beautiful present cost " *deux milles écus.*"

An extremely interesting English room, which is of eighteenth-century make, shows what we still call the. Queen Anne style of window ; whether there were other rooms to be attached to the sides, marks on the wood showing where hinges have been, we do not know. There has undoubtedly been a door which is no longer in its place. The furniture of this toy apartment is extremely interesting. An oak corner-cupboard has

brass candlesticks in it, Chippendale and other chairs
earlier in design are there, and benches for the doll
occupants of the house to rest upon ; a Jacobean table of
the kind known as a "gate table," with flaps to let down
and movable legs, stands in the centre ; a warming-pan
is hung on the wall. On a small round table is a
miniature chocolate service in red and white china; a tray
holds cups, saucers, and jugs. The beauty and accuracy
of make in miniature brass and copper objects, is as
remarkable as in the furniture and in the house itself :
pestle and mortar, but an inch in height, are made
in solid brass ; a tiny copper utensil for holding wood
is *repoussé* in elaborate design ; pierced work appears
in a charcoal holder and in a vessel for heating the
"brandy wine" of the Dutch, which was poured upon
hot raisins.

Of the famous Nuremberg kitchens there are few
specimens known ; these rooms were undoubtedly used
partly as educational toys, that the children, whose chief
occupation in after life would be the overseeing of the
housekeeping and culinary arrangements, might be early
accustomed to the use of the various implements through
their play.

Such rooms are exact models of the kitchen of South
Germany in the seventeenth and eighteenth centuries. We
have in our possession a specimen which might be a copy
to scale of that in Albert Durer's house in Nuremberg,
or of the kitchen belonging to Goethe's mother in
Frankfort, where the poet received the inspiration for the
great kitchen scene in *Faust*—the same wide chimney
reaching almost down to the big open grate ; even the
chicken-coops are there, in which the thrifty German

housewife always kept the next couple of fowls to be killed, that they might be fattened by all the kitchen scraps. These victims, when killed for the table, were at once replaced by another couple.

The completeness in the furnishing of these kitchens is remarkable ; the plates stand in rows, and are numbered in some cases by dozens. The jugs, tankards, drinking-cups are suspended from the shelves in quantities ; every variety of brass, wooden, and pewter pan, saucepan, stewpan, and preserving pan is represented in varying sizes. Strainers, meat-choppers, steak-beaters, ladles, and funnels are there, of every material and shape ; household implements for cleaning, such as mops, brooms, brushes, and whisks, are made in miniature ; and brass and copper warming-pans in *repoussé* work are to be found, besides cake and pudding moulds, spice-tins, candlesticks with snuffers complete, lantern, irons, and toasting-forks.

Shops were also made as toys in the seventeenth and eighteenth centuries. There is one in the Germanisch Museum at Nuremberg, and two at Frankfort ; these are most fascinating toys. A milliner's shop shows a fine display of miniature bonnets of the coal-scuttle shape of that period. Some are of the finest Dunstable straw plait, some of Leghorn, others of crinoline or buckram, and there are several in skeleton condition, of silk-covered wire. Dainty rolls of coloured ribbons, a few centimetres wide, are kept in some of the cardboard boxes which form the shop fittings ; in others, lengths of tulle, net, and hand-made thread laces, for though net was by then made by machinery, lace by the same process was not yet common. Tiny feathers are displayed in some of the glass-covered cases, and a few trimmed hats and bonnets are placed upon stands. A shop-woman stands behind the counter, and a file of bills and quire of wrapping paper testify to her tidy and business-like methods.

A grocer's shop at Nuremberg is completely fitted with jars, bottles, boxes, and miniature tea-chests; on the counter stand the weights and scales, sugar-loaves in their old blue paper wrappings stand in rows, while the shopwoman stands ready behind the counter expectant of purchasers. This attractive old toy measures sixteen and a half inches by nineteen inches.

The earliest doll's house of which we have been able to find an account is one constructed in 1558. An inventory of its furniture and contents was made forty years later. It had three floors: ground floor, first and second; there were four doors in the outside walls; the house was lighted by sixteen windows.

Of early dolls' houses of European origin there are very few in existence which still contain the original furniture and household plenishings. Of these known to us one is in the Bavarian Industrial Museum; five are in the German National Museum at Nuremberg; one in the Art and Industrial Museum at Berlin; one at South Kensington Museum.

Four of these were made in the seventeenth century, the largest and most beautiful probably in the eighteenth century; this measures five feet two and a half inches by five feet exclusive of the pitch of the roof, and is one of those preserved at Nuremberg. We are, fortunately, able to give an illustration of this unique specimen.

On the outside of the house there are strong iron gutters beneath the eaves, the gargoyles rival those of

Five XVIIIth Century Dolls' Houses and Miniature Furniture, in the Germanische Museum, Nuremburg. The largest measures 5½ ft. and was formerly in the possession of the Stromer family. It is sumptuously furnished with carved furniture, needlework hangings, carved silver and ivory candlesticks and other utensils, the walls of the best rooms are panelled in cedar and the floors of parquet.

Front of the "Stromer" Dolls' House at Nuremburg. The balustrade is of carved oak, the gutters, gargoyles and weather vane of lead. For the interior of the house, see opposite page 58.

Voltaire in his Study. XVIIIth Century figure from the Musée Carnavalet. Height of figure 9 in.

Notre Dame in grotesque elaboration, a dormer window
above the door shows some beautifully carved oak, the
bust of a man is at the top, above each attic window is
a brass star, a weather-cock is on each side wing.

Let us ascend in fancy the double flight of steps with
elaborately carved balustrade which leads up to the
panelled front door. We pull the wrought-iron bell
handle, near which the number of the house is painted,
and remove the whole of the outside of the house, which
divides in two halves, leaving each room in the house
displayed to view. There is ground floor, first and
second. The hall is in the centre and has two pillars,
and one sees a garden in the distance with a row of trees,
a summer-house and a fountain ; these are painted on the
farther wall. A curious old lamp and bracket candlestick furnish the artificial light. On the right, a door
leads into the shop or store-room where it was customary
in the seventeenth century, when large houses were almost
entirely self-contained, to buy, not only spices and every
comestible, but also dress materials. A large blue cupboard with side compartment contains the stuffs carefully
sorted in layers ; in the drawers and on a narrow side
table are pots, baskets, barrels, and hampers ; sugar-loaves
are on a shelf, and loaves brown and crisp-looking ; a
bunch of sponges hangs on the wall. A counter runs
down the middle of the room on which weights and scales
a ball of twine, and a till are standing.

On the left of the hall is the stable where two toy
chestnut horses stand feeding at their manger. The coachman, four inches high, is wheeling a barrow up to the
food-bin ; other stable accessories lie about ; a stable lantern
hangs from the ceiling. Through an open door one sees

into the coachman's bedroom, in which a bed, a table, with tools and baskets, are placed.

A narrow flight of stairs, a facsimile of the staircases to be seen in the old Nuremberg houses to-day, leads from the hall to the first floor; the landing has in it a spinning-wheel, a broom, and a miniature mangle. To the right we pass through (or should do if we were a doll) a door to the drawing-room, which has in it a fine green-tiled stove; tiny ornaments of men and animals are set upon the cornice. In the centre of the room is a round oak table; two small console tables are on each side of a painted panel; the chairs, of which there are six, are square in shape, reminding one of the Jacobean shape in England; they are upholstered in red plush; on one a finely-dressed lady doll is seated; her work basket is standing near with tiny reels of cotton, buttons, and tape; flowers are arranged in vases, and are also growing in pots in the windows. A fine pewter coffee-set is on a well-made stand, and a pewter bread-crock stands by.

Not only does the room contain all these useful and ornamental objects, but the decorations are perfect. The floor is of polished oak, the walls panelled in oak; a frieze rail or shelf supports tiny oriental vases; pictures and looking-glasses hang against the panelling; a daintily carved bracket in ivory holds ornaments and extra cups and saucers. A graceful glass chandelier is hung from the oak ceiling; the pendant crystal drops are most realistic. A clock stands on a side table, and a miniature silver watch hangs on a nail on the wall.

From this detailed description it will be seen that there is a value in old dolls' houses which new ones can never have; not only are we enabled to see the intimate

84

domestic life of the day, to peep, as it were, into the family menage, and see the people as they lived, but the miniature surroundings themselves are of great value, for all are made well and durable, in the most suitable materials, however costly. The rooms show the finest workmanship in panelling, carving, and ceiling decoration ; paintings hang upon the wall ; in some cases tapestry hangings are used. Real silver utensils, carvings of ivory, inlay of mother-o'-pearl are there, while the furniture is frequently of great intrinsic value. Such a house as we describe would have cost 1000 gulden to make and furnish ; its value now is enormous. Some of those at Nuremberg belong to the Museum, others are kept there by their owners.

A fine house measuring 4 ft. 9 in. by 4 ft. has twelve rooms, besides a spacious entrance hall and two landings ; this is dated 1639. It has pillared rooms and painted ceilings ; on the top floor is a bedroom containing, besides the bed and wash-stand, a spacious cupboard containing rolls of linen ; a brass chandelier of early sixteenth-century workmanship hangs from the ceiling ; another bedroom contains a tiny four-fold screen, a cradle and chest of drawers well and solidly made. This room also has a brass chandelier, and there is a wooden nursery stand for teaching a child to walk. A third room must be called a bed-sitting-room, for its plenishings are much more ornamental. On the table is a tiny chess-board, draughts, playing-cards half an inch square, and a basket made of the finest bead-work ; a stone clock stands on the chimney-piece ; pictures hang on the walls above the panelling. A passage-room contains a linen-press with piles of sheets, serviettes, and towels in bundles tied up with coloured ribbons ; in this room there is a rocking-horse two and a half inches high, a bird-cage, and a chair. The kitchen comes next, as we descend ; it is filled with the usual liberal complement of pots, pans, dishes, plates, cups and pots of brass, copper, pewter and earthenware, a rolling-pin, and a blackboard on which a list of the kinds of food in season each month appeal to the practical housekeeping mind.

The ground floor of this commodious family residence is divided into eight rooms, of which one is the larder, three are servants' bedrooms, one a cowshed, beer-cellar, store-room, shop or counting-house, and the last a well-equipped dairy. From our illustration it will be seen that nothing is left to the imagination ; the fortunate small owners did not have to " pretend " ; the cows even are there, the barrels and taps in the cellar, the plates and delft jars in the larder, the pans, cheese-press, and churn in the dairy,—all are in their places.

After this " patrician house," it is interesting to turn to a doll's house of the same period, which is the model of an artisan's dwelling. Though the building, furniture, and fittings are all on a more modest scale, they are of the perfect workmanship which characterises all the dolls' houses made in the Low Countries in the seventeenth century. Unfortunately the two houses are not side by side ; in fact hundreds of miles separate them, but our descriptions may be compared.

The artisan's house, which is dated 1673, measures 36 ins. by 36 ins., and is 18 ins. deep. It is divided into four rooms only, and has no entrance-hall or landings ; the staircase is placed against the kitchen wall. The seven windows are latticed, thin sheets of talc being

Doll's House, showing artisan's dwelling in Germany,
of the XVIIth Century.   36 in. in height, dated 1673.

Interior of above Doll's House, showing four completely furnished rooms.
Pewter plates are in the kitchen racks, pots, pans, kettles, milk pails, strainers,
knives, and every other household requirement, even domestic animals, are in
the kitchen, and stocks of clean clothes in the presses.

Japanese Doll's House, with all household plenishings complete.

The Doll's House of Queen Victoria, now at Kensington Palace.

carefully divided with leaded squares. There are also three open attic windows; the centre one resembles the door of a warehouse—this curious survival of the combination of dwelling-house and warehouse having been left in the domestic architecture both of the Netherlands and Holland.

There is one bedroom, kitchen, scullery, and sitting-room. The painted wardrobe in the bedroom is a curious reminder of the painted furniture of old Austria and Bavaria; in this room also is a baby's high chair, the only one we remember to have seen in miniature. There is the usual porcelain stove in the sitting-room, but it is extremely plain, as befits the rank of the occupant of the house. On the outside window ledges there are flower-pots in some of the windows.

With regard to the dolls' houses of other countries, many were made in Paris in the eighteenth and early nineteenth centuries, and in other parts, chiefly in the Departments of Seine et Oise, Moselle, and the Haute Rhine. This, it must be understood, was in the days when such toys were beginning to be made as articles of commerce, and not only as special orders when the finest workmanship alone would be employed. Now, we need hardly say that they are "turned out" by thousands, very pretty and complete they are, but as works of art or examples of fine workmanship in miniature, they need not be discussed.

In the middle of the nineteenth century in England there were houses "finished and unfinished, for dolls of all stations of life. Suburban tenements for dolls of moderate means; kitchens and single apartments for dolls of the lower classes; capital town residences for dolls of high estate. Some of these establishments were already

furnished according to estimate, with a view to the convenience of dolls of limited income ; others could be
fitted on the most expensive scale, at a moment's notice,
from whole shelves of chairs and tables, sofas, bedsteads,
and upholstery."

Such were the dolls' houses and furniture of Dickens'
time.

Fine examples of French and German Dolls' House Furniture, which includes elaborately carved bureaux, inlaid chests, upholstered chairs, and caskets of needlework. From the Bayeresches National Museum at Munich.

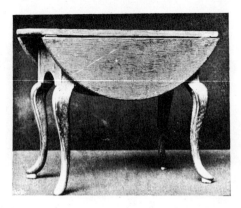

Oak Table, with two flaps, 7½ in., belonging
to a dolls' room of Queen Anne period.

Rosewood Bureau, with drawers and pigeon holes,
fine brass escutcheons. 13 in. high.

Marqueterie Corner Cupboard
fitted with 4 shelves. 8 in. wide

CHAPTER V

DOLL'S HOUSE AND MINIATURE FURNITURE.
BRASS.   COPPER.

WE have described much of the furniture and fittings **Doll's**
in our story of the dolls' houses of old times, but our **House**
subject would be incomplete if we omitted to mention **and**
those fine miniature specimens, many of which have **Miniature**
Furni-
undoubtedly been played with as children's toys, but **ture.**
which are too large for use in the rooms of dolls' houses. **Brass.**

So subtle is the distinction that it is extremely **Copper.**
difficult to differentiate between actual toy furniture
and small pieces of model furniture, which have been
made by skilful workmen in their leisure hours or as a
tour de force.   Such pieces are rare, but they are to be
found in every style and date ; we have even seen a
bureau in the remarkable Italian inlaid work of the
sixteenth century.   It stands seven and a half inches
high, the ebony and ivory inlay being used with extraordinary skill.

A marqueterie corner-cupboard of Dutch make also
shows inlaying of fine quality ; there are four shelves ; the
width of the door is eight inches.

93

Doll's
House
and
Miniature
Furni-
ture.
Brass.
Copper.

Another miniature bureau is in red lacquer of the Louis XIV. period ; it stands ten inches in height, and is ornamented in black and gold, the pseudo-oriental figures showing that this unique specimen belongs to that period when the Chinese wave of decoration was tingeing all the artistic productions of the day.

A talboy chest of drawers, of miniature size, is inlaid with satin-wood ; it is nine inches broad, and the pretty brass handles have been made to scale for the piece.

A very fine wardrobe of rosewood, carved and inlaid, is also in the possession of Mr. FitzHenry ; unfortunately the lower part of the side ornaments are missing ; the ten diminutive drawers are finely shaped at the sides to follow the curves of the wardrobe, and the larger drawers at the top and bottom are also shaped ; the handles and escutcheon are of brass and the cupboard is lined with old wall-paper of a pretty rosebud design, evidently of a make contemporary with the piece.

A beautiful English bureau with three drawers and sloping top, which lifts down to form a writing-desk, is of oak ; the four brass escutcheons are particularly finely carved ; there are Liliputian brass knobs for the drawer handles, and these are also on the wooden rests, which can be drawn out to support the desk flap, when it is let down.

An English bureau with one drawer stands seven inches in height and has drop handles in fine brass work. Another specimen of this kind of furniture is much more elaborate ; it is, in fact, the most highly decorated of any piece in miniature that we have seen ; it is carved as well as inlaid, and is probably Dutch ; the feet are of the claw and ball type, the sides finely curved ; there is carving on

94

Rosewood Wardrobe, finely inlaid. The shaped side drawers have brass handles; the lining of the cupboard is an old Rose Bud Wall Paper of contemporary make. 14 in. high.

ireau with brass handles and escutcheons. 7 in. high. the fine examples of Miniature Furniture on this page are the property of Mr. Fitzhenry.

Rosewood Tall Boy Chest of Drawers, inlaid with satinwood, handles of brass. 9 in. high.

Writing Table, veneered with kingwood and other woods. 9 in. high.
Ivory handles. Second Half of XVIIIth Century.

Miniature Chest of Drawers of XVIIIth Century, straw work with brass drop handles.
8½ in. The Toilet Glass of the same date is framed in green lacquer, and has three
drawers beneath. All the examples on this page are at South Kensington Museum.

the lower ornament; on the lid, which lets down for writing, there is marqueterie inlay work in several different kinds of wood. The forms of the design are floral, and birds which are amongst the flowers have mother-o'-pearl inlaid beaks. The brass handles and keyholes are well carved and designed. A looking-glass in an eighteenth century doll's house is of green lacquer ; it is eight and a half inches high, and has three drawers which open beneath the swinging glass ; the lacquer is painted in black and gold oriental patterns, and is of English make.

Another interesting toilet glass that we know of, is more fully described in our chapter on old silver toys. In this the glass is separate, the drawers open, and a tray also of silver and a tiny brush belong to this dainty toilet table ; a brush, not of the shape we now use for brushing the hair, but for brushing the powder out of the hair in the days when dolls and ladies " wore powder," is included in the set.

The chest of drawers which supports the green lacquer glass is of straw work ; it has the daintiest little drop handles of brass imaginable.

A very fine writing-table, veneered with King wood and other woods, is also in miniature ; it belongs to the second half of the eighteenth century, and is French, Louis XV. period ; its handles on the drawers, which are four in number, are of ivory. An oak table of the Jacobean period comes from a doll's house made in the seventeenth century ; its legs, made moveable in order to support the flaps at the side, are cabriole in shape ; this beautifully made simple specimen is seven and a half inches in diameter.

Doll's House and Miniature Furniture. Brass. Copper.

M. Bernard has, in Paris, a very remarkable collection of miniature *chefs-d'œuvre* in furniture, chairs of Louis XV. design, beds, above which finely carved cupids hold up the velvet and silken embroidered draperies, commodes

GROUP OF OLD DOLLS' HOUSE FURNITURE.
From the Bernard Collection.

of Louis XVI. whose inlaying is of the type which stamps them as "museum specimens." Empire furniture whose bronze gilt ornaments are of exquisite design and workmanship, miniature spinning-wheels, silk winders, Louis screens, Spanish leather-covered seats, and richly framed miniature mirrors — all show that no time and labour were spared in making these very beautiful specimens of the designer's, carver's, gilder's, and upholsterer's arts.

A remarkable set of dolls' furniture of the Empire period is in existence ; not only is the wood finely shaped and modelled in the Empire style, which suggests the Greek lines, but the gilt bronzes which ornament the pieces are made in a delicate and perfect manner, as finely as those for any full-sized example of the much prized furniture of this period. The console tables are delicately finished with the mirrors which usually accompany them, the bureau is ornamented with gilt bronze of bay-leaf design in Liliputian proportions, the clock is encircled with flowers supported on Doric columns ; a second clock, of lyre shape, stands on a bracket ; the chairs are of wood, upholstered and inlaid with brass, and the sofa has the correctly curved ends

OLD DOLL AND DOLLS' FURNITURE.
In the Bernard Collection.

which we are accustomed to associate with the *salon* of Madame Racamier.

Furniture of the Directoire period is equally correct in style, but less elaborately carried out, in that the

99

Doll's
House
and
Miniature
Furni-
ture.
Brass.
Copper.

real bronzes, which are such a remarkable feature of the Empire specimens, are represented only by gold paint.

Occasionally we come across simple specimens of dolls' furniture made of cardboard, the hinges, keyholes, and other details indicated by paint or in gilt paper, but on account of the fragility of such specimens they are not so often met with ; the more elaborate furniture of wood has stood the wear and tear of little fingers and of time better than those of card. We are fortunate in being able to give pictures of some of the finest miniature furniture which has ever been shown, and it may interest collectors to know that such pieces fetch prices very little below the cost of furniture of the same period, in full size.

At Munich there are some very beautiful specimens of French gilt-carving and needlework combined, some chests of drawers, whose curved lines and fine carving proclaim them to be of the early eighteenth century ; these measure about ten inches in height ; the embroidery in colours is done on pale-tinted satin and gives a very rich effect. Occasionally this needlework is to be found on rich silk velvet in gold or silver thread, and made up into tiny chair-seats, caskets, or miniature dower-chests. A very remarkable specimen of a doll's house console table is also at Munich, in which realism is carried so far as to show a marble top ; of stools, chairs, and lounges there are many specimens, some of the carved and gilt style, others on the more sober Dutch and English lines, when polished mahogany or oak is used with good effect.

Dressers, cabinets, and cupboards are occasionally to be seen ; a good specimen in painted wood is illustrated in our chapter on china. These were evidently made as separate pieces and belonged to no doll's house set or

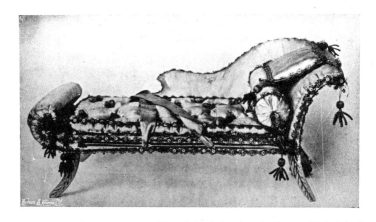

Toy Sofa, belonging to Queen Victoria, of
painted wood, upholstered in satin. 20 in.
long. Now at Kensington Palace.

Writing Bureau of the First Empire, of
glass, with gilt ornamentation.

ble, Stool, and painted Wardrobe. 7½ in.   From a Dolls' House representing the dwelling of a
ver middle class family of the XVIIth Century.   Made at Nuremburg.   Now at South
Kensington.

Fine Brass and Copper Vessels of domestic utility, from
Nuremburg Dolls' Kitchen of the XVIIth Century. The large
is 4½ in. in height. There is fine repoussé ornament on some
of these specimens.

Kitchen Dresser, 8 in. in height, with China
Jugs and Dinner Service.

Miniature Kitchen Utensils of Bronze. The largest measures 1⅛ in. in height. They
are amongst the toys in the Egyptian Antiquities Section of the British Museum.

suite. Sets of five or more shelves, too, are to be seen at
Munich. These generally measure eight to nine inches in
height, and are very dainty when set out with pots, pans,
and platters. Churns, stable-fittings, linen-presses, barrels,
spinning-wheels, and other household plenishings, interesting from their accuracy and shape, but of less intrinsic
value, may also be studied at Munich.

Of the toys in brass and copper there is a very
large variety amongst old specimens, for the household
implements and plenishings in the old dolls' houses were
largely made in these metals, and have been touched upon
in our chapter on that subject. There is no better way
of gauging the thoroughness and genuine methods in the
making of old toys than in examining specimens of this
special class. The solid brass pestle and mortars reveal
that here was no shoddy manufacture ; " anything will
do for the children to play with," was not one of the
sentiments of the sixteenth, seventeenth, and eighteenth
centuries. A mortar in the possession of the author,
though but one and a half inches in height, has quite
considerable weight ; it is of solid metal, beaten brass.

Brass candlesticks are to be seen in most old dolls'
houses ; whether tiny tapers were ever fixed in them we
do not know ; probably " let's pretend " was used as a
precaution in place of a too dangerous realism. We have
seen tiny wax candles in a miniature crystal hanging
chandelier of the eighteenth century, but never one in a
brass candlestick. An English grate with three bars in
front and comfortable " hobs " measures two and a quarter
inches in height, and has as solid an iron back and side
pieces, as if a hot coal fire was to burn in it constantly ;
doubtless some little housekeeper in embryo has learned

Doll's
House
and
Miniature
Furni-
ture.
Brass.
Copper.

to polish a grate on this little specimen, that one day she might overlook her own maids, and know when they performed their duties thoroughly.

Saucepans of copper and brass appear in every Nuremberg kitchen, not only because they were of the best, but because our latter day enamel pans had not yet been thought of; brass weights and scales, bird-cages, jugs, kettles, gravy-ladles, strainers, and pots are also to be seen. Of the copper pierced and *repoussé* work of the seventeenth and eighteenth centuries there are many beautiful miniature specimens; a warming-pan with a simple dotted pattern, with five holes, is in a seventeenth-century doll's house; it is mounted on a wooden handle painted in black and red.

A coffee-pot in the same well-furnished establishment has an ebony handle and stands two inches in height. A beautiful little receptacle for holding wood is ornamented in a rope design in *repoussé*; bands of an elaborate design of interlacing lines are also used, and a rose pattern is above the lid. A brazier evidently belongs to the same set, as it is similarly ornamented. A box with pendant ring handles measures two inches in height, and also has the rope *repoussé* pattern; it has a well-fitting lid of much rounded form.

A pierced dish on a pedestal also has the pendant ring handles; all these interesting specimens belong to the same doll's house of seventeenth-century make.

In some of the Nuremberg kitchens, cake, jelly, and pudding moulds are of brass—more often, however, they are of pewter. We have seen tiny shell moulds of brass and tiny tins of the same metal; each of these small objects has its ring fixed on to the side, so that it

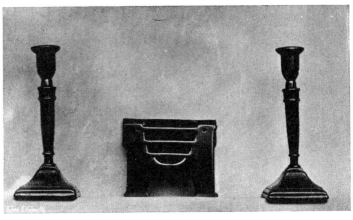

Brass Candlesticks and Brass Grate. From an XVIIIth Century Doll's
House.   3½ in.

ature Brass Candle-
ick and Snuffers.
2½ in.

per Kettle and Coffee Pot, Sweeping Broom, Mop, Warming Pan with pierced brass
d and hinged lid, Brush and Steak Beater.   Part of the kitchen equipment of a well-
furnished Doll's House of the XVIIth Century.

Elaborately wrought Lantern of Brass. 4½ in.
At the Germanische Museum, Nuremburg.
Beer Mug with Cover.

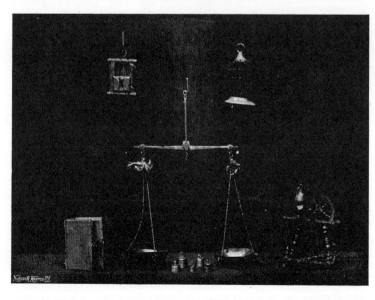

Scales and Weights of Brass, Miniature Book, Spinning Wheel, Bird-cage
and Mouse-trap. 1½ in. From South Kensington Museum.

may hang in its place on a wall or cupboard when not in use.

We have also seen, in brass and copper, rings of a dozen or more various spoons, knives, forks, choppers, hammer, and other small implements for kitchen use, such as are shown in an illustration in our chapter on silver.

Amongst the accessories of the kitchen we must not omit to mention the beautiful little specimens of miniature baskets occasionally to be met with. That these were made by skilled workmen there is not a doubt ; the flat baskets used for bread on the Continent are seen in the kitchens, large deep baskets are in the shops, sometimes measuring three inches in depth. Tiny work-baskets are on the tables of the *salons,* for holding the needlework of madame ; a string of baskets of Liliputian size we have found in a shop. The greatest variety of miniature baskets are, however, to be seen in the nativity and market groups of Naples ; here each kind of vegetable and fruit on the greengrocer's stalls in the market has its special basket ; wee hampers of vegetables stand by the side. The old pointed pottle used for strawberries is there, miniature punnets of chip and crates of osier wands. Miniature figures of women selling butter, eggs, and poultry have their baskets in proportion ; two good specimens of these are to be seen in the chapter on dolls.

CHAPTER VI

SILVER AND PEWTER TOYS.

Silver and
Pewter
Toys.
THE interest in the study of old silver toys, apart from the pleasure in their great beauty, lies in the fact that they are frequently faithful copies in miniature of those objects, which played a part in the ordinary everyday life of adults, so that they not infrequently throw a light on the use of an object whose association with the intimate home-life of a past century has become obscure ; moreover, they were made by the same worker who fashioned the larger objects. It is for this reason that we find specimens of silver toys in all the finest public and private collections of antique silver in Europe. Later we give a list of some of the best known examples at Stuttgart, Nuremberg, at the Ducal museums at Gotha, Anhalt, at St. Petersburg, and in other European collections.

In the Middle Ages the toy-maker, who made only toys, did not exist, for the modern tendency towards specialising had not arisen ; the silversmith who made a large silver sconce in the seventeenth century would probably make a replica of it in miniature to be sold as

Silver Bells and Coral Gumstick.
French (Louis XV.). From the Fitzhenry Collection.

XVIIIth Century Rush Bottom Chairs, reproduced in Silver. $5\frac{1}{2}$ in.
From a Dolls' House in the possession of Miss Swinburne.

Ring, 1½ in. in diameter, on which is hung 17 Kitchen Utensils, including steak beater, grater and funnel.   Tea and Coffee Set and Flower Pot.

Toilet Table of Silver with rope patterned edge.   4½ in.   Glass framed in silver, and powdering brush.   Of the same period (XVIIIth Century) is the silver Stove, Shovel and Frying Pan with silver Fish.   All these dolls' house furnishings belong to the Ashburnham family.

a toy; now all the silver toys are made by particular "houses" who specialise in this kind of work and em- ploy men who never make full-sized articles. At Furth, in Bavaria, and near Frankfort, quantities of the modern silver toys are made, sufficiently pretty in themselves to sell readily to that large class of the uninitiated who are satisfied with mere prettiness; mercifully so, for, if all were connoisseurs, there would never be enough of the genuine antiques to go round. By all means let us have replicas, duly acknowledged as such, made by skilled workmen, and place the originals safely in museums and in the cabinets of collectors.

Besides the twentieth-century "antique" silver toys of German and English make, there are others, cleverly made after models of "native" manufacture, so that in Ceylon and India, travellers are able to buy Shivas and sacred bullocks of Bavarian and English workmanship; in China and Japan, the most correctly made Buddhas and rickshas; in Paris, Louis XV. toys straight from Furth, which are charming in their delicacy of design, but in that only, are connected with the Louis period.

The collecting of antique silver has perhaps a higher educational value than that of any other art object, for in the imperishable material not only the workmanship of a period becomes familiar, but by means of dated specimens the gradual development of a style or ornament may be traced. The English and continental system of hall-marking silver enables us to use old silver-work as a key in dating other objects which are known to have been made at the same time, but which, without the accuracy of hall-marking, would only be assigned to a certain period or art epoch in a general way.

111

Silver and Pewter Toys. To the child mind a sequence in art history is most important. Show a child a "grown up" silver toilet-service, such as that to be seen at Knole Park, which is associated with the visit of King James ; tell her the story of his visit ; then give the little one a miniature silver puff-box (probably made in Bavaria or Manchester) for her doll's house, letting her know that it is a copy, and on her next birthday a tiny ewer and basin, and you will have given the child a lesson in collecting with understanding which will "go home" at that impressionable age ; she will never forget that the silver toilet-service is associated with the Stuarts in England, and will thus have acquired at any rate one correct fact with regard to the history of old silver, for silver toy services for the toilet were first made at this time when the growth of luxury demanded more costly accessories for domestic use. Their appearance coincided with the wave of Chinese and pseudo-oriental ornament, which implanted feathered and kilted Indian figures even in the needle point lace of the time.

Silver - framed mirrors, boxes for trinkets, tazza, receptacles for soap, powder, unguents, and sometimes basins and ewers, were made. These form the daintiest models imaginable in miniature, and on account of their minute size are by no means costly when purchased in reproduction.

Silver tables (not in the modern sense of the word, a table on which specimens of the silversmith's art lie at the mercy of the burglar, baby, dog, or any other destructive agency, but veritably tables made of, or rather overlaid with silver plates) were making their appearance at the time of Charles II.; the specimens in the possession of

112

Lord Sackville are of wood mounted with silver plaques. **Pedigree**
Other furniture is frequently to be found in miniature **Silver**
silver collections. **Toys.**

A most interesting toilet-table of silver is in the
possession of Miss Swinburn ; it measures four and a half
inches by three and a half ; round the edge is a design
of twisted rope pattern ; small galleries for holding candlesticks are fixed at each corner. This fine specimen of
English-made miniature silver is a small replica of one
made in the eighteenth century for Mrs. Crowly of
Barking Hall, Needham Market, Suffolk. A looking-glass
framed in silver stands on the little table, a tray is also
en suite, and a tiny powdering brush for the hair makes
the toy daintily complete. The set has a long and
authentic pedigree ; it was given by the original owner to
her granddaughter Lady Elizabeth Ashburnham, daughter
of John third Earl of Ashburnham. By her it was
bequeathed to Miss Swinburn, niece of Lady Jane
Ashburnham and Admiral Charles H. Swinburn, in
whose possession it now is.

Belonging to the same set, and made at the same time,
is a silver fireplace ornamented with *repoussé* work and
a pierced design. A shovel and gridiron, with a silver
fish in process of cooking, goes with the grate.

Two silver chairs of the straight-backed pattern, with
rush-bottomed seats, are also reproduced in silver. The
collection is also enriched by good antique specimens of
a miniature bureau or chest of drawers with wheat-ear
pattern, keyholes and handles chased. On a ring, but
one and a half inches in diameter, hang no fewer than
seventeen different kitchen implements in silver, including
frying-pan, nippers, chopper, strainer, spade, shovel, knife,

funnel, grater, and short handled scoop. These dainty little articles, finished and modelled with the utmost delicacy, are but an inch in length.

Of the silver toys in the FitzHenry collection the silver fire-dog is one of the earliest. These first appeared in silver at the end of the Stuart period. The single specimen in the same collection, measuring only two and a half inches, might be mistaken for a centre-piece or table ornament, did we not know that its full-sized prototypes are to be found at Windsor Castle and at Knole Park. A reproduction in facsimile of the latter specimen is at South Kensington Museum.

The great number of toys and miniature articles of utility to be found of the seventeenth and eighteenth centuries is accounted for by the magnificence of the revival in costly objects which took place at that time. They had already filled the palaces and villas of the merchant princes of Italy, and were spreading all over the north of Europe. Artists trained in the gold and silversmiths' arts were migrating to other capitals. The enormous quantities of precious metals coming into Spain from Mexico induced many who would have been content with humbler metals to use silver and gold for articles of household utility. In the northern beer-drinking countries toy tankards are found with handle, purchase, and hinges complete, showing that miniatures of these articles of everyday use were made in the precious metals. In several collections are the very artistic and beautiful hanging candelabra of the late sixteenth and early seventeenth-century pattern. One of this period measures four inches in diameter; a large globe of silver forms the centre ornament, round which hang branches of graceful

114

Dutch Cabinet of the XVIIIth
Century, reproduced in Silver.
7½ in.

Silver Chandelier, 4½ in. in diameter, Jam Jar lined with miniature blue
glass, Coffee Pot, Fire Dog, Casket and Tea Pot fitted with ivory
handle. All these objects belong to Mr. Fitzhenry.

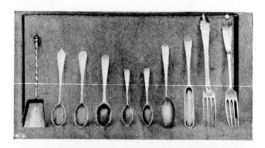

Toy Jam, Tea, and Marrow Spoons and Forks.
1¼ in.   Belonging to Mr. Fitzhenry.

Dolls' Plates of Pewter, belonging to a service in the
Industrial Museum, Nuremburg. 1¼ in. in diameter.

Fine Silver. Chandelier with a canthus ornamen-
tation. 4½ in. Candlesticks, Covered Vases,
Brandy Heater, Pierced Fruit Dish, and Coffee
Pot. All belonging to the Fitzhenry collection.

design terminating with the candle-holder. There are no separate fittings for the candles in this specimen; the holder is made in one piece. Another of rather later date measures five and a half inches; the central sphere has holes pierced in it at the top, and ornaments of acanthus leaf beneath.

In the seventeenth century silver toys were in very general use amongst the children of the wealthy. Whole services were ordered for special occasions; complete house furnishings were made as well as single pieces, which were sold separately. Not only was the furniture of the *salon*, the toilet, the nursery, and the kitchen reproduced, but horses, carriages, chariots, cabriolets, sledges, and trucks in miniature, though not always as children's toys, but simply as trinkets and cabinet specimens. Men and women daintily carved in silver were also made that the games of the children should want nothing in their realism. Cavaliers and richly-dressed dames ride in the carriages, men and women ride on horseback, valets attend their masters, and chamber-women their mistresses; milk-sellers, street-criers, porters with merchandise, sturdy sellers at the boothlike shops, ragged beggars, cripples with crutches, and half-clad ragamuffins, were all alike subjects for the makers of silver toys. Falcons dressed in their hoods and jesses, falconers holding the birds on gloved hands, hounds and lap-dogs, parrots, monkeys, and pigs—all are to be found, and as they were made by the same gold and silversmiths who worked on larger pieces, these toys often bear the initials of a well-known artist of the period.

There is an example of the work of Peter Winter in the Industrial Museum at Nuremberg; it is a very beautiful miniature box engraved with flowers and festoons ; this specimen of the master's work, which is dated 1702, is mentioned in *Der Goldschmiede Merkzeichen* by Dr. Marc-Rosenberg.

A large proportion of the silver toy-making was done in Holland, but special orders were carried out in Paris, London, Frankfort, and other centres of the silversmith's craft.

" Silver toys of the Queen Anne period and later," says the late Mr. Cripps, in whose work on *Old English Plate* several interesting toys are mentioned, " are common in England and still more in Holland throughout the eighteenth century." We may date their first appearance at about the end of the seventeenth century, though it is more likely we should be right in speaking of two centuries as the length of time before such small objects become lost or destroyed, for it is highly probable that articles were made in miniature after the models of the larger pieces in times much more remote than 1690. That is the date of a circular toy teapot, which measures two and a quarter inches including handle and spout. When we consider that tea was not introduced into England until 1664, that with the first chests of tea came small porcelain teapots in which it was to be brewed, and for the first decade of tea-drinking in England only earthenware teapots were used, it will be realised that this toy teapot, as one of the first metal teapots made, is a remarkably interesting specimen. The maker's mark on it is G. M. with a crescent beneath. A teacup or small basin belongs to the same set ; this measures one and one-eighth inches in diameter ; also a miniature cake-dish or tray which has a central foot ; a flat-handled spoon, two inches long, com-

Fine set of eighteenth-century ivory knives and spoons, wooden salt cellars shown on 7½ in. oak flap table.

pletes the set. This spoon has a handle which becomes The First Toy Teaspoon. broad at the extremity which is divided by two indentations into three points, slightly resembling the cleft in a hind's foot; hence the name given to this pattern by French connoisseurs : *pied de biche*. The bowl is round and elliptical ; such spoons were made until the time of George the First, but, during the later period of their manufacture, were slightly altered in shape, the outer points of the handle being omitted, so that the handle narrowed to the blunt point, thus losing much of the original characteristic shape of the spoon.

Though toy, as distinct from snuff, spoons are not uncommon, and the first teaspoon known, dated 1689, is a toy one, we are not aware of the existence of an early apostle spoon in miniature. These specially decorated spoons, which are rare before the sixteenth century, were made in large quantities during a century and a half afterwards, and as they were the most popular christening gift of the period, it would not have been surprising if some original or economically minded sponsor had made the present in miniature, or had caused a miniature replica to be made for the tiny recipient. If a silver spoon were given, the patron saint of the donor, or the name saint of the child, was frequently chosen to ornament the handle of the spoon.

All forks are of comparatively modern use, the earlier ones which came from Italy being made of steel and almost invariably two-pronged. There are toy forks of this pattern with silver handles ; the knives also with silver handles are of the shape with curved back, which we now generally use for the carving of fish. The oldest silver forks known are the three-pronged ones with flat plain

121

handle of 1667, which are at Cotehele, Cornwall; four-pronged forks were first made in 1726; specimens of miniature size are very much rarer than spoons.

A toy chocolate pot is known, in the lid of which is a hole to admit the stirring rod; this interesting piece is dated 1708.

Toy candlesticks of silver are frequently to be met with, more usually of the type which has a simple baluster stem and square base than those with fluted columns which are the earlier pattern. The Corinthian column towards the end of the eighteenth century, which was the first to have movable socket pans, does not afford a specimen in miniature that we know of. Possibly it was not considered necessary to make the separate pans for the tiny toy tapers; perhaps these minute adjuncts have been lost.

Of the rarer sconces which are seen in such variety and beauty at Knole Park in the King James I. room, there is a beautiful toy specimen by Anthony Nelme; it bears no date letter, but is spoken of as his work in " English plate." It bears the arms of the Russell family on the back plate in a lozenge. Perhaps it was made for the doll's house of some little girl of that family, so that by the laws of heraldry her arms are on a lozenge rather than a shield.

In 1576 an order was given by the daughter of Henry II. of France for a little silver toy set, composed of buffet pots, plates, bowls, and other vessels for the domestic menage, " such as they make in Paris," to be sent to the new-born child of the Duchess of Bavaria. Toys of great value are mentioned in the time of Henri IV. of France; a doll's set of table plenishings of silver set with diamonds figure in the accounts of his mother.   An interesting toy, once in the possession of the little son of Napoleon I., the King of Rome, is now in the Museum of Artillery in Paris ; it is a toy cannon and gun-carriage of ivory drawn by ivory horses with gold harness, which is encrusted with garnets and turquoise.

Some silver toy soldiers—now, alas, no longer existing ! —were made at the end of the seventeenth century for the Dauphin.   These succeeded a still older army which was made of cardboard by Henri de Gissey, who was designer of the King's ballets in 1670.   There is an old account in which a toy army is put down for payment : twenty squadrons of cavalry, ten battalions of infantry of cardboard, finely painted for His Majesty the King to give to Monseigneur le Dauphin ; the cost is 6000 francs.

Later the more durable army was made for the Dauphin, of silver, by Merlin the silversmith, after models executed by Chassel de Nancy.   In this costly little army, not only were cavalry and infantry represented, but various machines of war.   It is interesting to know that these little soldiers were, later on, melted down to provide armies of flesh and blood for the King's wars.   The reign of Louis XIV. was a time of great commercial activity amongst the artists and silversmiths ; the love of things beautiful, costly, and magnificent became almost overwhelming in its ostentation.   Colbert, to ensure good training for the artists, lodged gold and silversmiths at the Louvre.   Balm and Delaunay were the most skilful artists of the time ; Vincent Petit and Julien Defontaine were renowned for their works of art in precious metals ; it is calamitous that nearly all the

123

Silver and Pewter Toys. product of this group of splendid artistic genius went to the melting-pot with the poor little silver soldiers of the Dauphin. The silver produced three millions of francs ; it had cost ten millions ; its artistic workmanship is lost to us for ever, though the King ordered drawings to be made of the finest pieces, before they were melted.

Pewter vessels and platters were also made as replicas of the silver sent to the King's melting-pot at the time of royal necessity. Pewter is sometimes used in making toys. Many of the pots, tankards, mugs, cups, basins, and platters which appeared in silver in the seventeenth and eighteenth centuries we have also seen in miniature pewter ; the specimens are, however, rarer than those of the more precious metal, probably because their smaller value has caused them to be less well looked after, for when a little pewter dish was misplaced or mislaid the same anxiety for its recovery would not be felt. Very complete sets of pewter articles are sometimes found in very old dolls' houses. An artisan's dwelling, modelled on those at Nuremberg of the seventeenth century and contemporary with that time, shows rows of pewter dishes and plates, while pitchers and drinking vessels hang from the hooks. In the Nuremberg kitchens of the same period very complete sets of plates and dishes are found, each piece being usually marked with the maker's cypher. A beautifully made coffee equipage and table is in an eighteenth-century doll's house at Nuremberg ; the table measures five and a half inches in diameter, the cups half an inch.

Of silver toys in well-known European collections the following are some examples :—

A small box ornamented with flowers and foliage, height four centimetres, at the Museum of National

Antiquities, Stuttgart; this has the I. L. with S. beneath, which dates it the second half of the seventeenth century. Made at Augsburg.

Of the work of Peter Winter, 1702, there is an example at the Industrial Museum at Nuremberg, a miniature box engraved with flowers and festoons of fruit.

A tiny tea-service, with the T. B. hall-mark of Augsburg in the seventeenth century, is now in the Ducal museum, Gotha; the six enamelled cups stand but five centimetres high.

Two teapots in miniature in the same museum have oval medallions of enamel, and a tray with six tiny cups are enamelled and engraved; all these bear the Augsburg mark.

A miniature sugar-basin in the Ducal museum at Anhalt bears the same mark and is silver-gilt; it is ornamented with a picture of a woman on the lid.

At Frankfort-on-Maine, belonging to Herr J. Dreyfut-Pedels, is a miniature goblet, silver-gilt, with the mark L. R., dating about the middle of the eighteenth century.

In the same town, belonging to S. Goldsmidt, is a toy tumbler, silver gilt, with the mark of Philipp Stenglin, 1717, 1744.

Of John Christopher Traffler's work (1722) there is a miniature specimen at Mainz, consisting of three tumblers, silver-gilt and engraved with leaves. The J. C. with T. beneath is the mark.

The A. D. of Abraham Dreutwet the younger, 1785, appears in a miniature box, now at St. Petersburg.

The J. P. H. of John Philipp Heckenauer, 1765, is found on a toy beaker with medallions belonging to Professor

125

Segffer of Stuttgart ; it stands only six centimetres in height.

A miniature salt-cellar, oval in shape, in a private collection in Karlsruhe, bears the hall-mark of John Jacob Adam, 1762-1792, IIA in an oval being the form of mark.

A toy mug only two centimetres in height, belonging to Herr Moppert of Baden Baden, bears the same mark.

The H. R., the Luneburg mark in the sixteenth century, appears on a miniature pyx richly ornamented with engraving of Renaissance style ; it is in the St. Johannes Church at Luneburg, and measures but two to six centimetres in height.

Our account of silver toys would hardly be complete without a brief reference to the toy ships or " nefs " which have been made from very early times. These are, however, not toys in the meaning of the word for the purposes of this book, namely, playthings of children, though many of them are musical toys. The name " nef " is derived from the French word *navette,* a vessel in the shape of a boat in which incense is kept for the altar. They are highly elaborate pieces of plate, sometimes used as salt-cellars in the days when the salt-holder played an important part in indicating social status. In later times, when the place of the salt-cellar no longer indicated the rank of the diner, these nefs were used for holding spices and sweetmeats, and took the place of the epergne of the nineteenth century. Occasionally a nef was fashioned to hold a bottle of wine of some rare vintage.

Piers Gaveston in 1313 had amongst his jewels a ship of silver on four wheels enamelled on their sides. In the inventory of the jewels of Edward III. a silver ship is

mentioned, of elaborate design. It was on four wheels,
had gilt dragons on both ends, and was valued at £12:7:4 ;
both of these ships were probably used as salt-cellars.
Of the sixteenth-century nefs, which were made to work
by means of elaborate clockwork concealed in the interior
of the vessel, or in the figures, which had mast-yards,
shrouds, and often sailors climbing the rigging or clinging
to rope-ladders, a fine specimen is in Hotel Cluny in Paris.
It should be described, not as a piece of ornamental plate,
but simply as a mechanical toy. Another specimen is in
the British Museum. This formerly belonged to the Emperor
Randolph II. ; it is, however, less elaborate than that at
Cluny, which is of German make of the sixteenth century,
and belonged to the Emperor Charles X. ; it measures
from keel to the top of the mast 40 inches by 26 in length.
Its stand is artistically carved to represent waves in which
dolphins and other sea-monsters sport ; the sides of the
ship bristle with guns ; on deck there is a band of twelve
musicians in military costume ; on a raised platform
covered by a canopy of gold sits the Emperor; when the
toy is wound up, courtiers pass before him bowing low,
the Emperor bows to each as he goes by and moves his
hand, which holds a sceptre. There are seven sailors
attending to the masts and rigging ; each makes a movement controlled by clockwork concealed in the tiny
figure ; the ship is in gilt bronze and enamel, the King
and his throne only being in gold. Such elaborate toys
cost enormous sums, and were frequently the gift of one
sovereign to another; they were much sought after in the
sixteenth century. The one described above doubtless
amused the King as a relaxation after his researches into
politics, astronomy, alchemy, and other occult sciences in

127

which he spent so much time ; possibly he may have had it made for his son.   Another costly toy belonging to the King was a chess-board, for which the pieces were made of amber and jet ; the entry of their cost appears in the royal record of expenses.   Chess-boards and men constantly appear in the old archives, which record careful and minute details of expenditure.

The increase in the value of nefs, owing to their purchase by collectors, is very great.   His Majesty King Edward has several fine ones, and the collection of the late Duke of Saxe-Coburg was probably unique, comprising no fewer than thirty-nine specimens.   When it is considered that few museums can boast possession of more than one or two examples, it may be realised that such a collection of antique nefs is indeed rare.   One of the oldest nefs in existence is one presented by Queen Elizabeth, which is now in the Kremlin at Moscow.   One was made for Louis XIV. of gold ; its weight is 1200 ounces ; it is now at the Louvre.   Nefs were occasionally made to commemorate events ; such a one, showing the landing of Vasco di Gama at the Cape of Good Hope, is in the Duke of Saxe-Coburg's collection.

CHAPTER VII

WEAPONS AND SOLDIER PLAY.

BEFORE a child can articulate he shows his predilection **Weapons** for certain toys to the exclusion of others : the baby girl **and** holds out her hand for a doll, the boy for a horse, a **Soldier** whip, or a gun. As each successive age in the world's **Play.** history has gone by, the weapons of that age, made in miniature, have been in the hands of the boys. Bows and arrows, used by Anglo-Saxons and Danes not only in time of war as the most deadly weapon of destruction, but also in time of peace, in the chase, were doubtless given as toys to the lads ; the use of the bow was an essential part of a young man's education. The cross-bow was convenient for handling by women and boys, because the efficacy of the shot did not depend on the strength of the shooter, the arrows being discharged by means of a catch or trigger. Both the sons of King Henry VII. were excellent archers, especially Prince Arthur, who used frequently to visit the Society of London bowmen at Mile-end, and practised with them.

Bows and arrows appear to have been the favourite toy weapons of Chinese and Japanese children. In an early oriental painting of the fifteenth century there is a charming picture in which the mighty hunters are taking the pastime very earnestly. The bows are slightly made, and very unlike those in contemporary use in Europe. The toy bows of modern Japan are practically identical with those shown in the picture. The children wear long loose silk coats and have heads clean shaven, except for the tufts of hair on the forehead and at each side. This fashion seems to throw into prominence the cherubic roundness of face and skull.

Probably the slinging of stones was a favourite amusement amongst boys, where the tribe of Benjamin was celebrated for the skill of its slingers, and David slew Goliath with a pebble from the brook; the catapult of the boy of the present day is the survival of such primitive weapons. Later, slings of warfare were attached to a staff or truncheon and wielded with both hands; the wooden Y-shaped twig of the catapult dates its origin to about the tenth century. Strutt says, at the end of the eighteenth century: "I remember in my youth to have seen several persons expert in slinging stones, which they performed with thongs of leather, or wanting these, with garters, and sometimes they used a stick of ash or hazel a yard or better in length, and about an inch in diameter; it was split at the top, so as to make an opening wide enough to receive the stone, which was confined by the reaction of the stick on both sides, but not strong enough to resist the impulse of the slinger."

Every kind of military combat practised by the knights and their esquires from the twelfth century onwards was imitated by the boys. A charming picture of the three little boys tilting at the fixed quintain is

Curious XVIIIth Century Print of a Boy, with his back to the target, shooting with Bow and Arrow.

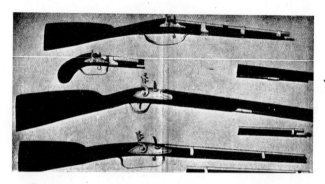

Toy Flint Lock Guns, from the pattern book of a toy maker in Paris in the First Empire.

Miniature Armour of the XVth Century. In the Munich Bayeresches National Museum. The larger helmet measures 2½ in.

Armour and Horse Trappings such a worn by the knights jousting in the by Burgmair, where such toys are s use. Only that part of the woodcut ing the toys is reproduced. See pa

taken from a manuscript in the Bodleian Library at **Early**
Oxford, dated 1344 ; two boys are dragging the wooden **Soldier**
horse along, while their mounted companion is prepared **Play.**
to strike at the quintain. Another picture from the

BOYS OF THE FOURTEENTH CENTURY IMITATING THE TILTING
OF THE KNIGHTS.

same MS. shows two boys practising with the movable
quintain. If the board was not hit by the striker he
was "laughed to scorn," and if he hit it full he was
struck heavily by the bag of sand which swung round

BOYS TILTING AT THE QUINTAIN.
From a manuscript in the Bodleian Library dated 1344.

with the blow, so that at any rate this toy afforded
discipline for both mind and body.

There is a fourteenth-century representation of three
boys who are tilting at a tub of water ; all three help

to support the pole which would be too heavy for their young arms singly, and they have taken off their clothes in anticipation of the ducking they will presently receive. The tournaments and jousts formed excellent subjects

BOYS IMITATING WITH BLUDGEONS THE SWORD AND BUCKLER PLAY
OF THEIR ELDERS.
From a fourteenth century MS.

for imitation by the youngsters, and persons of rank were taught from earliest childhood to delight in such exercises of a martial nature; toys were given them to encourage the love of the splendid tourneys they must frequently have witnessed. There is a picture of a toy on wheels in which a knight in full panoply appears; both knight and horse are of brass, and were at one time in the possession of Sir Frederick Eden; the wheels are wanting, but the hole in front for the insertion of a cord is there. This toy being of metal would stand the shock of the meeting of an adversary in the tournament, but another like it would be required for playing the game with success.

Two cavaliers in bronze, which are now at the Imperial Museum at Vienna, are set upon wheels, and are undoubtedly toys of the Middle Ages, when jousts and tourneys being the pastime of adults were the inspiration

for the toys of the children. Fortunately there remains
to the present day the representation of such toys in
use. We allude to the treatise entitled *Der wisz*
Koenig, which sets forth the doings of the Emperor
Maximilian I. This work, which was published by
Mars Trietzaurwein in 1775, shows a medallion in which
Maximilian is playing with the figures of armed and
armoured men on horseback. Five boys are at a table
in a wood ; two push from opposite sides of the table
the armed figures, so that they meet with lances, as in
the lists in the tourneys of the day ; the hands pushing
the toy figures forward are shown in our picture.

JOUSTING TOY GUIDED BY THE HANDS OF THE PLAYERS.
A woodcut by Hans Burgmair in the *History of Maximilian I.*

Such a toy in the Kuppelmayer collection was bought
by the museum authorities of Munich in 1895 for the
enormous sum of 47,500 francs. The armour of the
cavalier is complete in every detail : the helmet is
ornamented with engraved plaques ; the cuirass is
bordered by interlaced ornaments of metal ; on the
breast is a medallion with A engraved upon it ; on
the back R is shown ; the figure on which this armour

135

Weapons and Soldier Play. is placed is of wood articulated at the knees, wrists, and shoulders, in order that it could be made to effect all the desired movements; the horse is covered with a gorgeous cloth such as was used at tournaments; it is in the act of galloping, the hind legs only resting on the ground. Two such figures are at Munich; the wooden stand, which shows imperfectly in our picture, as it is sunk into the pedestal on which it is erected, has a ring in it for the child's string to draw it along. Fragments of such toys are to be seen occasionally in collections of fifteenth- and sixteenth-century armour, but a perfect specimen is almost unique; a single figure of a man armed *cap-à-pie* is shown in a wood-cut of 1587, where children are represented playing various games; the armoured man is made to ride astride a little dog by one of the urchins. This picture refutes the theory that such small figures were always made merely as workmen's patterns or *tours de force*. Popguns and squirts are also shown in this same series of pictures, which belongs to the *Recieul des jeux*.

The military toys of Louis XIII. mentioned in the *Memoires* of Heroard in 1604 include a little arquebus, a musket with a bandolier embroidered in gold and silver, a pistol, a little cannon of silver given to the boy by Sully when he visited the arsenal, a little bow and arrow, an ivory ring to attach to the bow, a poignard set with rubies, and many other costly and beautiful toy weapons.

In an engraving by Silliman of the sixteenth century, the central group of children, who are surrounded by many others playing with the toys of the period, are enjoying a most elaborate war-game; a bandmaster heads the procession, staff in hand ; immediately behind him drums and flutes are being played ; the halberdiers,

EX NVGIS kinder-spel. SERIA

SOLDIER PLAY OF THE CHILDREN IN THE SIXTEENTH CENTURY.
From an engraving by Silliman.

flagbearers, and bearers of lances, staves, and pikes come behind, while the proud possessor of a shield takes a

137

prominent position. It is interesting to note that both boys and girls figure in the martial procession, and carry the swords or banners promiscuously. Some excited onlookers stand on their heads with infantile delight at the spectacle. On the extreme right of this fascinating picture an animated game at blindman's-buff is going on, while in the foreground on the left a group of four girls are playing with a delightful selection of household toys, such as pokers, tongs, spoons, a miniature strainer, a dish-cover, pail and mug, salt-cellars, and a tiny sugar-basin with its cover. An elaborately dressed girl, whose neck-ruffle, cap, and apron are edged with the pointed lace of the period, with which the pictures by Vandyke have made us familiar, is preparing a wicker bassinette for the reception of a doll, who wears a neck-ruffle and puffed sleeves which are replicas of those of the little mother. At the back a nurse carries a baby-boy muffled in a shawl, and another child carries a doll. Two boys are flying kites, another holds aloft a stick on which is a little paper mill, such as may be bought at fairs for a penny, a boy is bowling a hoop, others walk upon stilts. One of this *troupe*, in a three-cornered paper hat, has just fallen, and is overtaken by a band of leap-frog players; a boy flies a paper flag, while another wields a skipping-rope. There are boys playing little musical instruments; the violinist stares at a companion, whose attention is engrossed with what Miss Florence Upton, in her inimitable "gollywog" series, calls a "scissors-boy," the movable crossbars of wood, screwed together as the lazy tongs of a confectioner, achieve the rapid growth or diminution of the puppet fixed on to the extremities; two mites are blowing into a bladder; the cheeks of one are distended,

while another holds the bladder and watches his play-
mate's operations; an urchin close by whips a top, and
one of the eldest children in the picture, promoted to the
dignity of the shoulder-knots and drooping hat feather
of his elders, plays at cup and ball. If the picture were
redrawn and the children clothed in the costumes of the
present day, no toy would need modernising. Replace
the Flemish architecture of the houses, church, and
fountain with an English country mansion, and one
would have a perfect representation (as far as the children
and their toys and games are concerned) of a joyous
band of little ones playing with the toys of the twentieth
century. Surely our children are the most conservative
of beings in their tastes with regard to toys! Where is
the progress boasted of in other arts and trades? The
toys of to-day are practically the same as those in the
sixteenth century. By all means let them remain so,
for the miniature steam-engine, electrical toy, and hydraulic
crane are essentially the playthings of the elder children,
whose reasoning powers and faculties of observation are
either abnormal or are well on the way towards maturity.

In an interesting print of the eighteenth century by
Chodowiecki, a young urchin, in long coat and vest, is
shooting at a bird perched conveniently on a branch
above his head; the bow is heavy in make, the string
stretched to its full capacity before the arrow flies. Three
other boys appear in this print: one in the pointed shako
of the French army at this period, and a moustache
pointed or marked in charcoal; their weapons are
wooden swords, and they are worn even by the two
bandsmen who are playing respectively on a flute and
a drum; these are less glorious in apparel than their

officer, for they lack the shako and moustache, but the animation of their goose-step is undeniable.

Paris has always been one of the principal centres for the manufacture of toy accoutrements; early in the nineteenth century quantities were made in the Quartier

SOLDIER PLAY OF THE EIGHTEENTH CENTURY.
From an engraving by Chodowiecki.

St. Martin, and the large trade in cards, bearing a helmet, cuirass, sword, and perhaps a sabretache, was begun, which has since flourished exceedingly. The little town of Plombières, in the department of Vosges, makes a speciality of this variety of toy, as also the gun and pistol which are so necessary in the modern toy equipment.

In China, popguns are called paper-guns, on account of the wads of paper which are used as pellets ; the gun itself is of bamboo. Blow-guns, through which pebbles are expelled, are also used, and sometimes a needle fixed in a tiny section of reed makes a more dangerous projectile. Toy squirts are known in China.

In Japan the boys feather their darts with paper. They call their popguns blow-arrows, and their bamboo squirts are water-guns.

The origin of the child's popgun is obscure. It may either be derived from the blow-pipe of the savage, or have been invented as a harmless form of the weapon which succeeded the bow and sling. Certain it is that big, bouncing words are compared to popgun reports (or potguns, as they were sometimes called, on account of the clay pellets in general use) in a comedy called *The Knave in Graine*, written in 1640. "Blow-point" occurs as the name of a game in a description of children's play in the sixteenth century, an arrow being blown through a trunk or tube at certain numbers in a child's lottery.

In *The Amusements of Aix*, by Pierre Mortier, 1736, we first hear of that pretty weapon of play warfare, confetti, which forms the ammunition for many a mock battle at fête or fair. He says that near to the Tivoli baths at Rome great quantities of small hard stones are gathered. They are so smooth and polished that they resemble to a remarkable extent tiny sugar sweetmeats. Most people are taken in by them, especially when they are mixed with real sweetmeats. These are called *confetti di Tivoli*, or *dragées de Tivoli*.

The obvious objection to hard ammunition in too zealous hands, even in play battle, caused the substitution

141

of the paper discs now chiefly used in place of the stones. A quantity of the once useless cuttings from perforated cards and papers were stored in a toy warehouse awaiting destruction, when the employees used handfuls in a friendly encounter ; the proprietor, watching the contest unnoticed, made a note of the pretty effect of the vari-coloured and harmless ammunition, and utilised the idea thus given to him with true commercial instinct.

What pleasure the game of soldiers has given, and what infinite variety of playing is possible ! Sometimes the children themselves are the generals, lieutenants, bandsmen, or artillery-men, and even the baby is recruited in war-time in the nursery ; sometimes the miniature army comes in full war-strength out of a wooden box. Louis XIV. paid 6000 francs to Henri de Gissey, designer of the King's ballets, for an army of cardboard soldiers finely painted, for his Majesty the King to give to Monseigneur le Dauphin ; this miniature army consisted of 20 squadrons of cavalry, 10 battalions of infantry, and were, later on, replaced by the little silver army made by Merlin the silversmith in the seventeenth century from artistic models, when not only were the men and horses made, but also guns and other machines of war. Would that these little silver toys had not joined the silver treasure of the King in the oblivion of the melting pot, so that we could see them as they were in those days !

Though ancient specimens of toy soldiers, dating almost from prehistoric times, have been described from time to time, we believe them to be chess-men which were frequently fashioned in the form of mounted warriors, rather than toys of children, the immediate ancestors of the lead or wooden soldiers of to-day.

It is extremely likely that the children of ancient Greece and Rome had playthings, representing, in miniature, the warriors whose forms were so often before their eyes, and whose deeds of valour were so frequently in their ears ; doubtless such deeds constantly formed the basis of their games, and we may look upon the little model of Caesar discovered in a tomb, as the forerunner of the soldiers now moulded in thousands of dozens, complete in every detail, accurate to the pattern of a button and the arrangement of a shoulder-strap.

The tilting and jousting toys of the Middle Ages form another link in the chain of warrior toys, together with the miniature St. George and other militant saints whom we are accustomed to class with the toys connected with religious observances and pilgrimages.

Considering the later achievements of Louis XIII. of France, when war was no longer a game to him, but a stern reality, it is amusing to hear that in 1606 the future King of France played in the palace garden, attaching his silver cannon with a garter, and his garter to the string of his pinafore, and so walked pulling his cannon after him. Like his successor, Louis XIV., he learnt how to move his battalions of flesh and blood, while playing at soldiers with his army of metal.

The soldiers of Louis XIV., given to him when he was but twelve years of age, were designed by the sculptor George Chassel, who produced models of infantry, cavalry, and also guns and other war machines. These models were afterwards executed by the silversmith Merlin with great skill. " The little army with the boxes for keeping them in safety cost," says M. Allemagne, " *cinquante mille écus.*"

Weapons and Soldier Play.

For the eldest son of Louis XIV. Colbert sent to Nuremberg for soldiers in 1662. In his correspondence with his brother Charles Colbert, occurs the following passage :—" I beg you to remember the little ornaments, such as pieces of artillery, figures of men and horses, that I have asked you to have made by the most industrious masters of Augsburg and Nuremberg, to serve as playthings for Monseigneur the Dauphin."

It is to be regretted that the cardboard soldiers, such as one sees in such variety and such perfection of detail in the Museum at Nuremberg, should be no longer made. Certainly they compare most favourably with the productions of lead which are now so popular. The " tin soldier " has always been essentially the product of Germany, and the headquarters of the industry from earliest times has been at Nuremberg. The army of Frederic the Great was the first complete lead army to be placed upon the market for purchase by the general public; it was Jean Georges Helpert, who died in 1794, who first produced leaden soldiers as toys at Nuremberg, and the principal uniforms of the Russian army were reproduced by him with great exactitude. The army of Napoleon followed; Wellington and his generals found their way into the nurseries of Great Britain ; Crimean heroes succeeded those of the Peninsular war, and the men in khaki are now the favourites together with the heroes of Japan. The same toy, but in a different dress ; the same marshalling of troops in line, but with different generals; and the game goes on interminably. Every European war has left its mark in the toy-boxes of our children, and the Imperial Yeomanry in South African war, with the C.I.V. and Remington's scouts, are still first

144

Toy Soldier. 3½ in. Made in Pewter. At the Germanische Museum, Nuremburg.

Curious Wheeled Soldier blowing Trumpet. Early XIXth Century.

Feudal Toy of Knight in a complete suit of armour. The helmet is engraved, the cuirass is bordered with interlaced ornament. There is a ring in the wooden stand for the insertion of a string when the child drags the toy along. 47,500 francs was the price paid for this toy by the authorities of the Bayerische Museum, Munich.

Splendid Mechanical Toy, with outriders and postillions.   XVIIIth Century.

Tin Soldiers of minute workmanship, Trumpet Blowers, Standard Bearers,
and Roman Gladiators. $1\frac{1}{2}$ in. high.   From the collection of early
specimens of Toy Soldiers at the Industrial Museum, Nuremburg.

favourites, though Japanese and Russian warriors are more up to date.

In Germany, where the play of children is so much utilised for educational purposes, toy soldiers are taken very seriously ; not only do the best Nuremberg makers employ good artists to make their models, but men of letters to furnish details as to past wars, archaeologists to secure accuracy in details of arms and accoutrements, and writers to furnish short accounts of the wars in which the soldiers were engaged. Nearly every war of any importance in the history of the world has contributed to the furnishing of " copy " and models to fill the delightful glass-covered boxes, which contain the famous toy soldiers of Nuremberg.

Of the two distinct types of toy lead figures, the flat, rather than the rounded kind is the oldest, and was, no doubt, derived from early cardboard models ; a good example of the early flat lead figures is the set of Italian actors now at South Kensington Museum. They stand one and a half inches high, and are brilliantly painted in colour ; the attitudes are somewhat extravagant ; several of the figures wear masks. The flat figures lend themselves much more readily to the marshalling in line, forming squares, and other warlike manœuvres, which are so important a feature in the play of soldiers. The rounded soldiers are heavier, less easily moved, and very much more expensive, besides being much more difficult to arrange in military formation. The thin chip boxes in which the cheap flat soldiers of Germany are packed are very largely made in France in the Vosges district ; these boxes are also made in Sonnenburg in Thuringia.

147

Weapons and Soldier Play.

In the eighteenth century, flat soldiers were chiefly used. The earliest specimens are blackened with age, as no particular attention was paid to the mixing of the alloy in order to ensure continued brightness. Age no longer brings discoloration, since modern science has found a remedy for such chemical changes which obscure the chief charm of the lead soldier. The later development of the lead soldier army, the figure rounded and perfect in form, was, we believe, first produced in France. The different limbs are made separately and soldered together, instead of the whole piece, man and horse, being made in a mould. Commissariat-waggons, ambulance-waggons, and ammunition-carts are also moulded in pieces and united afterwards.

The war game, played on a space marked out with mountains, rivers, forests, and habitations, such as might be found in any country where troops are to be manœuvred, is not the pastime of children. The *Kriegspiel* is the game of experienced soldiers who take pleasure in pitting their brain and experience against those of their *confrères*, and delight to seize upon a natural feature in the mimic country, or to show their powers of invention or resource, thus laying up a store of experience in miniature, which may some day be useful in ordering the manœuvres of a real army.

Besides the armies in lead of which we have been writing, there are numerous objects, such as forts, tents, hedges, etc., in which materials other than lead are used ; these are frequently sold with the soldiers. Galleys or transport ships are occasionally to be seen amongst eighteenth and the early nineteenth century specimens.

In the early years of the nineteenth century, soldiers

were made, like the irreversible Buddhas of China, mounted on a rounded leaden base, so that on their being knocked down, they righted themselves ; these were called the invincible army.

A primitive variety of toy soldier is made of folded paper. A large number of these attractive home-made members of the military profession, dating from the latter half of the eighteenth century, are now at the Nuremberg Museum ; they are elaborately painted, and show little signs of age and wear.

Nearly all the early toy soldiers, whether of paper, lead, wood, or pewter, are larger than those of modern make. They measure from five and a half to seven inches in height. This is also about the size of the peasant groups and models figuring in village festivals which were also made in the eighteenth century. These latter figures are occasionally to be met with in composition, which is coloured with great accuracy. The elaborate dress of the late seventeenth century is well shown in a bridal procession, where the priests, musicians, choristers, and bridal party are all represented. Such figures were also made in sugar, marzipan, gingerbread, and a mixture of flour and honey—edible toys being great favourites with the little ones, and largely purchased as " fairings."

A fine collection of old wooden, lead, and cardboard soldiers, owned by M. François Carnot, extend over a period of a century and a half. An officer of the Guard of Louis XIV. is the earliest of these. Grenadiers of the Guard of Frederick II., 1744-1750, show the elaborate facings and high peaked hat with red bow. French light infantry of 1797 have the turned-back skirts of the coat, high gaiters, and three-cornered hats. The infantry of the early years of the nineteenth century, models of those who fought in Spain, recall to one's recollection the drab and black hats of Napoleon. A fife and drummer of another regiment which served in the Peninsular war, have the short frocked coat and red and yellow facings, which gave a gaiety wanting in the drab uniforms. Doubtless, however, they were surer food for powder, if our recent experience with khaki-clad men, rather than the red coats of Crimean date, count for anything.

The sober garments of a sapper of Peninsular war date, in Mr. Carnot's collection, could not be bettered for invisibility by our present War Office, and his miniature hatchet and varied kit hanging from his belt gives him a most workman-like appearance.

Lancers of the Guard of 1810 make a brave show with their brown horses, lances in rest, yellow housings, scarlet and blue coats and trousers, while the high, flat-topped helmet is most accurately carried out in miniature. It is interesting to note that these lancers are in the act of reining in their fiery steeds, which rest upon lead stands for the hind-legs only. The fore-legs are pawing the air in a truly martial manner.

Infantry of the time of Louis Philippe, and bandsmen of a line regiment in the middle of the nineteenth century, bring us up to the date when we cease to examine our subject of early toy soldiers.

Though all these soldiers in this collection represent members of the French army, it is almost certain that they were made in Germany, probably at Nuremberg, which has always been, and still remains (as a recent visit showed us), the headquarters of the world for toy soldiers

150

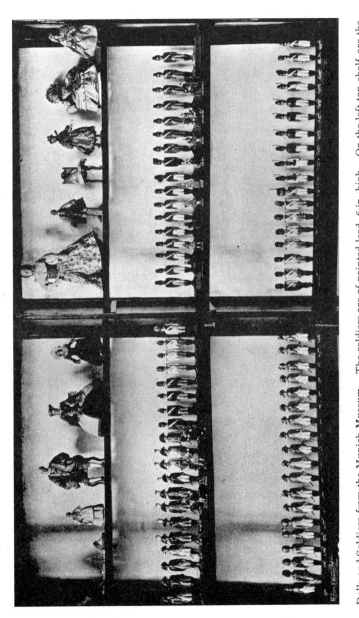

Dolls and Soldiers from the Munich Museum. The soldiers are of painted lead, 6 in. high. On the left top shelf are the Prussian Guard under Frederic II., 1744-1750; next, Prussian Light Infantry, 1797. On the lower shelf, Fusiliers under Napoleon; Prussian Guard, 1750, Grenadiers, 1800 to 1815, and French Soldiers under the First Empire.

Pewter Figures. 1½ in. From the Industrial Museum, Nuremburg. Frederic William III. of Prussia, Frederic the Great, and a Hussar.

Group of Toy Soldiers. 2 to 4 in. in height. At the top are five soldiers of the time of Frederic the Great. In the centre of the second row is a kneeling peasant shooting, a French soldier of the Revolution and a Prussian volunteer. Below there is a mounted German at the time of the war with Turkey, a keepsake in remembrance of the homage done to Frederic William III., and a trumpeter of the time of Wallenstein, 17th Century.

of tin or lead. Sailors we hear of comparatively little, and a toy of early date showing sailors is a comparative rarity. In the Exhibition in Paris of 1855 there was an exhibit of toy sailors, shown by a Berlin exhibitor, but we can find no special description of them. At Nuremberg there is an early mechanical toy boat, but of the sober canal-boat type, and it is drawn by three horses.

In the middle of the nineteenth century a patent was applied for, to register the idea, that any toys hitherto made of lead or tin in moulds should be made in cardboard, composition, or papier-mâché. Some of these curious toys exist. The weapons of the soldiers only are of tin; they are of the date of the Crimean war. An episode of the siege of Sebastopol is one of the scenes represented. The figures are thicker and clumsier in make than their metal proto-types, as would be expected. They stand firmly upon platforms of the composition, and each of the figures shows a different attitude, so that the effect is extremely lifelike and animated. Such composition toys are still made, but less elaborately, and are sold in regiments or in single specimens by the cheap toy-vendors of France and Germany.

Toy soldiers have frequently figured in the political caricatures of the day—the tin and leaden variety, and also those which are mounted on movable wooden crossbars, and are drilled with a single movement of the hand of the manipulator. One drawn by Gustave le Petit, published in 1807 in Paris, is headed " Le déménagement du Roi de Suede." The King's crown is falling off; he holds in his hand wooden soldiers in the uniform of the Swedish cavalry and infantry.

Another caricature refers to the siege at Antwerp in

Weapons and Soldier Play. September 1832. Louis Philippe is shown kneeling before a table where he arranges his toy army; Marshal Soult is shooting beans out of a toy cannon, and Admiral Rigny swims paper boats in a basin.

At the time of the Crimean war, in England, quantities of toy soldiers were sold in wood, the uniform and accoutrements of the meagrest simplicity, the whole get-up vastly inferior to the silver soldiers of an earlier time, of which none, indeed, remain to show us how a Dauphin was amused and educated in the art of war. This cheap wooden type still survives.

Away in a lonely Yorkshire parsonage, early in the nineteenth century, were a set of such wooden soldiers, interesting on account of their ownership and the delicate fancies which were woven round their unbending frames. Some strange little girls amused themselves by writing little dramas, poems, and romances, and playing their little secret plays with their doll's-house soldiers, which were mostly titled, and generally either statesmen or men of genius. "Mine was the prettiest of the whole, and the tallest, and the most perfect in every part," wrote Charlotte Bronte. "He was the Duke of Wellington."

CHAPTER VIII

ANIMALS, CARRIAGES, CARTS.

IN all ages of the world's history children have loved **Toy** their toys to be in the shapes of animals. Mules appear **Animals** among the toys of pottery from Cyrenaica, made in Athens ; **beloved of** spotted cows from Egypt, a boy riding on a swan, a goat **Children.** from Cyprus, made before the Christian era ; rams, pigs, ducks, fish, all bear witness to the love of the children of early times for animals in miniature, as playthings.

To come down to comparatively modern times, amongst the treasures of the Wollaston Franks collection is to be found a Kakemono, measuring $81\frac{3}{4}$ by $49\frac{7}{8}$ inches ; on its silken surface is painted in colours, as yet un-dimmed though laid on four centuries ago, a brilliant scene in the child-life of the China of the day. A pedlar's stall is gaily decorated with tiny flags and trophies, such as the Chinese excel in making with bright silks, scraps of tinted ivory, wood, and other trifles so attractive to the little ones. The stall is set out with toys and lanterns of every description ; a row of tiny, duck-like birds occupy a conspicuous place ; sweetmeats, cakes, and tempting-looking parcels, possibly the "surprise

155

packet" of the Ming period, are piled on it. A round-cheeked urchin is bargaining with the pedlar, and holds out his pierced coin. In the foreground is a pretty group of street children attracted by the show: one has purchased a duck, others are clutching flowers and necklaces, and what we feel sure are sticky parcels—so well beloved of children now, and surely equally delightful in the third month of the cyclical year Ping Isze, when the picture was painted by one Tsze Chung under the seal of the Ming dynasty. In another picture on silk, of the same period, we see the identical hobby-horse of modern times. The head and neck are of painted wood, a stick passes between the legs of the child, two wooden wheels facilitate the movements of the rider. Such is the toy seen also in an early European wood-cut, again in England in the time of Queen Anne, and in an elaborate engraving by Chodowiecki, where a little lad, in long, full-skirted coat and hair tied *en queue*, straddles a wooden stick held up by the bridle and reins and attached to the carved head of the horse.

In this interesting eighteenth-century engraving, a form of rocking-horse is shown, which is most whimsical. Instead of the prancing animal with legs apart with which we are all familiar, this noble steed is in a crouching position upon the rockers, with which it is cut in a solid block of wood from the back downwards, the legs being marked in outline only upon the rockers. In a lithograph by Marlet, of the Empire period, a child rides a horse of large size and finely modelled; there are no rockers attached to this toy, but solid wooden wheels facilitate the transport over the rough cobble-stones of the Pont Neuf. The child riding it flourishes a single lash whip and clasps a large

156

figure of Punch ; the proud father dragging the little one is dressed in the light trousers, swallow-tail coat, and high collar of the fashion associated with the elaborate dandyism of Count d'Orsay.

There is a story that Henry IV. of France was dis-

PLAY OF THE EIGHTEENTH CENTURY.
From a print by Chodowiecki.

covered on his knees playing at horses with his children by the Spanish ambassador. "Are you a father, Monsieur ? " asked the King, holding his little son still on his back. "Yes," said the Spaniard. "Then I will ride once more round the room before we commence our business," said the King.

"Playing at horses" seems to have been attractive to royalty, for the first hobby-horse game that we know of, was that indulged in by King Agesilaus, who, we are told, made a horse of reed and rode with his children.

In a vignette by Huquier of the eighteenth century we see a hobby-horse with insignificant head, but sufficiently long stick for three children to stride it. The first holds the reins, the second the arm of the first rider, and the third clutches the stick itself and brandishes a single lashed whip.

In a book of models for a toy-maker of the First Empire period in France, elaborate horses are represented made of carved wood, saddled, and caparisoned ; mounted on them are riders, military and otherwise, in the dress of the period. These representations are coloured, and the wooden stands are mounted upon wheels, to facilitate the drawing along of the toy by a child.

Rocking-horses were also much in vogue at this time ; the little King of Rome was shown on one, in an engraving which was brought out under the title "La première course de l'Enfance." This picture, published in 1813 after a drawing by Condé, was lithographed by Ruotte.

Mechanical horses also were not unknown ; patents were applied for them in 1822, and again two years later ; one of these horses was mounted on three wheels, and could be guided by the hands of the rider by means of two handles placed one on each side of the animal's neck ; these handles controlled various mechanical appliances in the body of the animal. The second was similar in its working, and we see in such toys the idea of the bicycle in embryo. Horses of moulded cardboard were made in large quantities in the neighbourhoods of Sonnenburg, Ulm, Stuttgart, and Nuremberg, and were painted with

Fragment of Egyptian Spotted Cow. 5 in. long. From the British Museum.

Toy Mounted Figure, made before the Christian Era. Greek. From the British Museum.

Chinese Children riding Wheeled Hobby Horses. From the "Roll of the Hundred Children," painted on silk by an artist of the Ming Dynasty.

Wheeled Carriages and Animals, which include Punch with an early Tricycle. From a coloured trade catalogue of a toymaker of Napoleon's time.

rough realism. Such animals were largely imported into England, France, and other European countries, together with the roughly carved wooden toys which are more universally known as toys made in the Black Forest districts. The wooden or chip boxes are generally oval in form, and contain the sets of animals. Farm-yards, poultry, or what not, vary in size from the 13 or 14-inch box, which contained a farm-house, trees, fences, and animals, down to the 2 or 3-inch box, which held but a couple of animals or half-a-dozen wooden soldiers.

IMITATION OF AN ANIMAL WITH BELL ACCOMPANIMENT.
From a fourteenth century Bodleian MS.

The chase, not only of men in pursuit of animals, but also of one animal after another, has not unfrequently inspired the form of a toy. Mechanical toys of the Empire period show a dog pursuing a hare, a cat chasing a mouse. The distance between the pursuer and the quarry did not vary, for, on the turning of the key, the wires regulating the movement by clockwork move the two animals equally.

Hobby-horses were used by morris-dancers in the fourteenth and fifteenth centuries, and later, the head found in children's toys was supplemented by a light wooden frame

Animals, Carriages, Carts. for the body, to which a tail was attached, and over which trappings were fixed, which reached the ground, effectually concealing the feet and legs of the person who was performing the double character of horse and rider. Thus equipped the players curvetted and pranced about, sometimes using bells and such embellishments as are seen on

SAXON GLEEMAN AND JUGGLER.
From a frontispiece to the Psalms illuminated in the eighth century.

country farm-horses. In the seventeenth century morris-dancers and riders of these hobby-horses are frequently mentioned. Strutt gives a delightful anecdote of Prince Henry, the eldest son of James I. "Some of his Highness's young gentlemen, together with himself, imitating in sport the curvetting and high-going of horses, one that stood by said that they were like a company of horses, which his

162

Highness noting, answered, ' Is it not better to resemble a **Tumbling** horse, which is a generous and courageous beast, than a dull, **and** slow-going ass as you are.' " Strutt adds with delightful **Juggling.**

TUMBLING.

From an illuminated MS. of the fourteenth century.

naïveté, " The Prince was exceedingly young at the time he made this reply."

In the ancient celebrations by the Lord of Misrule, the master of merrie disports was not only elected at court at Christmas time, but also at the houses of wealthy citizens ; in some country parishes hobby-horses were constantly used in the revels. Jugglers and jesters also appeared at such times. The vielle, a small musical instrument, was nearly always used with the jugglers' art, for minstrels, jesters, and jugglers were of the same class, and appeared at revels or were regular members of the households of the wealthy.

JUGGLER PERFORMING WITH SWORD.

From a fourteenth century MS.

Tumbling was sometimes practised by them, both men and women taking part in

163

such feats of skill. They performed with cups and balls, swords, plates, eggs, or some simple contrivance, for the display of their skill, walking on their hands, rope-dancing, etc. A juggler was sometimes called hocus-pocus, a term equally used for a pickpocket.

There is a curious variant in the form of a hobby-horse

JUGGLING AND BALANCING.
From a fourteenth century MS. in the Bodleian Library.

in a French print of the sixteenth century, the horse being in a crouching position. In an earlier representation a youngster, well-equipped for the tournament, sits astride his hobby-horse, the reins in one hand, in the other he poises a lance in the correct attitude before the striking. A little wooden mill is at the end of the lance instead of the shapely pointed weapon, a wise precaution of a fifteenth-century mother.

Such hobby - horses are mentioned in Ben Jonson's *Bartholomew Fair* as one of the children's toys. " A fine hobby - horse to make your son a good rider." The hobby-horse is represented in a cavalcade of the time of Charles I.

In the *Dictionnaire de Commerce* by Savary, 1723, are mentioned as toys, dolls, cardboard horses, little chariots

164

and coaches, monks ringing their bells, street porters to hold bonbons.

At that time there were two sorts of toy knick-knacks: the first consisting of little models made of tin or of lead, such as the toys which furnished the children's dolls' houses; the others of linen, stuffs, and other materials of which such toys are made, as dolls' carriages. " Drapers sell the latter ; glassmakers, spectacle-makers, knick-knack sellers sell the others." An engraving of this period shows an itinerant seller of paper-mills attached to little sticks. They are of many patterns, and the woman selling them

DOMESTIC SCENE.
Printed in 1493.

carries a supply in her basket, where they are so disposed as to best catch the wind and the eye of the possible purchaser. She has also a goodly supply in a stick in her hand.

Such poor inexpensive toys were called *bijouterie de*

165

Animals, Carriages, Carts.

saint claude. Trifles made of box-wood, maple, or yew, such as are carved in Switzerland, also came under this name.

In the delightful reminiscences of the childhood of Princess Mary Adelaide, Duchess of Teck, some of the memories of the old days, spent by the Royal household at Kew, cluster round the children's play with the rocking-horse, "when the princess delighted to ride on Prince George's rocking-horse, which, though long since discarded by its owner, had been carefully stored away. When Miss Clark and Lady Arabella came (Lady Arabella West, youngest daughter of the fifth Earl

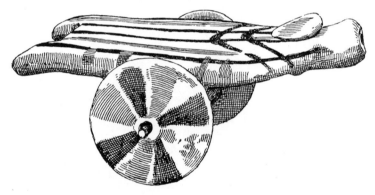

EARLY WHEELED TOY IN BAKED CLAY.
From Athens. 2½ inches.

Delaware), there were fine romps in the old nursery. Mary (the schoolroom maid) had to get out the rocking-horse, and all three children mounted it at the same time, to the great glee of the little princess. One day she had been naughty during her morning lesson, and the duchess directed she was to have bread and water for luncheon, a punishment Princess Mary particularly disliked. But she **The First Wheeled Toy.** was not going to let any one see it, and when the bread and water were taken up to her in the school-room, the princess was sitting on the piano, with her legs dangling in the air, and singing to herself as though she were quite happy."

A cart and a chariot, the one from Athens, the other from Thebes, show us the first wheeled toys that we have been able to find, dating from archaic times ; they measure respectively two and a half and three and a half inches ; we can imagine the little boys playing at the Olympian games with

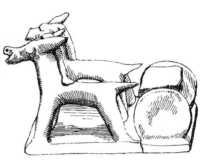

CHARIOT IN BAKED CLAY.
Found at Thebes. 3½ inches.

the toy chariot, after their elders had taken them to see the great show, just as our children will play at fairies, dragons, clowns, and pantaloons after their first visit to the pantomime. When the boys discarded the toys of their childhood, they repaired to the temple of Mercury, and consecrated to the god the playthings which had been the delight of their boyhood.

Tiny carriages for the use of children have been known from very remote times and driving-games have always been most popular. In a picture of 1587 we see a dog harnessed to a tiny cart in which a child is seated, other children urging the steed with a whip and pushing behind ; in front of the cavalcade is a dog led by a boy, and a

167

curious figure of a knight, armed *cap-à-pie*, is seated on
the dog.

Square carts or cages used for teaching children to
walk are of great antiquity, and are frequently represented
in old miniatures and prints. One of great beauty is
mentioned in the inventory of the toys and silver posses-
sions of Louis I., Duke of Anjou ; it is described as a
chariot of silver to teach the children to walk. It was
chased and carved, and had enamellings of great value.
Louis XIII., when an infant, received as a gift, a carriage
with four dolls, one representing the Queen, the others
Madame and Mademoiselle de Gieve and Madame de
Guercheville.

Little carts for children were the first to foreshadow
the automobile of the present day ; as early as the seventeenth century toy-carriages were made to move on a
round table, and gradually the mechanism employed was
applied to larger carts, capable of holding children
instead of dolls. In 1663 such a one is described
as being seen at Nuremberg. It had been ordered by
the King of Denmark, and could be made to move
backwards, forwards, or to turn simply by the use
of two handles, worked by children, seated in the little
carriage.

There are numerous records of the tiny carriage drawn
by white lambs used by the son of the first Napoleon. It
was made in 1812 from designs by Antoine Carasse,
executed by Tramblay, a coachbuilder in the Rue Duras ;
a print of the little King of Rome in this carriage was
executed by Boltzer ; the carriage itself was shown in the
Exhibition of 1900 at Paris. One of the most elaborate
toy-carriages ever made is now in the possession of a

private collector, M. Allimagne, to whom we are indebted for this description. He attributes its date to the reign of Louis XV. The frame is made of iron, and the body of the carriage elaborately decorated with a painted trellis design, while an ornamental lozenge is placed at the intersection of each line ; five pieces of glass form the windows, through which the occupants, a lady and gentleman in Venetian glass in the court dress of the period, are able to admire the beauty of the country ; two lackeys (niggers) are standing behind; the coachman, in three-cornered hat, is seated on the box seat, and a postillion guides the foremost pair of the six dapple grey horses, which are richly harnessed in red leather ; plumes of feathers are on their heads. Unfortunately the owner omits to mention the dimensions of this wonderful coach, which is worked by clockwork placed in the interior of the carriage. The mechanism is of sufficient power to move the back wheels, which alone are practicable, and bear along the coach and team of six horses.

The neighbourhood of the Jura produced the less elaborate automata of the eighteenth century : such a specimen as that described above would probably be of French make ; others were made, in which the mechanism which turned the wheels, caused the carriage to advance, and the occupants to incline their heads in greeting the passer-by.

Some of the French chariots and coaches are most elaborate and beautiful toys. It must be remembered that coach-building had attained a very high standard of perfection in the days when Martin worked and invented his inimitable varnish, which has added to so many of the toys and trifles of the period of Louis Quinze, and, on

account of its fineness, has given the name Vernis Martin
to boxes, fans, or any painted article which is painted
over with the perfectly hard clear varnish.

In the great collection of antique French toys, owned
by M. Bernard, we see perfect little coaches, with stately
coachmen in full liveries and three-cornered hats, which
differ in no particular from the state liveries at the present
day. The footmen standing behind, and the horses
modelled in wood, make the toy complete. Other specimens show the older form of cabriolet, that popular vehicle
which was the mode for so many years.

A very beautiful carriage of elaborate build is amongst
the toys which belonged to Queen Victoria. It is hung
on Cee-springs ; the hammer-cloth has been a magnificent
affair, richly fringed ; there are no figures on the box, nor
in the dickey behind ; nor are there any horses attached
at the present time.

A fine toy with six horses, coachman and postillion in
the cocked hat and liveries of the eighteenth century, is of
carved wood, finely painted and gilt. It is now in Munich.
In the same Museum is an earlier German toy of rougher
design ; the coach has a heavy top and large clumsy
wheels ; the original box made for keeping the toy in, is
also at the Museum.

The toy-carts of India and Ceylon are most elaborate
models of bullock - waggons, handcarts, and trolleys,
vegetable baskets on wheels, fruit-trucks and barrows piled
with flax and other farm produce in endless variety ; even
from Yarkand there is what is called a watchman's cart,
the low body of the vehicle being balanced on two wheels,
which are constructed on the primitive principles adopted
by that brilliant caricaturist, Mr. Reed, in his designs of

L'ENFANCE.

Painted by Lancret, engraved by Foudrenée.

Wheeled Chair or Perambulator, painted by a Japanese Artist of Chinese
subjects, in the XIVth Century.

Toy Sleigh and XVIIIth Century Coach, with six Horses ridden by Postillions,
carved and gilt wood, with Original Putting Away Box. Also Carved and Painted
Animals and Birds. German.

paleolithic times, a section of the round trunk of a tree being simply sawn off and used as a wheel.

A child's go-cart or wheeled-chair of the fourteenth century occurs on a painted record of Chinese children's toys and games. The little one is seated at ease in her chair, which is closed in with sliding bars like the baby's swing of the present day. Older children drag it, and the Oriental taste for simplicity, which seldom fails of effect, is shown by the child who holds a large and spreading leaf over the little rider's head for shade. That the procession is of some considerable state is shown by the fact that the two children walk before, holding banners fringed at the edge and mounted on a stick, like the children's flags of the present day.

The toy used as a chair, in the charming picture by Lancret, is really a frame for a child learning to walk ; this shows us that the little ones of the seventeenth and eighteenth century in France were well provided for in this way ; the wide outspreading base will rejoice the mother's heart, for it would be almost impossible to upset the frame which is so firmly set on the wheels. This square wooden frame made for a child learning to walk, the feet just touching the ground, the wheels of the frame facilitating the progress, we have seen in miniature in many antique dolls' houses ; in one, the nursery of a dolls' house, the doll is in the frame and wears the elaborate lace cap of the seventeenth century. Such a chair forms the subject of a Chelsea " toy " of the eighteenth century, the wide square base making the head of the seal in the dainty coloured porcelain.

A toy to be pushed in front of an infant who is learning to walk is to be seen in a representation dated 1493.

Animals, Carriages, Carts. A square frame of about twelve inches has a solid wooden wheel at each corner ; a handle and crossbar are built on one side, for the child to hold.   In an eighteenth-century print there is a charming group, showing an elder sister or nurse, who drags a young child in a little go-cart ; the solid wooden wheels and springless frame seem to render the cushion, on which the child is resting, a most necessary luxury.

CHAPTER IX

RATTLES, BELLS, BAUBLES, MUSICAL INSTRUMENTS,
TOYS OF PERCUSSION.

MUCH ingenuity has been expended on the toys whose **Sound in** use is primarily to produce a noise for **Baby's** the joy of young children, and which, **Toys.** incidentally, torture and distract adults. The plaything which produces sound is the first to be given to a child in the form of a rattle or jingle, and even before this has been used, a delighted relative, anxious to make the baby "take notice," has probably rattled keys or some such object in front of the wide-open baby eyes.

The primitive instinct is strong in the newborn infant. Is not the passion for loud sound shown by every uncivilised race in the world? Gongs, drums, and clappers are the accompaniment of native dances; warriors shout and yell, as they don their paint and feathers, while the women beat gongs and clash cymbals. The war-whoop is as old

TOY FIGURE WITH
MUSICAL INSTRUMENT.
From Ancient Greece.

175

Rattles,
Bells,
Baubles,
Musical
Instru-
ments,
Toys of
Percus-
sion.

as humanity itself; drums of every size and shape are found amongst primitive peoples.

Toys of percussion, whistles, and squeakers are amongst the most favoured playthings all over the world, and there are few toys even in civilised countries which have not some simple contrivance attached to them to produce sound, though such sound be the secondary object of the toy. Dolls with squeakers in them can be had for a penny; tops are fitted with a contrivance which produces a humming or whistling sound; models of animals have squeakers or whistles, or have hard pellets inside them which produce a rattling sound. Rabbits beat drums as they are drawn along; even the children's hoops in the days of ancient Greece were made with spokes on which were threaded discs of metal, which clanked and jingled as the wheels went round; and now our baby's hoop, which is pushed along with a handle, has a bell and clapper fixed to the hub, while skipping-ropes have tiny bells attached to the handle.

Several toy bells have been found in the tombs of the children of early Christians at Rome; it will be remembered that toys were buried with the little ones, not only by the Egyptians and pagans of Greece and Rome, but also by the Christians, in accordance with the quaint and beautiful idea that the objects, which had given happiness in life, should be left with the owners in death. These bells, which measure about one inch in diameter, are of the ordinary shape, open at the base; they are made of metal, and the rings which suspended them in two cases remain intact. Since their removal from the Catacombs in Rome they have been kept in the Vatican Museum.

176

The finding of bells, which in this shape are said in **Silver** Hawkins' *History of Music* to have been invented by **Baubles.** Paulinus, Bishop of Nola, at the commencement of the fifth century, is interesting, as they must have been some of the first to be made. According to the ritual of the Romish Church, the bells were not only blessed and exorcised, but baptized and anointed with holy oil, in order that evil spirits lurking in the air might be driven away.

Some very beautiful silver toy bells of sixteenth-century workmanship have a whistle attached ; these are of Spanish origin and are now in the Musée Cluny in Paris.

Rattles and bells have always been made of great beauty and costliness ; gold, silver, crystal, coral, enamel, agate, and other precious or secondary stones, have been used in their fabrication, and fine workmanship has been expended upon their design and make.

Rattles were used in the Middle Ages not only to assemble the congregations, but also to mark the different offices in the services of the Roman Catholic Church.

Drums, trumpets, whistles, flutes, clarionets, and other more complicated musical instruments, are amongst the favourite toys of childhood ; and with reference to the primitive delight in sound, it is interesting to note that directly the play of adults becomes less decorous and self-conscious, a return is made to the childish delight in making a noise. When holiday-makers return after a day of pleasure, the modern trumpet, concertina, or tambourine are much in demand. In the noise, combined with that produced by nature's own whistle, the fingers or teeth, and shouting from healthy lungs, the

Rattles,
Bells,
Baubles,
Musical
Instru-
ments,
Toys of
Percus-
sion.

most enthusiastic seeker after musical instinct must be disappointed, for surely such manifestations are prompted only by the primitive love of noise.

The rattle dates from the most remote antiquity. Many are found amongst the primitive peoples, but careful investigation is necessary to determine whether these are the playthings of children, or are war-rattles used to exorcise devils and demons, intimidate the enemy, or call together the heads of the tribe.

A toy rattle from the West Indies is made of cane ; another from Queen Charlotte's Islands has a handle thirteen inches long ; the ball at the top is seven inches in diameter ; enclosed in it are the pellets which produce the sound.

An interesting rattle for adult use from North Africa is shaped like a hanging meat-safe. There is also a fetish whistle used by the medicine men for frightening away the devil of sickness.

A child's rattle of the Niger Coast Protectorate is shaped like a dice-box, and measures six and a half inches in length. Indian toy rattles from Yarkand are made of cane, which is roughly plaited together like the cheap toy rattles of English make ; they have long handles for the child to hold. Many of the earliest specimens of rattles, produced as children's toys by the civilised races of Western Europe, have two uses : a gum-stick of coral, agate, ivory, or some other hard and insoluble material, serves to soothe the gums of the child during dentition, and bells, whistles, or rattles to amuse and distract it with noise.

Several of this latter kind have been found at Pompeii, of somewhat original form : a circle of metal mounted on

178

Silver Whistles and Bells, with Agate and Coral Gum Sticks; the first is of the Georgian period, the second has Pagoda decorations. In the Fitzhenry collection.

Baby's Baubles with Whistle and Bells. Spanish. In the Musée Cluny.

Native Drum and Fife Band. The accompaniment of a masked show in Japan.
From a drawing by Hokusai.

an ivory handle has bells at intervals ; a small ball at the **Rattles.**
top holds the circle firmly in its place. At the Louvre
there is a miniature systre of Egyptian origin ; on two

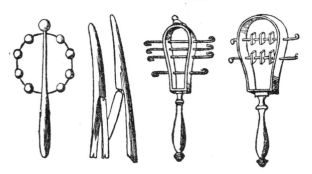

RATTLES, BALLS, AND SYSTRA.
Found at Pompeii.

bars of metal are threaded small blocks which, knocking
against each other, make the rattling sound which was
used in the elaborate Egyptian religious ceremonial in
connection with the worship of Bacchus and Isis. Toy
systra in clay exist, stamped with the figure of Orestes,
who, with the Gorgon, possessed
the special privilege of frightening the little ones. The reason
that a large number of toy
pigs are found as rattles and
other playthings, is due to the
fact that sucking-pigs were
sacrificed for the special preservation of young children.

EARLY GREEK RATTLE OF
BAKED CLAY.

Rattles of baked clay in every variety of shape have
been found wherever excavations have been carried out, and
they are made to this day in many kinds of coarse pottery.

181

Rattles,
Bells,
Baubles,
Musical
Instru-
ments,
Toys of
Percus-
sion.

Of the baby's bells there are many of great artistic merit.   The Georgian bauble in the FitzHenry collection measures seven and a half inches in length ; the silver-gilt body of the toy is carved in a pagoda pattern and richly chased ; a bulbous-shaped whistle is at the top ; two tiers of covered jingling bells, four in each tier, hang on with tiny rings ; a piece of red coral forms the gumstick. Another rattle in the same collection is of unusual shape : a richly chased crescent of silver has the bells suspended

ENGRAVING OF THE SIXTEENTH CENTURY.

Showing rattle.

from it ; an agate handle supports the bells ; there is no whistle on this pretty toy, which measures seven inches in length.

A rattle and coral in the same collection is silver-gilt with fine repoussé work on the stem, and a rounded body, which holds the eight bells in two tiers ; an unusually large whistle is at the top.   Vandyke, Velasquez, Rembrandt, Holbein, and other great masters of portraiture have all used the rattle and gumstick as suitable toys in the hands of their baby sitters.

Though by no means a child's toy, we must briefly

182

mention the bauble of the jester, which formed so im- portant an item in the outfit of the fools who, in the fifteenth and sixteenth centuries, were always to be found at the Courts of Europe, and also amongst the retainers of the great nobility. Without his silver or carved bauble this witty amuser of kings would have been poorly equipped for his work, for the toy, not infrequently made in the form of a head, was often used as a pretended counsellor or inspirer of the jests. Sometimes a blown bladder or silver filigree ornament appeared at the end of the baton, and a bunch of gaily coloured and embroidered ribbons tipped with bells did duty as the symbol of the office of jester.

This character, so often introduced by Shakespeare, not only relieved the strain of a too lugubrious plot, but also gave a correct touch in the representation of incidents taking place at a time when a fool with his bells and bauble was numbered amongst the retainers of every great household. During the Middle Ages buffoons and jesters made their bow to the public in that portion of pantomime fun of a rough-and-tumble nature, which was strangely brought into the most solemn of Mystery and Miracle plays—perhaps to render such serious performances " palatable to the vulgar taste," suggests Strutt. Beelzebub seems to have been the principal comic actor, assisted by his merry troupe of under-devils, who, with a variety of noises, strange gestures and contortions of the body, excited the laughter of the populace.

Two of the early Chinese toy musical instruments of the fourteenth and fifteenth centuries are shown in the paintings on silk of the period, and seem to have been very generally used by the little ones as an accompaniment

Rattles,
Bells,
Baubles,
Musical
Instru-
ments,
Toys of
Percus-
sion.

to many of their games. For instance, we see them while a puppet show is going on, and also when a tumbler of infantile proportions is showing feats of agility on a carefully spread reed mat. The child tumbler is almost nude ; the softness and roundness of the limbs, the texture of the baby skin, is exquisitely rendered in the still fresh and beautiful colouring, painted so many centuries ago. For the tumbler, the usual " band," consisting of tambourine player and clapper, is increased by the addition of a small rounded drum, which is being played by a third child, who stands watching the proceedings.   The child manipulating the clapper is also standing.   This instrument consists of a dozen or more thin slabs of wood about twelve inches long by four inches ; at one end the pieces are joined together, at the other they hang separated, and it is the noise of the pieces knocking together that forms the sound which may have been used to mark time. We have seen such instruments used during the fun of carnival time in continental cities. The third instrument in the Chinese group is played by a child in a crouching position.   In shape it is like a tambourine, and is raised on three sticks placed tripod-fashion ; the player strikes the parchment with sticks like those of a drum.

A curious musical toy of Korea is in the form of a bird ; this has a hole in its back, a tube fitted into the tail is blown by the child, and the sound of a dove's note is produced.

In Japan and India the favourite toy instruments are the tambourine and the drum ; every shape and size are used by the children ; sometimes the drums are struck by sticks with leather-covered knobs like gong-sticks, some-times with simple wooden sticks, occasionally they bang

184

Village Scene in Japan. From a drawing by Hokusai. A large drum is set up so that the children may satisfy their love of noise.

Toy Shop in Japan, where the children's wants are gratified in a very special manner.

on the parchment and get the much-loved noise with their own little fingers and knuckles.

In Japan there is an accompaniment of drum-beating at every show, whether it is a peep-show, a marionette performance, or the antics of a masked man, or a couple of performing dogs that are being displayed. Occasionally an enormous drum is set up in a village ; on this all the youngsters are allowed to bang under the superintendence of an adult.

In all countries where the bamboo is common, the flute is a favourite amongst the children, for in the ever-useful stems they find a ready hollowed instrument which only needs the holes for the notes and a mouth-hole to be made ; even the solid end is grown by nature for the little ones, so that they have but to cut above the cross division and each section makes a perfect flute. We have before us the picture of two little Japanese boys—one plays on one of these home-made flutes, the other on a drum ; they are playing a game called Kangura, in imitation of the real maskers who come round on New Year's Day with a band of cymbals, flute and drum, and perform various antics to the accompaniment of music. Another little boy has a tiny drum the size and shape of a saucer ; this is fixed on to the palm of his hand with a loop, in the other hand he holds a large stick padded at the end with which to beat his little drum.

Amongst the antique toy treasures preserved at Munich is a very beautifully made organ ; the case is of perfect proportion and elaborately carved. Twenty-six pipes are used in the construction of this bijou instrument, which doubtless once ornamented a doll's house ; it stands fourteen inches in height.

187

Rattles,
Bells,
Baubles,
Musical
Instru-
ments,
Toys of
Percus-
sion.

Wood, metal, glass (in the old harmonicon), and the skins of animals are the most common materials used in making toy musical instruments ; horn, bone, pottery, and gut have also been used.

In South Kensington Museum there are several whistles in the agate ware which was made during the first half of the eighteenth century, in some of the Staffordshire potteries ; a pair of birds which form whistles are coloured brown and blue ; they stand four inches in height. Toy whistles are sometimes made in extraordinary and most unexpected shapes, the tail of a bird being a very favourite mouth-piece ; the body of the bird containing the whistle is sometimes intended for holding water ; the note of the whistle is then altered and softened considerably. The handle of a toy jug also is made as a whistle. This device is frequently used in Belgium and in Spain.

In Japan, the jack-in-the-box is made still more alarming by the shrill whistle emitted, as the huge paper balloon is freed from the tiny box and is filled with air, which passes through the whistle by means of two orifices blown into, by the opening of the toy. A laughing face is generally painted on the reverse side. Sometimes these jacks of the Eastern hemisphere emerge from a pipe instead of from a box. Whistles are frequently combined with rattles in Japan, as with us ; their form generally inclines towards the grotesque.

Toy musical instruments of lacquer are made with great care in Japan. A pretty reed-like toy, which can be made to give chord harmonies, is to be found amongst the old toys.

In Sicily and Italy whistles are frequently made in

THE JEW'S HARP.
Painted by Wilkie, engraved by Burnet.

A RECRUITING PARTY.
Engraved by C. White.

the coarse pottery which is so often used for articles in **Whistles.** miniature for children's use. Animals, jugs, birds, cups from Palermo—all have their pierced tails, heads, or handles, which make the delightful shrill whistle beloved of the little ones.

An essentially French toy is the little clapper of the eighteenth century preserved at a museum in Paris ; this is a miniature of the wooden instrument with iron knocker which strikes sharply on the iron knob when shaken by the seller of the little wafers or *plaisirs* beloved of French children. Like our muffin-bell, the clapper announces the arrival of the cake-seller to his little patrons at the Bois, the Parc Monceau, or wherever the laughing crowds of French children most do congregate at the hour of *goûter*. Doubtless the little miniature " tick-a-tick," preserved in the collection of old toys, was specially made for a child who loved the dainty *oublies*, and who delighted in selling to her dollies piles of the ephemeral *gateaux*.

This delicacy is sold by a simple kind of lottery in many parts of Europe. Fixed to the top of the tin box in which the wafers are kept is a dial and pointer ; when the sou is tendered the purchaser spins the pointer, and according to the number at which it stops the child receives her portion of one, two, or perhaps a dozen cakes.

The jews' harp, the favourite toy of boyhood, is a very widely distributed musical instrument ; it is found not only in Europe and America, but also in the hands of the Khergis and in Eastern Thibet. Such specimens are made of cane, and have neatly made cases for carrying the delicate toy.

Amongst the playthings which are musical as a

**Rattles,
Bells,
Baubles,
Musical
Instru-
ments,
Toys of
Percus-
sion.**

secondary attribute, we must speak of the Korean board on which the game which is practically identical with the Japanese *Go* is played. This board is made in the form of a small hollow table, and is resonant; by an arrangement of wires stretched within, a musical note is emitted when a piece is played; these pieces or men are small polished black pebbles, irregular pieces of polished white shell furnishing the necessary variation.

In many of the mechanical toys music is a secondary

EIGHTEENTH-CENTURY AUTOMATIC MUSICAL TOY.

attraction, while some of the most elaborate are for the production of music only. Musical boxes, as these are called, reproduce the sound of all the instruments in an orchestra, and though more intricate effects are produced every year, they had already been brought to great perfection in the eighteenth century. In our chapter on mechanical toys we mention forms in pageants, which produced sound by means of a flow of water, also figures in which were concealed special contrivances for the production of musical notes.

Dancing figures in the peep-shows were sometimes

contrived so that music was produced while the puppets
moved ; sometimes it was supplied by a small hurdy-gurdy,
or some such instrument played by the showman. Nearly

DRUM ACCOMPANIMENT TO FIGURE DISGUISED AS A STAG.
From a fourteenth-century MS. in the Bodleian Library.

every show had its special instrument : drums with
mumming and juggling. The whistle or squeaker is now
identified with Punch. Formerly such
an instrument for increasing the volume
of sound in the human voice, or disguising it, was used by those actors in the
plays of Aristophanes and others,
whose parts necessitated the wearing
of masks, which would have muffled
the natural voice of the speaker.
The drum and pandian pipes are
now used by Punch and Judy showmen. Who could imagine the possibility of a harp or clarionet prelude
to this show? The drum and cymbals

From a manuscript of the
tenth century.

for obvious reasons call the public to the shows of
tumblers, jugglers, and other small exhibitions, which are
the delight of children, and which formed the chief

193

Rattles,
Bells,
Baubles,
Musical
Instru-
ments,
Toys of
Percus-
sion.

feature at the great fairs, now almost entirely abolished. Again, the fool has his bells, the nigger his tambourine. Who would tolerate a jester with a cornet, or a nigger with a harp?

The simple mechanical toys emitting sound were much used in the early nineteenth century ; animals were made to growl, bark, or mew, according to their nature, by the pulling of a string beneath the body; others, of roughly carved wood or moulded card or composition, were mounted on a board placed on a squeaker. These were sufficiently popular to form a very large item in the exports of the toy-making districts in Germany and France. Realism was still further achieved by the movement of the tongue or jaw of the animal ; this was effected by the current of air which worked the bellows of the squeaker.

A later artifice used for reproducing the noises of animals has existed only, we believe, since the introduction of " skin " animals—those having dressed leather or skin, generally chamois leather or calf-skin stretched over composition models. The sound is produced by the movement of the head of the animal, which, being suspended, is in connection with a contrivance so superior to the old squeaker that the *miow* of a cat, the bark of a dog, the *baa* of a sheep, or the roar of a lion is made to resemble the sound in a really remarkable manner.

At the end of the eighteenth and beginning of the nineteenth century, when Cruchet was designing the cheap mechanical toys which were to bring such things within reach of the people, many excellent effects were achieved, such as the walk of a sentry along a board and back to his sentry-box, on the turning of a handle, the bugle-notes sounding in the interior of the machine; again, a band Cheap consisting of officer with drawn sword, two fifes, and two Mechanical Toys drummers marched to the tinkling sound of music inside with the stand, when a handle was turned. Such designs and Music. many others we have seen in a toy-maker's pattern-book of Napoleon's time.

A large-sized single figure of a drummer in the huge shako of the Peninsular war makes an alarming tatoo on his drum, when wound up.

Of Vaucouson's wonderful musical automata, the first important work was the flute-player, exhibited in Paris in 1738 ; its height was fifteen feet six inches. The idea for the figure was suggested to the maker by a statue of a faun playing on a flute in the gardens of the Tuilleries, says M. Allemagne. Vaucouson's uncle tried to dissuade him from making the toy, and for a time the clever youth gave it up, but during his enforced idleness, on his recovery from a serious illness, he resumed his calculations, and so correct were they that, on having the different parts of the machinery made by several workmen, the figure worked perfectly on their being first put together. From the same source we learn that this earliest effort is the only automatic toy made by Vaucouson which still exists ; it is preserved at Vienna.

Soon after, this remarkable inventor made a tambourine player of equal ingenuity ; his efforts were afterwards used in the direction of other toys not specially musical, described in our chapter on mechanical toys.

Peep-shows and mechanical dancing-dolls frequently had musical contrivances attached to them. We have before us the picture of an Italian organ-grinder, who, as

Rattles,
Bells,
Baubles,
Musical
Instru-
ments,
Toys of
Percus-
sion.

he turns the handle of his organ, sets in motion the figures of some dancing-dolls.

Amongst the toys of the royal children recently sent from Windsor Castle to Kensington Palace, to make room for the new belongings of King Edward VII. and Queen Alexandra, is a little toy musical-box, which, on being wound up, merrily grinds out the tunes in vogue in the middle of the last century, while three tiny dolls, but two and a half inches high, elaborately dressed in silks and satins of brightest colours, dance round and round to the tunes.

Another musical toy, once belonging to the Princes and Princesses of our royal family, shows a somewhat cadaverous-looking woman at the piano, whose head has nearly fallen off ; on winding up, the "Roseta Waltz" is played. This little toy, which is in a black case measuring nine by eleven inches, was made by Bouchet in Paris. The picture is painted in colours, the curtain a brilliant red.

The celebrated spinet-shaped instrument of the time of Louis XIV., which mystified the whole of Paris with the ravishing airs played by apparently mechanical process, was discovered afterwards to be manipulated by a little child-player concealed in the body of the instrument. The ingenious inventor of this contrivance, M. Jean Raisin, was the first to organise amongst his own and other children a little troupe of comedians, who played their pieces with great success in Paris and elsewhere.

CHAPTER X

BALLS, BALL-PLAY, SWINGING, AND OTHER GAMES.

THE ball shares with the doll the distinction of highest **Man** antiquity amongst toys, but it bears the palm of **a Ball-** popularity ; for while the doll appeals essentially to girls, **playing Animal.** the ball is the plaything of everybody, irrespective of age and sex.

Are we taking our subject too seriously in pointing out the Seven Ages of ball-playing ? At first when the sphere must be of woolly softness lest it should hurt baby fingers ; then the rubber or leather ball bounces and rebounds, while chubby legs totter in pursuit ; next the sturdy five-year-old, thirsting for more definite sport, rolls a wooden ball to knock down his group of nine-pins ; while bat, trap, and ball or rounders engages his attention when at seven years he is promoted from the nursery to a dame school ; cricket and football, in turn, mark separate stages in the development of youth ; these games, together with tennis and fives, being sometimes prolonged until manhood has long been reached. In mature age, enthusiasm in the pursuit of the ball reaches its apogee in the fascination of billiards, polo, and the " royal and ancient game," for the golf enthusiast is eager to tramp many a mile after the ball of what composition the future alone knows.

Certainly man is a ball-playing animal. Can there be a doubt about the importance of playthings while the skilful manœuvring of an inflated leather sphere by twenty-two men attracts a crowd of 60,000 onlookers in England, and 100,000 are drawn to see a base-ball match in America?

Quite a large number of balls can be seen at the British Museum, which it is safe to conjecture were the means of amusing the little ones 4000 years ago ; these vary in size, from the tiny marble, of which there is a saucerful of specimens, half an inch in diameter, to the well-preserved remains of a leather-covered ball sewn in sections like the tennis-ball of the present day, and stuffed with husks of grain tightly packed ; the stuffing of the balls of ancient Egypt vary greatly, some being stuffed with pliable reeds which are wound and rolled up tightly like a ball of string, over which the leather covering is sewn.

There are many earthenware balls painted in light and dark shades of colour, generally blue ; others are slightly flattened like the cheese-shaped bowls, as if they had been used for bowling along the ground. A very interesting antique Roman ball was found during the excavations in 1896 at Behnesch ; it should be described as Egypto-Roman ; it is covered with coloured wools as fresh in hue as if wound yesterday, instead of in the third century before Christ ; the arrangement of the wool covering is in interlacing bands ; it is one and a quarter inches in diameter.

Woollen Ball, 1¼ in., of IIIrd
Century before Christ.

Egyptian Ball of Wool and Flax
Threads. 2½ in.

Ball of tightly twisted Papyrus
Fibre. Egyptian. 2½ in.

Blue and Grey Ball of Pottery.
Egyptian. 2½ in.

Bouncing Ball of Split Cane
from the Malay Peninsular.
8 in. diameter.

Mediæval Ball Play. From a miserere seat in
Gloucester Cathedral.

Covered Tennis Court with protected gallery for spectators. French.
Late XVIIIth Century.

A glazed porcelain ball of about the same period was **Ball-play** found at Cairo ; this is two and a half inches in diameter. **for Old** The ball-play of antiquity was not confined to children, **and Young.** for from Egyptian, Greek, and Roman records we have abundant proof that, like the moderns, they ceased playing with balls only when age rendered their limbs too stiff for active movement.

With the Egyptians, the mere amusement of throwing and catching was considered suitable only for girls ;

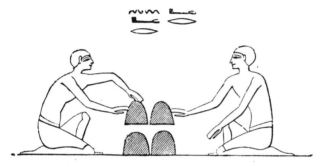

EGYPTIAN EQUIVALENT FOR THIMBLE-RIG.
From a fresco.

Greek and Roman records, however, prove that boys and men participated in the sport.

The riding on the back of an unsuccessful catcher by a second player in Egypt was considered as a punishment or forfeit ; this was redeemed when the next player missed the catch. The distances between thrower and catcher were carefully regulated by rules arranged between the players before the commencement of the game. Forfeits were also used by the Greeks as well as the Egyptians in their elaborate ball-catching games.

Sometimes the mode of catching was regulated and

201

Balls, Ball-play, Swinging, and other Games. hands were clasped over the breast or behind the back. Besides ball-throwing to an opponent, high throwing was indulged in ; this was common in Egypt. A game is

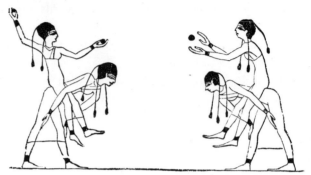

AN EGYPTIAN BALL GAME.
From a fresco.

described by Homer in which one player threw the ball high in the air, and the other, watching its fall, leapt high

BALL-CATCHING WITH THE ARMS CROSSED.
From an Egyptian fresco.

in the air and caught it before his feet touched the ground again.

Though there is no reason to doubt the possibility of

some ancient form of ball game where the equivalent of **An**
the modern racquet or bat was used, no pictorial record **Inflated**
of such a game exists, nor have we been able to find any **Ball.**
allusion to a bat or racquet in early writings. The *follis*,
or inflated ball, like our football, was struck with the
arms, and a smaller inflated ball was struck with the hand,
on which a kind of gauntlet was worn. We see, from an
Etruscan vase picture, that the protective gauntlet was
strapped below the elbow and covered half of the hand
like a mitten ; it was worn on the right forearm only ; on
it one of the players is supporting the large sphere, which

BOARD AND HOOP OR DISC GAMES OF THE GREEKS.

is considerably larger than the player's head ; its lightness
is shown by the fact that another player is supporting
a similar ball on his finger-tips.

What we should call juggling with balls—that is,
throwing up three or four in quick succession, catching
them and throwing them up again, keeping the whole
number in play at the same time—was brought to great
perfection by the Egyptians, and there are Anglo-Saxon
records of this game.

The Greeks had a game in which balls were rolled down
a sloping board, and apparently fell into a hole in the
ground a few feet away. We know of two bas-reliefs
representing children engaged in this pastime.

203

Balls, Ball-play, Swinging, and other Games.

At what time the ball as a toy was introduced into England it is difficult to decide. A manuscript of the fourteenth century belonging to Trinity College, Oxford, mentions it in describing the life of St. Cuthbert : "He pleyde atte balle." Fitzstephen, writing in the thirteenth century, describes how annually upon Shrove Tuesday the London schoolboys go

A BALL GAME WITH SLOPING BOARD.

into the fields after dinner, and play at the celebrated game of ball, every party of boys carrying their own ball and playing with the youths of their own school, but not competing with the other scholars. Stowe thinks this to have been a kind of golf or bandy-ball ; but Strutt

AN EARLY SAXON CLUB AND BALL GAME.

does not consider such an assertion is justified, as there is no mention of a bat or cudgel.

The origin of the *jeu de paume* in France was in the palm play, for when the game was first introduced the ball was driven by the palm of the hand. To avoid injury to the

204

naked skin a glove was used, which, in some instances, had a knotted lining. Later, cords were wound round the hand to accelerate the speed of the ball, from whence the racquet evolved. As early as the reign of Charles V. large sums were lost and won at the *jeu de paume*; a century later, tennis courts had appeared in every quarter of Paris and at Versailles, besides which many of the great nobles had tennis-courts attached to their houses. Such places were the fashionable rendezvous of the day ; we have a picture of one before us, in which there is a gallery or lounge running the whole length of the court, where gentlemen-at-arms and their friends are talking to each other or watching the game. These courts were covered with a roof, so that the game might be played irrespective of the weather ; this is one of the reasons, doubtless, of the rapid advance of the players in skill. The vigorous nature of the exercise is indicated by the doffing of the players' cloaks, coats, and hats. This engraving is by Crispin de Passe. It will be remembered that it was while watching a game of tennis that Charles VIII. of France expired.

By the sixteenth century covered tennis courts existed in England ; an early one still stands at the historic home of the Cecils, Hatfield House in Hertfordshire. In the record of the expenditure of Henry VII. these items occur : " for the king's loss at tennis, twelve pence ; for the loss of balls, three pence." Henry VIII. had special tennis coats and tennis slippers. That the game was played by young boys as well as men is certain, and a French writer speaks of a woman, named Margot, who in Paris in 1424 played hand-tennis with the palm and also the back of her hand " better than any man."

**Balls,
Ball-play,
Swinging,
and other
Games.**

No less an authority than J. J. Rousseau writes in praise of ball-play, as an exercise for children ; he says, "To spring from one side of a tennis court to another, to judge of the rebounding of a ball while it is in the air, and to return it with a sure and steady aim—these are diversions less adapted to the amusement of grown persons than proper to form them in youth."

This game of tennis must not be confounded with the lawn-tennis of the present day, which was introduced in the middle of the nineteenth century.

The reasons for the playing of special games at special seasons of the year when not obviously prompted

CHILDREN PLAYING AT BALL.
From a fifteenth-century MS.
in the British Museum.

by the state of the weather are always difficult to assign. Certainly there seems no particular reason for the playing of hand-ball during the Easter holidays. Strutt is our authority for the assertion that hand-ball was played by children of both sexes during the Easter holidays, and tansy cakes were given as prizes. A learned authority has suggested that the nature of the reward may be traced to the Jewish custom of eating bitter herbs at the time of the Passover.

Fives, the surviving form of hand-tennis, was played in Queen Elizabeth's day. This is one of the games still recognised at Eton. In 1765 a manuscript list of games played at Eton gives "cricket, fives, shirking walls, scrambling walls, bally cally, battledore, pigtop, pig in the ring, goals, hop-scotch, heading conquering cobs, hoops, marbles, trap ball, steal baggage, puss in the corner, cat, gallows, bictes, cloysler, tops, humming-tops, hunt the hare, hunt the dark lanthorn, chuck sinks, stare caps, hurtle cap." No games are now recognised but cricket, football, and fives.

In a manuscript of the fourteenth century there is an illustration of a game which Strutt calls balloon ball.

BALLOON BALL OR FIVES.
From a Harleian MS. copy of the romance called
Histoire de Lancelot ou S. Graal.

This resembles the inflated ball game of the Greeks and Romans. It was struck from player to player with the naked hand, or by the hand and arm protected with a covering of wood or leather ; the ball is not so large as that of the ancients.

The above is quite distinct from the inflated ball game played with the foot. It is amusing to read how this enormously popular game of football is spoken of in 1830 : " Football is so called because the ball is driven about with the feet instead of the hands. It was formerly much in vogue among the common people of England, though of late years it seems to have fallen into disrepute and is but little practised. . . . The goal is usually made with two sticks driven into the ground about two or three feet apart. The ball, which is commonly made of a blown bladder, and cased with leather, is delivered in the midst of the ground, and the object of each party is to drive it through the goal of their antagonists, which being achieved, the game is won."

FOOTBALL IN THE STRAND IN THE EIGHTEENTH CENTURY.

In the time of James I. a rule was made to " debarre from this court all rough and violent exercises as the football, meeter for laming than making able the users thereof."

The game was much played in the streets of cities. **Antiquity of Football.**
At Chester, from earliest times, on Shrove Tuesday a
football of the value of three shillings and fourpence was
played from the Cross to the Common Hall. In 1540
this old custom, " productive of much inconvenience," was
discontinued. Football was played in the Strand as late
as the eighteenth century. We have an old print showing
an assemblage of apprentices enjoying the game.

It is related that football was first played in Japan at
the time of the Empress Kogioku, A.D. 642, but as there
was a woman on the throne it was not played at court
until an emperor reigned about the year 1184. It was
at this period that the rules for the game in Japan were
made, and from the first the great generals appear to
have taken part in it, and used the kicking of a huge
football as a test of strength and ability in their
soldiers.

Gods and goddesses play an important part in the
history of the Eastern football. The spirits of football,
three in number, have the faces of children and the
bodies of monkeys. On their foreheads are the names
respectively, " Spring willow blossom, Summer forest,
and Autumn garden." They visit all football grounds
and are its presiding divinities. Words which are used
as cries at certain points of the game are their names.
They are worshipped on one of the days dedicated to
the monkey, and their shrine is at the ancient seat of
Lord Marimetsee, a famous patron of the game.

Football was always a favourite pastime at the
Japanese court, and there are many pictures of the
Japanese nobles of high rank playing the game. The
Mikado and his court, during the time of extreme poverty,

**Balls,
Ball-play,
Swinging,
and other
Games.**

added to their income by giving lessons in the art of football.

The description of the games of boys and girls in the reign of Henry II. is delightfully given by William Fitzstephen. " We may begin with the pastimes of the boys. Annually on the day which is called Shrove Tuesday the boys of respective schools bring to the masters, each one his fighting cock, and they are indulged all the morning with seeing their cocks fight in the school-room. After dinner all the youths of the city go into the field of the suburb and address themselves to the famous game of football. The scholars of each school have their particular ball, the particular trades have most of them theirs. The elders of the city, the fathers of the party, and the rich and wealthy come to the field on horseback in order to behold the exercises of the youth, and, in appearance, are themselves as youthful as the youngest, their natural heat seeming to be revived at the sight of so much agility, and in a participation of the diversions of their festive sons." Every Sunday in Lent " . . . the lay sons of the citizens rush out of the gates in shoals furnished with lances and shields, the younger sort with javelins pointed but disarmed of their steel. They ape the feats of war and act the sham fight, practising the antagonistic exercises of that kind. If the king happens to be near the city, many courtiers honour them with their presence, together with the juvenile part of the households of the bishops, earls, barons, such as are not yet dignified with the honour of knighthood, and are desirous of trying their skill. At Easter the diversion is prosecuted on the water : a target is strongly fastened to a trunk or mast fixed in the middle of the river, and

210

a youngster, standing upright in the stern of the boat
made to move as fast as the oars and current can
carry it, is to strike the target with his lance."

On holidays in summer the pastime of the youth
is to exercise themselves in archery, in running, leaping,
wrestling, casting of stones, and flinging to certain
distances.

In the winter holidays the youths are entertained in
the morning with boars fighting to the last gasp, ". . . and
when that vast lake which waters the city towards the
north (the districts of Moorfield and Finsbury) is hard
frozen, the youth in great numbers go to divert themselves
on the ice." After describing the sport of sliding, the
author goes on to say : "Others there are who are still
more expert in these amusements on the ice : they place
certain bones, the leg bones of some animal, under the
soles of their feet by tying them round their ankles, and,
taking a pole shod with iron into their hands, they push
forward by striking it against the ice and are carried
along with a velocity equal to the flight of a bird or a
bolt discharged from a crossbow."

There appear to have been two ways of playing
stool-ball. Dr. Johnson says it is "a play where balls
are driven from stool to stool"—a somewhat vague
description. We believe that a certain number of stools
were set up in a circle at measured distances from each
other, each one of them occupied by a player ; the ball being
thrown to one, each must alter his position as at rounders,
and if he who threw the ball can regain it in time to
strike one of the players before he reaches his stool, the
person touched must throw the ball. The second mode
of playing resembled cricket, one stool being used instead

of the wickets, the player defending it by striking the ball with his hand, the thrower of the ball doing his best to strike the stool.

Hurling is a very ancient form of ball play, but as it was never, we believe, a children's game, we must not go into it fully.   It was played in Cornwall; goals were used, and matches were frequently arranged between different parishes.

Golf, cambue, or bandy-ball, on the other hand, was frequently played by boys.   It is practically the same as

BANDY.

From a fourteenth-century MS.

the rustic pastime of the Romans, played with a ball stuffed with feathers.   In the reign of Edward III. the name cambuca, from the crooked club or bat, was given to it.   We have an illustration of bandy-ball in the fourteenth century taken from a manuscript of that date : two boys are playing, the ball is large in size, the clubs more like the hockey-sticks of the present day.

A delightful golf anecdote is given by Hove concerning Prince Henry, eldest son of James I., who was "playing at golf, a play not unlike to pale-maille, whilst his schoolmaster stood talking to another, and marked not his highness warning him to stand farther off.   The prince, thinking he had gone aside, lifted up his golf club to strike the ball ; meantyme one standing by said to him, 'Beware that you hit not Master Newton,' wherewith he, drawing back his hand, said, 'Had I done so, I had but paid my debts.' "

Stow-ball seems to have been not a distinct game, but another name sometimes given to a golf-ball.

The game pale-maille mentioned above was something like golf, the ball being struck with a mallet or club, but different, in that the ball must fall through an arch of iron, thus resembling the modern croquet. At the

PALL-MALL IN ST. JAMES'S PARK.

interesting exhibition of Les Primitifs in Paris recently, a fine piece of tapestry showed this game in progress.

It was fashionable in England in the reign of Charles II., the walk in St. James's Park now called the Mall having been appropriated to the use of the King and his courtiers for practice. Such was the origin of the name of the famous thoroughfare Pall Mall.

213

**Balls,
Ball-play,
Swinging,
and other
Games.**

In a rare book entitled *The French Garden for English Ladies and Gentlewomen to walke in*, published in 1621, one lady says, "If one had paille-mails it were good to play in this alley, for it is reasonable good length straight and even." In Sir Robert Dallington's *Method for Travell* he writes this reflection : "I marvell among many more apish and foolish toys which we have brought out of France, that we have not brought this sport also into England."

A variant of the game played by children was called rug-ball, where a rug as well as an arch of iron must be passed over before the game could be won. Like pall-mall and golf, the fewest number of strokes in accomplishing the round declared the skilful player.

Club-ball, mentioned in an edict in the time of Edward III., was played with a curved and a straight bat held respectively by two players. It was played by boys and • girls, and is represented in a manuscript in the Bodleian Library dated 1344, as well as in a genealogical roll of the Kings of England to the time of Henry III. It is considered that from this ancient game of club-ball, cricket was evolved, a name derived from the three-legged stool or cricket whose use we cannot trace farther than the commencement of the eighteenth century. Brand describes it as "most usual in Kent with a cricket ball, bowl'd and struck with two cricket bats between two wickets." The name is from the Saxon *cricce*, a bat or staff, which also signifies a support or prop, whence a cricket, or little stool to sit upon. Cricket play among the Saxons was also called staff play. In a description of the game written at the beginning of the nineteenth century the remark is made : "It is called a run, and one notch or score is made upon the tally towards his game." It would be interesting to compare an old cricket tally of 1800 with a modern scoring card. Strutt says in 1838, "Cricket of late years is become exceedingly fashionable, being much countenanced by the nobility and gentlemen of fortune, who frequently join in the diversion." With the modern aspects of the game we are not dealing, our record of pastimes being up, roughly, to 1838.

Trap-ball is an earlier game than cricket, more probably coeval with club-ball. A manuscript of the fourteenth century shows that the old mode of playing differed slightly from the present game of trap-ball. In this picture the "trap" is so elevated that the player is in the

BAT, TRAP AND BALL, AS IT WAS PLAYED IN THE FOURTEENTH CENTURY.

From an old manuscript painting.

upright position when he strikes the lever which raises the ball in a position to be struck away. In the modern game the trap is a shoe-shaped box with a wooden lever, placed upon the ground, and the player must stoop low to strike. Village boys make a round hole in the ground and use the flat brisket bone of an ox as a lever on which they place the ball; boundaries are made, and six or eight players sometimes take part in the game. The bat varies considerably in shape, but was generally short and wide, like a short-handled tennis racquet; sometimes only a stick was used, this requiring much more skill on the part of the player.

215

Balls, Ball-play, Swinging, and other Games. There are very many games in which a ball plays a minor part, though not being thrown or struck, as the chief implement in the display of skill on the part of the player, but simply being used as hostage, forfeit, or gage. There are varieties of children's pastimes which

FROG IN THE MIDDLE.
From a Bodleian MS.

have come down to us, inspired by the courting customs, the oracle or divination rites, or the robbery and treasure hiding, which were the serious occupations of the adults of the day. Such a game is Queen Anne, or Lady Queen Anne; as Chambers's *Popular Rhymes* has it, at the lines—

> I choose you one and I choose you all,
> And pray, Miss ——, yield up the ball,
> The ball is mine and none of yours, etc.,

the ball is passed from one to another of the players, Queen Anne, the chosen head of the game, pointing to the player on the opposite side whom she thinks possesses the ball. In many games the carrying of the sport to a successful issue depends on the hiding of a ball, but any other small object would do equally well.

Mrs. Gomme suggests that the leading figure is that

216

of an oracle, and the hidden ball represents stolen treasure, Games in which Balls represent a Prize or Goal. or that a bride and her damsels were the characters taking part in the game. Undoubtedly these are represented in many of the advancing and retiring games, such as nuts and May, and in other games when boys and girls choose sides and two lines are formed.

It were interesting to study further the subject of children's games and their origins, the forfeit and punishment games such as hot cockles, when the hand of the victim is smitten and the name of the buffeter must be guessed.

In hoodman blind an important element of the game was the buffeting of the blinded player ; this we see in a

HOODMAN BLIND.
From a fourteenth-century MS.

miniature from the margin of a fourteenth-century MS. This feature of the game is now happily repressed. We must forbear to touch further on this subject, however, for it is with the implement of play rather than the play itself that we deal.

Tip-cat, though not exactly a ball game, is played in a way so resembling the ball games we have been describing, that we must include it in this chapter. Two figures of children engaged in this pastime are frequently represented in the woodcut initial letters used in some of the smaller books which were issued from the Gioldo press at Venice during the first half of the sixteenth century. Like hop-scotch, or Scotch hoppers, as the old name reads, tip-cat is played by native children in India, where it was introduced by the Portuguese.

The stick or cudgel held in the hand of the child is used to strike one end of the shuttle-shaped "cat," which is about six inches in length ; this causes it to rise into the air with a rotatory motion ; it is then beaten away by the stick. Sometimes a ring is drawn upon the ground and players measure the distance with the eye ; sometimes a more elaborate game with several holes, each occupied by a player with his cudgel, is played.

The game of marbles was originally played with nuts, small stones, or spheres of pottery ; these latter have been excavated with other toys of antiquity.

Taw, the best-known form of the game, can be played by any number of boys who aim at marbles placed within a ring, using other marbles as ammunition, and shooting with the fingers, the thumb being the ejector ; he who succeeds in beating most of his opponents out of the ring is the conqueror. There are many other variants of the game, " nine-holes " and " hit " and " span " being the best known.

Span and counter is a game like marbles, but played with counters or stones ; French boys may often be seen playing it.

Brand says that " marbles no doubt had their origin in bowls, and received their name from the substance of

PULL DEVIL, PULL BAKER.

F. Bartolozzi, R.A.   After Wm Hamilton, R.A.

HOT COCKLES.

F. Bartolozzi, R.A.   After Wm. Hamilton, R.A.

which the bowls were formerly made"; another old
authority mentions that marbles had taught him percussion and the laws of motion.

A large number of marbles were found in the
eighteenth century near Hythe, and it was alleged that
they were of prehistoric origin ; this assertion was, however, disproved, and it was shown by the make of the
pottery that they were not more than a century old ;
they are of marbled brown and white clay.

Bowling-greens were known in the thirteenth century
in England ; the representation of one from a manuscript
shows a small cone-shaped object as the mark. The
French game *carreau* of the Middle Ages appears to
have been similar, but there appears no mark at either
end of the alley. In most country towns bowling-greens
are still to be found, and formerly bowling-alleys were
attached to noblemen's houses. The somewhat similar
game of *nine-pins* is the form most patronised by children.
This was originally called *kayles*, *cayles*, or *keiles*,
from the French word *quilles*. It is difficult to say
when the number of the pins was decided upon ; certainly
in the fourteenth century a number short of nine was
used, and their form varies more than in modern times.
In early representations of this game, club kayles is
played ; it was not till a good deal later that the pins
were knocked down by the bowling of a ball instead
of the throwing of a short stick or club. *Closh* or *cloish*
is the name sometimes given by old authorities to the
game where the pins are overthrown by a ball.

Kayle—kayle-pins or kettle-pins—is a game derived
from the ancient kayles,—the pins, of whatever variety,
being bowled at by the player, standing at a distance

**Balls,
Ball-play,
Swinging,
and other
Games.**

settled by mutual consent. Skittle-pins were sometimes made of bones. The Dutch pins are more slender
than the English, especially the central king pin ; the
balls used are larger and of a very light kind of wood.

In *four corners* the balls used are large and very
heavy ; " the excellency of the same, " says Hove, " consists
in beating down the pins in the fewest casts of the
bowl."

" Half-bowl," prohibited in the reign of Edward IV.,
like kayles and closh, is played with a half-bowl of wood.

THE ANCIENT GAME OF KAYLES.
Ancestor of kayle-pins or skittle-pins.

Nine-holes, or " bubble the justice," has an interesting
history : it is the game which the boys played when,
at the end of the eighteenth century, the magistrates
caused the skittle alleys to be destroyed ; it is a variant
of skittles, and could not be set aside by the justices as
it had not been mentioned in the statute.

The old children's game of fox and geese or solitaire
is said to have been invented by an unfortunate man
kept in solitary confinement at the Bastille ; but it is
probably of much older date, being a simpler form of
the " odd squares " or Pachisi, the national game of
India. The great Akbar played it in a truly regal

222

manner, the court of the palace having been inlaid with marble to form the board, young slaves from his harem wearing different colours representing pieces moved according to the throw of the dice. Traces of such "boards" in the courts of the palaces are still to be seen at Agra and Allahabad.

Solitaire is also called nun's play, and much artistic skill was expended on the making of some of the boards and spheres or men, which were beautifully carved and decorated, in France and Italy in the seventeenth and eighteenth centuries.

Wooden balls are made in India of a light wood called Veppolai, which is skilfully turned by the natives, and while revolving on the lathe, sticks of various coloured lacs are applied to the surface. The heat of the friction melts the lac, and causes it to adhere to the wood with a polished surface ; these balls are extraordinarily cheap.

Cup and ball, that most excellent game for the training of the eye and hand, was well known in India at a very early date. This toy also has had much skill lavished upon its decoration. Ivory carving of the most elaborate kind frequently renders the implements of the game of great artistic value. Such toys were played with, not only by children, but also by adults at the French, Italian, and Spanish courts of the seventeenth century. Heads, hearts, flowers, and fruit sometimes replace the ball in elaborate specimens.

Two Indian toys of this description are amongst the playthings of Queen Victoria, now to be seen at Kensington Palace.

The Esquimaux play an interesting variant of the game. A piece of walrus ivory, the size of a man's fist, is pierced with holes at irregular distances ; an ivory pin, about two inches in length and half an inch in diameter, at the thickest end, is attached by a cord, and the player must show his skill by jerking the pin into the air and catching it in a hole in the ivory. The cord is only four inches in length, which greatly adds to the difficulty of the game. Another way of playing with this toy, is to hang the pierced piece in the centre of the room, and then throw the dart from given distances, aiming at the holes ; this form of game has the advantage that many are able to take a part in it.

In China, Japan, and Korea a bat and ball game is now played by children, but, as in the case with so many other games, it was formerly played also by adults. Two lines are drawn on the ground a few feet apart, there is a dividing line mid-way. A wooden ball is placed on it, and the players, eight in number, are divided into two sides ; each endeavour to knock the ball with wooden clubs across the opposite line ; of course spirits and demons are mixed up with the play as with all games in the East, and the sticks or bones used are called in Chinese, " The bow for driving evil spirits away."

The ball is not much used in Korea ; small oranges are sometimes thrown, but the popularity of the sphere as a toy is not great. The cash, or money of very small value with a square hole in the centre, is far more used in playing games both there and in China,—not necessarily for gambling, but as the actual toy or implement of the game.

In a measuring game a stick is cut, three inches in length, a hole is made in the ground, and throws are

TRAP BALL.

F. Bartolozzi, R.A.   After Wm. Hamilton, R.A.

Japanese Ball Game played by Girls. Elastic or a cord is attached to the ball and
depends from the finger of the player. From a drawing by Hokusai.

made as near, or into the hole if possible; cash is used, and no throw counts which is outside a three-inch radius. Other games, which in Western countries would be played by children with their marbles, are all played with cash.

The Japanese girls are devoted to the ball with elastic attached, which is caught up and pushed away from the hand incessantly; sometimes the ball, which is usually of light make and wound round with silk, is bounced on a wall or the ground; sometimes its fall is limited only by the length of cord attached.

An interesting account is given by M. Leo Claretie of a somewhat similar game in vogue at the terrible time of the French Revolution; it was called l'Emigrette, after the nobles who, despairing of the fortunes of the monarchy, emigrated to other capitals, leaving their splendid houses unoccupied and ruined. An old print exists which shows the toy to have been made of a double disc of ivory; it rose and fell by the aid of a narrow cord or ribbon which wound or unwound round a small spring. Four figures are represented using the toy; the last one has one in each hand.

History has stamped itself on other toys besides the Emigrette of the Revolution. The subject is treated amongst the special toys of special seasons and epochs.

So accustomed are we, of modern time, to the use of indiarubber that it is difficult to think of the means used for obtaining the elasticity which is so desirable in a ball. Inflated bladders covered with leather for strength, served the purpose; but the most perfectly bounceable ball we have seen, made without the aid of indiarubber, is the

**Balls,
Ball-play,
Swinging,
and other
Games.**
hollow ball of split cane made by the natives of the Malay Peninsula ; these are about six inches in diameter, and are woven in an open pattern. Exquisite neatness and finish is shown in the welding of the cane, so that the ball should not split asunder.

CHAPTER XI

MARIONETTES, PUNCH AND JUDY, DANCING DOLLS.

AMONGST the patrons of the Marionette Theatre may be Distincounted, not only the children of the civilised world, but guished "grown ups" such as Plato, Aristotle, Horace, Marcus Audiences. Aurelius, Galien, Tertullian, Shakespeare, Cervantes, Ben Jonson, Molière, Pope, Swift, Fielding, Voltaire, Goethe, Byron, and hundreds of other distinguished men, who, taking their places amongst the crowds of happy children, through successive ages, have watched with innocent delight the antics of " the little wooden folk."

Le Sage and other brilliant playwrights have produced dramas for representation on the miniature stage ; every popular footlight favourite in opera, ballet dance, and comedy, has been exploited in miniature ; each artifice and accessory of the stage has been bent to the purpose of the Showman of Marionettes, from the *sifflet pratique* used in the days of ancient Greece in the production of the plays of Aristophanes, when artificial means of assisting or disguising the human voice were used (this still lives in the Punch's whistle of to-day), down to the newest method of electric lighting, with

**Marion-
ettes,
Punch
and Judy,
Dancing
Dolls.** which the few remaining modern marionettes' " wings "
are fitted.

The light thrown on the history of serious drama in
tracing the history of marionettes is considerable.   In
the children's puppets, on a stage five feet square, we
see the antics of the great tragedians and comedians, as
it were through an opera-glass held the wrong way.   We
hear echoes of the opera in the voices and review the
ballet in the grace of the performers in miniature.

The marionettes described in this chapter are the
figures of wood, bone, ivory, cardboard, or linen which,
representing persons, real or imaginary, are made to move
by means of an invisible hand, with or without the aid
of strings or wires.   Those puppets, which move by clockwork or any device other than strings, we describe
amongst mechanical toys.

Charles Nodier, writing in the *Revue de Paris* in
1842-43, traces the origin of the marionettes to a child's
doll, for he argues that the child herself supplies the
dialogue suitable for her game, thus standing in the place
of the showman.   Does she not, if endowed with dramatic
instinct, alter her voice when different dolls are speaking,
giving us a foretaste of Punch's squeaker?   Is not the
doll set to her lessons, scolded as a naughty child, put in
a corner, shamed with a Dunce's cap, pardoned again and
taken into favour, thus providing a whole drama, unwritten,
but sufficiently dramatic to shadow forth the plays of the
marionette stage?   The analogy is close, but we think that
M. Magnin, in his brilliant *Histoires des Marionettes*, has
proved without a doubt that marionettes derived their
origin from the animated statuary of the ancients, rather
than the doll of childhood.

When, to complete the illusion of life in the figures of **Two** Greek statues, artificial movement was added, there were **Methods** two means used for endowing the inanimate form with **of pro-** the superficial appearance of life—one when clockwork, **ducing** counterbalance, or the expansion of metals was used and **ment.** hidden in the figure, the other when strings of cord or wire were attached to the limbs, which being pulled by an unseen hand, a semblance of life was given to the immobile muscles. To these last the Greeks gave a name which embodied in it the fact that the movement was effected by strings. It is in Egypt that we first find an account of moving figures. Herodotus writes of a fête of Osiris when mechanical means were used to imitate the natural movements. Later, the statue of Jupiter Ammon, when carried in a golden car on the shoulders of twenty-four priests, indicated by a movement of the head the route he should take. Several of the Greek oracles were made to impress the worshippers and wisdom-seekers, by a movement of the hand or arm, as the words were spoken. Aristotle admits that the movement of the famous wooden statue of Venus was accomplished by a quantity of quicksilver placed in the body.

In the Middle Ages we again meet, this time in the service of the Christian Church, animated figures associated with the tricks of priests in impressing an ignorant and gullible population.

In the semi-religious processions in Rome which wended their way to the circus on festive occasions, monsters were borne by attendants, partly to inspire awe, partly to amuse the multitude ; the monsters opened and shut their mouths, gnashing their teeth by means of a hidden string manipulated by a hidden person.

231

While such uses, religious and otherwise, were made of the simulation of life by string-pulling, the same principles were applied to less ambitious efforts. In private houses the custom of carrying a mummy amongst the guests at a feast obtaining with the Egyptians, was made still more impressive by enduing the statue, which in some cases replaced the actual mummy, with movement. Xenophon mentions, in an account of the amusements at the famous banquet of Callias, that a showman of marionettes attended with his puppets; such a man would probably have a small theatre in which his display could be seen to advantage (for some of the marionettes were already housed in their own theatres); he would also attend the houses of the rich when hired.

When the reproof of the Church, and of Clement of Alexandria especially, was called down upon all other theatrical performances of the day on account of obscenity and vulgarity, the harmless pleasantries of the puppet-show were immune; and after the suppression of the Chorus, the Athenians obtained permission for the appearance of their favourites in the theatre of Bacchus.

The name of the manager of this early marionette show has survived; one Pothin it was, who catered for the theatrical tastes of the Athenians, as interpreted by the animated puppets.

At Rome the delight of the populace in marionette shows knew no bounds. There is no word alone which in Latin stands for the animated dolls; several are used which explain it sufficiently. It is undoubted that the Romans, on coming in contact with Greek and Etruscan civilisation, applied the use of animated figures, not only to religious rites, but also to the providing of popular and

232

Articu-
lated
Figures
of Ivory,
Wood,
and Clay.

domestic entertainment, though we have no foundation for thinking that there was ever a permanent public show such as that of Pothin at the Athenian theatre.

In the Louvre, the British Museum, and amongst other well-known collections of antiquities, there are articulated figures made of ivory, wood, or baked clay; one of bronze is spoken of by M. de Caylus in his *Recueil d'Antiquités*, but we have not seen such a specimen. Such articulated dolls are generally about seven inches high; they are unclothed to the waist. On the head there is a coronet-shaped head-dress, or the hair is dressed very elaborately. In some cases the legs and arms are missing, but one sees the holes at the shoulders and hips where they would be fastened by means of wires.

ROMAN FIGURE
OF BAKED
CLAY USED AS
MARIONETTE.

Showing holes
for the strings.

The frequent allusions in the works of the early poets and philosophers to dancing puppets, and the use of the simile in which the passions of man are likened to the strings which guide his actions, leave no doubt that the marionettes were perfectly familiar to the Romans. Marcus Aurelius, in no fewer than seven of his remarkable reflections, exhorts man to oppose his will to the passions which would guide his movements like the strings of puppets. Horace puts similar words in the mouth of a slave.

It would be extremely interesting to know how the miniature stage was arranged at this early period, when the theatres were always built as are our circuses of the present day, the stage being in the centre with raised seats

**Marion-
ettes,
Punch
and Judy,
Dancing
Dolls.**
round it. How could a show take place whose essential
requirement was a hiding-place for the manipulator of the
puppets, unless we conclude that all the illusion of the
entertainment was done away with, and the puller of
the strings was exposed to the full view of the audience
(as in a picture of a Chinese performance of the fourteenth
century). We are reluctant to believe this was the case.
The only solution is that in Greece and Rome the stage
was built up on a skeleton framework, so draped that the
figure of the wire-puller was hidden.

This brings us to the familiar little stage of the latter-
day Punch and Judy shows, the " baraque " of the French,
the form adopted by all the itinerant puppet showmen of
later times in Greece, Italy, Spain, and Portugal. We
believe such to have been the permanent stage of the early
marionette theatres.

In India, Japan, Java, and all Eastern countries
puppet-shows have been known from very remote times.
The Chinese picture mentioned above shows us the play
at a very perfect stage of development ; it is in " The Roll
of the Hundred Children," painted at about the time that
Albert Dürer flourished, and forms one of a series of the
pictures showing games of the children of the day.

A table a few inches high forms the stage. On it is
spread a piece of fine matting ; a low drapery shows up
the puppets, and is the only attempt at scene-setting. In
this early representation, three children are holding the
strings and guiding the movements of the dolls, which are
elaborately dressed, and are doubtless being made to
perform some special scene,—for there is no meaningless
dance such as the puppet of the eighteenth century was
made to execute. An elaborately dressed man, whose

234

Elaborate Marionette Show, where numerous strings are manipulated by means of wooden bats to prevent entanglement. The puppets wear the valuable heavily embroidered dresses always used on the Chinese stage. From a Chinese painting on silk of the Ming Dynasty.

太々神樂

Grotesque Mask on head of Showman.   From a drawing by Hokusai.

splendid green coat indicates that he is a person of high rank, holds himself proudly erect ; his hands are hidden in his voluminous sleeves in the conventional Chinese attitude ; at his feet is a figure with almost lifelike humility expressed in the prone and supplicating form. There is no audience visible ; but the inevitable music or clamour, the invariable accompaniment of Eastern shows, is furnished by a kind of tambourine raised upon a tripod on to which the round skin-covered instrument fits like the top of a table. A child is beating the parchment with small drum-sticks ; another child is adding to the din or perhaps marking time with the instrument often seen in the paintings of the Ming dynasty, and still used in China. This is fully described in our chapter on toy musical instruments.

In another Chinese painting a half-clothed pedlar at a toy stall holds aloft a very perfectly made puppet ; a row of other figures of the same kind, supported on sticks, is by his side. The dolls are well dressed, and each face is carefully modelled, so that a very animated, and in some cases almost comically ferocious, expression is obtained.

It is interesting to see from a fine specimen of a Chinese marionette in the collection of M. Maury that the rich, semi-regal clothing of a bygone day, which is the traditional wear of the Chinese actor, is also worn by the puppets ten inches high ; such suits are often a hundred years old, being handed down as valuable heirlooms amongst the stage properties.

In Java there is a kind of pantomime, in which men are dressed to imitate wild beasts ; these appear in procession or combats, and give a performance especially for children ;

**Marion-
ettes,
Punch
and Judy,
Dancing
Dolls.**

it is accompanied by the beat of a gong and drum. The marionette show proper is, however, a very elaborately developed affair. Some of the puppets, which are ten inches high, are made of wood; they represent historical characters of a legendary nature. From such puppet - plays Sir Stamford Raffles, the author of *The History of Java*, has obtained much of his materials for the incidents in the careers of the old inhabitants of the island, such being the themes of the little dramas, which are, in consequence, of great historical value.

Many of the Javanese nobles of the present day still have one or more sets of such puppets in their possession, and number a stage-manager of puppet-shows amongst their retainers, as did the Spanish and Italian nobles of the seventeenth century.

While the marionettes at most periods of their history, in both the Eastern and Western hemispheres, were supposed to speak the words belonging to their part, the custom of action and voice being located in separate persons some-times obtained with the wooden puppets as with the real actors in the full-sized stage, the dialogue was frequently entrusted to an orator who explained the action of the players ; thus we have speaking marionettes, by which we mean those which were supposed to speak through the voice of the showman, and pantomimic marionettes, whose actions were interpreted by an orator or chorus standing at the side and visible to the audience.

In the seventh, eighth, and ninth centuries the play of the marionettes in Europe was mostly in dumb show, a reciter at the wings declaiming a legend verse or history, frequently of Biblical origin. Such performances took place at fairs or often in the porch of a church, as did the

Moralities of the same epoch; the slightly elevated position formed an excellent " pitch."

Such plays as the Canticle of Judith and Holophernes and the legend of St. Nicholas were performed by the little wooden actors. Other dramas of the day, half-fabulous, half-historical, were given at the great European fairs, and on other occasions when " moralities " and " miracles " were acted. In M. Maury's fine collection of antique marionettes there is a St. Anthony, the Devil, and other figures required for representing the temptation of the famous saint.

In a manuscript of the twelfth century preserved at Strasburg, which has been published by M. Christ, there is an illuminated miniature showing two men armed *cap-à-pie*. The combatants are marionettes, the strings which govern their movements are visible, and the moral pointed out in the text is illustrated by this parody of a duel.

The first writer on the subject of marionettes was Jerome Cardan, born at Pavia in 1501. He gives a full description of these most simple of all mechanical toys, which he says were made of wood, the string being attached to the side. There was no dance, he continues, which they could not render perfectly, making at the same time the most surprising gestures, moving the feet, legs, arms, and head. The writer cannot understand how these complex movements can be accomplished by means of one thread only, and considers them much more surprising than that other kind of marionette, which is commonly seen when many strings are used, one being attached to each limb of the puppet.

It is probable that the thread which appeared to be solitary was in reality a very small tube, in which many

**Marion-
ettes,
Punch
and Judy,
Dancing
Dolls.**

fine threads were concealed.   Cardan ends by saying that
if he wished to tell all the marvels performed by Sicilians
with their marionettes, a whole day would not suffice to

PUNCH AND BABY.

write how the little figures are made to play, fight, hunt,
dance, blow a trumpet, and cook.   At Palermo elaborate
shows may still be seen.   An excellent description of
these latter-day puppets may be found in Mrs. Alec
Tweedie's *Sunny Sicily.*

At Constantinople, in the sixteenth century, amongst
the shows enumerated as playing in the highways are " the
magic lantern, Chinese shadow-play, and marionettes, such
as are to be seen at Naples and at Rome."

At the end of the sixteenth century, Buratino, the

240

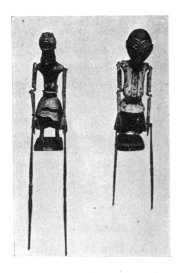

Grotesque Marionette Figures from Java. Handles for manipulation. 14 in. high.

Finely ·Carved Marionette, in habit of a Monk. 12 in. high.

Peep Show Group in Biscuit China at South Kensington Museum.

A Marionette Princess, Don Cæsar de Boger, Pierrot, Harlequin, Marquis Incroyable.

Marionettes of the Theatre Seraphin.   From the Maury Collection.

celebrated actor, caused such a furore of enthusiasm, that the entire personnel of the marionette theatres became named after him. The itinerant dancing-dolls or fantoccini of the roads were never called buratini, the name was owned exclusively by the little wooden man who had attained the dignity of a permanent home in one of the large towns, where for 5 or 6 sous a seat could be obtained.

Polichinelle or Punch was by this time first favourite. A domino sometimes covered the upper half of his face, a

" WHERE'S THE BABY ? "

mitre-shaped white cap upon his head was worn with a white gown, which made him half-harlequin, half-pierrot. As to his origin there are many theories.

243

Marionettes, Punch and Judy, Dancing Dolls.

In the *History of Punch and Judy* illustrated by Cruikshank we read : " We take it for granted that Silvio Fiorello invented Pulcinello, and first introduced him as a

THE BEADLE AND HANGMAN CAPTURING PUNCH.

variety in the list of buffoons required to represent the impromptu comedies of Naples ; but although he may date his separate existence from about the year 1600, it is a matter of much doubt whether he was not, in fact, only a branch of a family of much greater antiquity." In support of this theory the discovery, in the year 1727, of a Roman statue of a mime, with humped back and large nose, is brought forward, with the Vice or clown of the Moralities, whose business it was to relieve the graver part of the play with jests and buffooneries.

With regard to the supposition that Punch represents Pontius Pilate, Judy, Judas, and so on, we are rather inclined to believe that the characters have been gradually built up and endowed with the characteristics of each successive age, borrowing the bonhommie of an Italian actor here, the roguery of a popular knave there ; than that the famous characters are taken complete from any one person in history, sacred or profane. It is extremely likely, however, that in the old Morality plays Pontius

PUNCH HANGS THE HANGMAN.

Pilate was made a Vice or clown, the character *pour rire* ; and in this way is one of the ancestors of the Punch of to-day, for Punch belongs to the Harlequin family, of

245

**Marion-
ettes,
Punch
and Judy,
Dancing
Dolls.**

which the clown, the Vice, Pantaloon, Maccus, the fool,
the jester and Pulcinella, all belong.

Dr. Johnson, in a note on *Hamlet,* asserts positively
that " the modern Punch is descended from the ancient
Vice." According to some, the name Pullicenello is derived
from turkey cock, an allusion to the length of Punch's
nose and the beak of a turkey cock ; others say Pulcinella,
the Italian for hen or chicken, refers to the squeaking note
of his voice.

With regard to the clothing of the marionettes of
Western Europe, it is likely that their religious origin gave
the character to the dresses, but we do not doubt but that
their later use for lay purposes, introduced a fantastic and
grotesque element, of which we now see traces in Punch's
costume.

The origin of the motley or particoloured habit of the
clowns, harlequins, and of Punch himself is probably
associated with the idea, that the ancient harlequin was a
poor fool or dolt, whose dress was composed of patches.
This was certainly the summary of the character of the
domestic fools of the Middle Ages. Cardinal Wolsey had
a fool amongst his retainers who was known by the name
of Patch. The pointed fool's cap has come to Punch in a
slightly different form, but is clearly derived from the old
model. In Richard Doyle's representation on the front
page of *Punch* the journal, the artist has retained the bell,
which is part of the jester's livery.

The fantastic was certainly represented on the ordinary
adult stage at the time of the comedies of Aristophanes
and other writers of the same period, and it is likely that
on the miniature stage of the marionettes, such grotesque
figures were copied from the larger buffooneries. It is in

246

Greek Mask of
Terra Cotta.

Queen Victoria's Peep Show.
It is made of cardboard and opens at the top

Children playing with a mask.   L. Schiavonelli, Sculpt.

O'RAREE SHOW.

Mezzotint by L. Smith, from a painting by Kirk. The subject
of such pictures in relief was always chosen from the lives of
Saints, Martyrs, and Devils.

Simple type of Dancing Doll, used
by itinerant showmen.

Jointed figure with hole in the
head for insertion of wire.
Greek.

this tendency towards fantastic disfigurement that we find the first indication of our old friend Punch, who reached England about the time of Queen Anne. M. Magnan mentions two fragments of vases, drawings of which had been sent to him by M. Muret ; he describes them thus :—
" Le premier est une figurine de terre cuite du musée Campana ayant à la fois les épaules et le ventre très prominents ; le second est une figurine appartenant à M. Comarmont, représentant un personnage accroupi par derrière d'une bosse et par devant en guise de contre-poids d'un autre genre de déformité."

A small bronze found at Rome, 1727, which is engraved in the *History of the Italian Theatre* by Riccoboni, shows the prominent paunch, the humped back, and the tunic tightly drawn in at the waist, which are the leading features in Punch's make-up.

From the writings of the ancients we gather that a little instrument of metal or ivory was used in the mouth of the showman to change the voices of the various puppets, and especially to emphasise the speaking of the principal actors. Some writers identify this *sifflet pratique* as the French call it, the *puvetta* of the Italians, with a similar instrument used by the priests to give a mystic intonation to the utterances of the Oracles. Something of the kind was also used by those actors whose parts necessitated the wearing of masks, through which the human voice, unaided by artificial means, would not have been sufficiently loud.

One of the antique vases whose decoration so enlightens us on the subject of domestic life of the Ancient Greeks, shows the fearful joy to be obtained by covering the face with a mask, and the alarm of a young child at the trick

249

Marion-
ettes,
Punch
and Judy,
Dancing
Dolls.

played by an elder brother.   Doubtless the little Greek boy
was well spanked for frightening the baby, and we feel
sure the ever-fresh, "Boys will be boys," was brought
forward as an excuse for the evildoer by the overlenient
mother.   It is impossible that the large quantities of
masks of every size and expression which have been unearthed by excavation should all have been used as toys ;
but that the mask was used as a plaything is proved by
pictures such as that mentioned above and others that are
equally graphic.   Schiavonetti's charming rendering of the

CHILDREN'S PLAY WITH A MASK.
From a Greek vase.

same subject brings us up to the end of the eighteenth
century.

A beautiful intaglio on cornelian shows love, with an
old man's face as a mask, held before his own laughing
and joyous features.

In another drawing, shown in *Recueil des Monuments*

250

de la Villa Mattee, an artificial serpent is seen to be protruding from the mouth of the mask, in order to still further alarm the little victim of the joke; artificial serpents are known to have been used by actors, and in the performance of the rites in the worship of Bacchus, and it is probably one of those which is used by the chubby boy who is inside the large mask.

CHILDREN'S PLAY WITH A MASK.
From a Greek vase.

Punch made his appearance upon the marionette stage very soon after his success at the large theatres. Le Sage was writing pieces for Pulcinella and other puppets in 1721, but the ancestors of Punch, Harlequin, Clown, and Vice of the Moralities were represented by the little wooden men long before.

In a painting of the sixteenth century a group of Italians stand round a little puppet-show: two Roman women and several men are crowding nearer to gain a better view: there are some peasants: one seated on an ass is thoroughly enjoying the spectacle from his elevated position. Such a picture might have been painted at any time during the sixteenth and seventeenth centuries in any of the large Italian cities, Rome, Milan, Florence, or Venice on the Quai des Esclavons, at Naples on the Lago di Castello, at Turin, at Genoa or Bologna.

The superior fantoccini, which were not shown in the open air, were at this time partly made of cardboard, or what is called statuary pasteboard, which could be

**Marion-
ettes,
Punch
and Judy,
Dancing
Dolls.**

moulded into shape. The head was of this material,
the shoulders and legs of wood, the arms of card, the
hands, feet, and neck of lead, or garnished with lead so
that they obeyed the least motion of the string without
loss of balance. At the top of the head a little ring of
iron was fixed, for attaching the suspending string ; a fine
net with perpendicular threads was stretched across the
opening of the proscenium, so that the wires suspending
the puppets were confused with these lines and were
scarcely visible. Another clever device was the arrangement that the threads affecting all parts of the body
should, by means of a tube, pass out at the top of the
head. Later on, another system was introduced, by one
Neri, a distinguished painter and mechanician, which
consisted in embedding, in grooves in the floor, the
supports, in which the marionettes ran noiselessly, and
were worked from below. Sometimes these two systems
were worked together, and very perfect effects were
obtained.

At Milan, the fantoccini theatre "Fiando" was
considered as important a place to visit as any of the
other great sights in the town ; there, ballets were given,
and the dancers at the opera being closely watched, their
style was imitated by the manipulators of the miniature
performers.

Numerous are the accounts in the eighteenth-century
journals of travel, and in private letters, of the remarkable and perfect marionette shows, which astounded and
delighted the spectators, not only in public places of
amusement, but also in the houses of the noble and
wealthy citizens, many of whom possessed perfectly
appointed marionette theatres. One of these we have

been fortunate enough to examine. These private theatres were used every evening for the entertainment of the guests ; and the chaff and slang of the moment, the " on dits" and the railleries of the market, the bourse, or the court, were introduced into the dialogue of the plays, provoking much friendly laughter and enjoyment. At Rome, the marionette theatre enjoyed special privileges ; it was allowed to open from the last days of the Carnival till Easter, when all other places of amusement were closed. Here the whole repertoire of Rossini was sung by the little wooden men and women, or rather for them, by concealed vocalists ; not only comic, but serious operas, such as *Othello*, were given with ballets, orchestra, and song in the nineteenth century.

There is an account in a French journal of 1835 of a presentation of grand opera by marionettes at the house of the Abbé Dubois. The puppets were four feet high and were called Bambocchie ; the voice of the singer was heard through an opening in the floor in the tiny stage.

Undoubtedly it was the Italians who brought the fantoccini to the highest perfection, propagating the love of the little entertainers by introducing them to all the cities of Europe.

The Italian influence on the marionette shows in Spain is clearly traceable, even in the dresses and appointments of the theatres, while, at the same time, subjects and characters interesting to the Spaniards are made use of. Polichinelle becomes Cristoval, and Moors, enchanters, conquerors of the Indies, characters from the Old and New Testaments, martyrs and hermits, all make their appearance on the marionette stage of the Peninsula.

Marion-
ettes,
Punch
and Judy,
Dancing
Dolls.

Punch's whistle in Spain is called *peto* or *cerbatana*,
and is sometimes used when the marionettes are made
to speak in the voice of their showman ; but those shows
where the action is explained by a second person standing by the side of the miniature stage, such as that
described by Cervantes, are the most usual kind.

A somewhat elaborate theatre is spoken of in the
journals of travellers of the seventeenth and eighteenth
centuries at Seville, and by the beginning of the nineteenth
century there was no important town in Spain or Portugal
where this amusement, for the little ones and adults, was
not to be obtained—generally in a room in a convenient
centre of the town.

The scene in *Don Quixote*, when the marionette show
is displayed at the inn, will be remembered : — " The
Show set out, filled in every part with small wax candles
so that it made a gay and brilliant appearance. Master
Peter, who was to manage the figures, placed himself
behind the Show ; and in front of the scene stood his boy,
whose office it was to relate the story and expound the
mystery of the piece, holding a wand in his hand to
point to the several figures as they entered."

The thrilling story of how " Don Gayferos delivers
his spouse Mislisendra, who was imprisoned by the Moors
in the city of San Sausuenna, now called Saragossa " ; the
calling to order of the boy reciter, when his flights of
fancy led him to stray from the narrative ; the annoyance
of Don Quixote when bells were rung, which were not
known to the Moors, instead of the dulcimers and drums
which were used at the time of the story ; the final
destruction of the show by Don Quixote in a fine frenzy
of chivalrous knight-errantry ;—all these are amongst the

most amusing episodes of the inimitable history of the **Don** **Quixote** knight of La Mancha. **and the**

Such shows were almost invariably owned by Italians **Marion-** who travelled the country, usually accompanied by a **ettes.** monkey ; sometimes a little stage was erected and the movements were effected by strings, but more often the hand of the showman was concealed beneath the clothing of the dolls, or the puppet was mounted on a stick and moved by the man from beneath, as in the Punch and Judy shows of the present day. Occasionally a still simpler method was resorted to, a single string attached to the knee of the showman producing crude and spasmodic movement.

Amongst other itinerant shows the most important were the rare or raree show, when quaint and lifelike figures, sometimes stationary, sometimes moved by the showman, were taken round the country, and evoked wonder and surprise in the villages.

Scenes from the lives of the saints, biblical subjects and legends, formed the subjects, which were much more elaborately worked out than in the later peep-shows. These have always been in the hands of Italians or Frenchmen. They have also been made as toys for children themselves to act as showmen, as in the Punch and Judy shows of our day.

In the provinces of France, especially at Marseilles and at the great fairs, such subjects as the Mysteries of the Passion, the Nativity, and Samson and Judith were played on the marionette stage, reciters standing at the side explaining the pantomime of the puppets. In 1840 Punch had his theatre in Paris, on the left bank of the Seine, opposite the Louvre at the

Marion-
ettes,
Punch
and Judy,
Dancing
Dolls.

Porte de Neste; the proprietor was the famous Jean
Brioché.

With regard to Dame Gigogne, as she is called in
France, she is contemporary with Punch, but has not
always appeared in feminine guise. In 1602 she was
first introduced as a woman under the name of Madame
Gigogne, to give further interest to the escapades of
Punch and his companions, Harlequin and Pantaloon.
She soon achieved popularity, and appeared at every
puppet-show, sometimes attending to a prodigiously large
family, sometimes fortune - telling and divining the
future, if astrology were the craze of the day, or selling
salves and medicine-waters to the audience : her part
in the present-day tragedy of Punch and Judy is of
comparatively recent origin.

Amongst the most famous French directors of
marionette shows we must place Jean Brioché, who
during the reign of Louis XIV. combined the professions
of tooth-extracting and marionette-showing at the Pont
Neuf, in company with his famous monkey Fagotin.
His monkey was the forerunner of the dog Toby, now the
invariable attendant on Punch and Judy shows : it was a
clever monkey, it will be remembered, who arrived with
the showman in Cervantes' account. Fagotin was afterwards
engaged from Brioché as a lackey by the mad Cyrano
de Bergerac, who eventually killed the unfortunate beast,
and the pamphlet " Combat de Cyrano de Bergerac contre
le singe de Brioché " appeared in 1655.

La Fontaine mentions this monkey in his amusements
of the Carnival. The marionettes of de Brioché were
frequently commanded at court to amuse the dauphin and
his young companions ; the price is given in a register of

THE PEEP SHOW.

Painted by F. Wheatley.   Engraved by F. Bartolozzi.

Marionettes of the early 19th Century from the Bayerische National Museum at Munich. The figures are from 12 to 15 in. in height.

the royal expenses—" for performances at St. Germains en Laye during the months of September, October, and November 1669, to amusements of the royal children of France, 1,365 livres." Another entry gives the sum of 20 livres per day from the 17th of July to the 15th of August 1669 to François Dablin, marionette showman, to amuse the dauphin ; he was at this time nine years of age, and apparently allowed to indulge largely his taste for marionettes. Doubtless in the following year, when Bossuet became his preceptor, such diversions were stopped, as Bossuet did all in his power to put down such shows.

Other famous owners of marionettes in the seventeenth century were Archambault Jerome and the brothers Feron, who had a small circus, a troup of marionettes, and a tennis-court at Cercilly at the sign of the Fleur de Lys. The Theatre of the Pigmies, or the Theatre of Bamboches, was opened by La Grille about 1676, and everything was managed on a most lavish scale.

At the Pont Neuf also, waxwork shows were to be seen, besides tumbling, juggling, performing animals, and circus entertainments. It was at the fairs, however, notably those of St. Germains and St. Laurent, that the marionette shows of the seventeenth century were chiefly appreciated by the little ones, whose sous were not sufficient to gain entrance for them at the permanent marionette theatres : these, at the time of the fairs, did not disdain to leave their established homes to take up temporary quarters in the booths of the fairs, lowering their prices considerably.

John Rivers, an Englishman, went to Paris at the beginning of the eighteenth century and opened a salon for rope-dancing, tennis, and marionettes. Punch took an

Marion-
ettes,
Punch
and Judy,
Dancing
Dolls.

important part in the entertainment, and a complete record
of his dialogue has been preserved, in which the war
waged between the Comédie Française and the shows of
foreigners in the capital, besides other current topics, were
discussed : these must have been extremely dull for the
children amongst the audience.

Ballets, parodies, serious dramas, and shortened editions
of the pieces performed at the great theatres were given,
and Ragonde, the ill-used baby of the Punch family, whose
woes are the chief theme of the Punch and Judy of to-day,
first makes her appearance in Paris at this time, which is
the grand climacteric of marionette history.

In the eighteenth century we find our old friends the
marionettes under a new name. "Les Comédiens pratiques,"
such was the grandly sounding title given to them under the
patronage of the dauphin, but their beauty and popularity
were already declining, and the elaborate title could not
hide the decadence : already mechanical figures other
than those moved by strings had begun to usurp the
stages once occupied by the little wooden men.

A permanent fair at the Boulevard du Temple led the
way for its more aristocratic descendant at the Palais
Royal, constructed by the Duc de Chartres. Here the little
comedians of M. le Comte de Beaujolais opened in a well-
fitted theatre in 1784, and it is interesting to note that in
1810, after the eclipse of such places of amusement during
the Revolution, the marionettes again reappeared under
an Italian named Dumersan, who played pieces with the
old puppets of the Comte de Beaujolais, which had been
stored in the cellars for twenty years.

During the sinister years of the French Revolution the
spirit of frivolity at the Palais Royal was condemned :

while the guillotine was running with the best blood in France, Punch and Judy continued their innocent follies, but at the peril of their owners. The Marquis of Custine tells that in 1794 his mother was imprisoned in the same chamber with a poor marionette player and his wife, who perished on the scaffold because their Punch was too aristocratic.

Madame de Maintenant writes in 1713 : "Madame la Duchesse de Maine contributed much to the pleasures of Paris by giving a ball and a marionette entertainment at which the siege of Douai was presented."

Voltaire tells us that in 1746 the Comte du Eu gave a marionette entertainment, directing the puppets himself ; he writes a four-verse compliment to the Comte under the name of Polichinelle.

The celebrated Théâtre Seraphin was founded in 1771 by Seraphin Dominique François, who opened a small theatre for Chinese shadowgraphy in the Jardin Lanion at Versailles, where various small shows and fêtes took place. The first advertisement of Seraphin ran thus :—

> Venez garçons, venez fillettes,
> Voir Momus à la silhouette.
> Oui, chez Séraphin, venez voir
> La belle humeur en habit noir,
> Tandis que ma salle est bien sombre
> Et que mon acteur n'est que l'ombre,
> Puisse, Messieurs, votre gaîté
> Devenir la réalité.

The show was most popular, and was frequently commanded at court, so that the name of " Spectacle des enfants de France " was assumed for it by Seraphin.

After twelve years we find Seraphin established in the Palais Royal in a booth of wood in the garden of the

**Marion-
ettes,
Punch
and Judy,
Dancing
Dolls.**

Duc d'Orléans. In 1797 marionettes were added to the
Chinese shadowgraphy with which the show had begun.
Seraphin died in 1800, and his nephew Joseph François
continued the show, adding many novelties. He was
succeeded by Paul Roger, a singer of some note ; he first
enlarged the little theatre and then moved to more
ambitious premises in Montmartre. He died in 1868.
At his death the show passed to M. Plet, who replaced the
well-known and time-honoured name of Seraphin with
that of Theatre Miniature. From this time it ceased to
flourish. A new Théâtre Seraphin was recently opened in
the Boulevard des Italiens by the well-known collector and
savant M. Maury, but, notwithstanding lavish expenditure
on puppets, decorations, and stage accessories, its doors
were open but a few months.

In the prosaic twentieth century the popularity of the
little people has waned ; if we see them at all in the houses
of the great leaders of society in England, Germany,
France, or Italy, they are there to amuse a party of
children ; and though the adults seem to enjoy the antics
of Punch, Judy, and the unhappy baby, it is *à propos* of
the children's pleasure. They are now considered only a
childish amusement.

Though in London, Amsterdam, Moscow, and Berlin
the marionettes never achieved the enormous popularity
which was theirs in Greece, Italy, France, and Spain, yet
they were well established in the sixteenth century.

Later, in London, the poet Colley Cibber opened the
Grand Marionette Theatre in St. James's Street. Smollett
describes the show as a "modish diversion" of the time.
The extraordinary medley of laughter, murder, the super-
natural, and the trivial, which jostle each other in the

modern story of Punch and Judy, appealed strongly to Lord Byron.

The Desirability of a Marionette Revival.

Would that an artist, an enthusiast, and a man of means, might appear to restore its past glories to the marionette theatre in England, that this daintiest of all shows might again afford innocent amusement to the little ones, and a piquant sensation to the " children of a larger growth " !

CHAPTER XII

SPECIAL TOYS FOR SPECIAL OCCASIONS AND THOSE
SUGGESTED BY SACRED HISTORY.

Special Toys for Special Occasions and those suggested by Sacred History. THE line which must be drawn between material representation of religious subjects, playthings made in the form of objects connected with religious history, and those used in the performance of religious observances, is a very subtle one. With the former we have dealt, with some fulness, in tracing the history of marionettes worked with strings, and mechanical toys, whose motive power is concealed within the body of the puppet. In this chapter we intend dealing with toys, the playthings of children, whose form has been suggested by sacred history or the observance of religious rites.

With the ancients, worship was not looked upon as a cult separate and distinct from secular acts of daily life, as is too frequently the case now. It was an integral part of the life itself. Certain toys, even, were dedicated to the use of the gods themselves, as, for instance, the ball and the rattle of the infant Bacchus.

Children dedicated their toys, the girls to Diana, the boys to Mercury, when, having arrived at the state of

womanhood and manhood, they desired to use them no **Toys**
longer. Toys were placed in the tombs, not only of **dedicated**
the pagans, but also of the early Christians, miniature **to Diana.**
bells and dolls having been found in the catacombs
at Rome.

With savage peoples also the playthings of children
have often a double use—as toys, and also as charms
against evil spirits and malignant deities ; while between
the doll of primitive races and the dreaded or idolised
form in human semblance, there is a similarity of attitude
almost interchangeable.

It is difficult to separate the religious idea from the
love, fear, and superstition which have always surrounded
the presentment of the human form in whatever guise.
In Persia, on the birth of a child, an image of it is placed
in a temple, which is considered a kind of talisman, and
on its remaining within the sacred precincts depends the
welfare of the child. When human sacrifices were discontinued, mannikins or dolls replaced the human victims.
Natives of Central Africa still dress up a gourd in leaves
and rags, and use it for exorcising the demons of sickness
and loss. Savage tribes have the greatest horror of
seeing their reflection in water, and look with terror on
rocks, mountains, or crags which by accident or nature are
formed in the semblance of a human figure, attributing to
them superhuman power.

Numbers of cases of witchcraft in the Middle Ages,
and at later dates amongst uneducated people, have for
their basis evil, supposed to be wrought through the
making of a puppet in the form of the victim, upon which
the evils of sickness, deformity and maltreatment could be
inflicted. Injury to the puppet was in some occult way

supposed to bring injury to the person in whose likeness it was made.

It is strange then, that, notwithstanding the terror, superstition and mystery surrounding the presentment of the human form in the minds of primitive peoples, the doll is undoubtedly the best beloved of all toys when used purely as a plaything. Certainly it inspires the greatest love and tenderness in the minds of girls of all ages and nationalities.

A vividly-written page in the life of Maggie, the heroine of *The Mill on the Floss*, shows the survival of this belief in the child's half-frenzied mind. " She kept a Fetish which she punished for all her misfortunes. This was the trunk of a large wooden doll, which once stared with the roundest of eyes above the reddest of cheeks, but was now entirely defaced by a long career of vicarious suffering. Three nails driven into the head commemorated as many crises in Maggie's nine years of earthly struggle ; that luxury of vengeance having been suggested to her by the picture of Jael destroying Sisera in the old Bible. The last nail had been driven in with a firmer stroke than usual, for the Fetish on that occasion represented Aunt Glegg."

This passage is interesting from the fact that it is an open secret that, in writing of Maggie, George Eliot was writing autobiography.

To the sweepingly severe Protestantism of Reformation times, to the grim and gloomy doctrine of Calvin, holding all pleasure sinful, we must attribute the extraordinary modern attitude with regard to the relations between toys and religious observances. In the nurseries of the early nineteenth century all toys were taboo on Sunday : true,

266

as the day specially set apart for praise and worship, our **Sunday** chief care should be to train our little ones in worship and **Play; its** prayer on Sundays, but to tell a child that it is wicked to **Regulation.** play on Sunday is a doctrine abhorrent to all thinking minds.

Let us keep clearly before us the fact that our children will best love the Sabbath, and all that is connected with that holy day, if they learn that, though there is nothing wrong in playing on Sunday, there are other more beautiful and lovely things to do, which should be of first importance.

Undoubtedly the most popular toy in England suggested by sacred history is the Noah's ark, beloved alike of boys and girls from earliest infancy. What matter if the animals are of rudely shaped pine chips, unornamented with paint or varnish, or if, in the glories of highly glazed colouring, the elephants stand forth with more gaiety than veracity in glaring pink coats, and the zebras are striped beyond all possibility of animal endurance! What pleasure lies in the marshalling of a Mr. and Mrs. Noah and their family, rendered so steady by the extraordinary cut of their coats; how cunningly Shem Ham, and Japheth with their wives can be made to bring up the rear or lead the way into the spacious and comfortable ark, which serves the double purpose of an important feature in the game and as a most satisfactory "putting away" box!

Dickens's description of the Noah's arks in Caleb Plummer's room is delightful :—

"There were Noah's arks in which the Birds and Beasts were an uncommonly tight fit, I assure you; they could be crammed in anyhow, at the roof, and rattled and shaken into the smallest compass. By a bold poetic

Special
Toys for
Special
Occasions
and those
suggested
by Sacred
History.

licence most of these Noah's arks had knockers on the doors : inconsistent appendages, perhaps, as suggestive of morning callers and a postman, yet a pleasant finish to the outside of the building."

It was at the beginning of the eighteenth century that the art of carving the cheap toys, which now come in such abundance from the valleys of South Tyrol, was begun as an industrial enterprise. The trade has increased to such an enormous extent that the district may now be said to be the capital of the cheap toy world.

It is strange to meet, in a foreign country, amongst strange faces, all the most intimate friends of our childhood. Here are the wooden-jointed dollies beloved in all nurseries from that of Queen Victoria downwards. There are the extraordinary arboreal growths whose bright green chippy leaves we took so very much as a matter of course, before we had reached the less happy age of keen criticism. There is the typical Tyrolean homestead in a boat, which brings us back to our Noah's ark. The cottage workers, who carve the animals by the hundred dozen, achieve their astonishing rapidity and skill by working continually at one model ; hundreds of them do precisely the same things, and not only have they been doing them all their lives, but their mothers were doing them also, and they have probably taught their children the simple methods of their own immediate branch. Mrs. Edwards describes this point in her *Untrodden Peaks* :—

" In one house we found an old, old woman at work, Magdalena Paldauf by name. She carved cats, dogs, wolves, sheep, goats, and elephants. She has made these six animals her whole life long, and has no idea of how to cut anything else. She makes them in two sizes, and

Display of Antique Dolls and Furniture prepared for the Girls' Festival in Japan. The centre figures are those of the Emperor and Empress; they are surrounded by figures from the Imperial Orchestra and other attendants. Rice and bowls of sake are offered, after which the Toys are put away until the following year.

Jack in the Green.   The Village Festival on May Day, which probably has
its origin in tree worship.

she turns out, as nearly as possible, a thousand of them
every year. She has no model or drawing of any kind to
work by ; but goes on steadily, unerringly, using gouges
of different sizes, and shaping out her cats, dogs, wolves,
sheep, goats, elephants, with an ease and an amount of
truth to nature that would be clever if it were not so
utterly mechanical. Magdalena Paldauf learned from
her mother how to carve these six animals, and her mother
had learned in like manner from the grandmother.
Magdalena has now taught the art to her own granddaughter ; and so it will go on being transmitted for
generations."

Another centre for very cheaply made wooden toys is
that of Kalpodi in India. In this place the wood is turned
out on the primitive native lathe ; a very light white wood
is used, and domestic vessels in miniature, toy carts, cups,
wheels, bottles, goblets, and balls are made in thousands.
They are ornamented with coloured lacs, which are applied
while the wheel is still turning ; the heat of the friction
melts the stick of lac, and sufficient adheres to the wood
to give a shining line of colour.

The fact that special toys are used at special seasons
is noticeable in every country. Sometimes the reason is
obvious, for no one can use skates except in winter, nor
play cricket except when the ground is dry. Sometimes the custom is traceable to certain fixed dates of
festivals with which the toy is more or less remotely
connected, as in the case of the girls' festival in Japan,
described in our chapter on dolls, when dolls are the
special toys played with, presented as gifts or displayed
as inheritance.

Fashion occasionally rules the games of children—

Special Toys for Special Occasions and those suggested by Sacred History.

doubtless the toy merchants know well how to regulate it —and for a few months a " Puzzle craze " will " catch on " ; or a grasshopper, or some such trifle, will make its appearance ; green and gigantic in form and voice, it will spring and squeak in every quiet boulevard, in the Bois de

EMIGRETTE TOY OF THE FRENCH REVOLUTION.

Boulogne or in the Parc Monceau, for such passing fashions in toys are especially noticeable in Paris. In a few months the furore will be over, and in a year's time a green squeaking grasshopper will be unobtainable in Paris toy-shops ; the fashion will be as dead as last year's bonnet or hat, and the children will all be catching bouncing balls, which are attached to their fingers by elastic, while the passer-by, a tree, or a wall are used impartially as the resistant surface from which the ball shall be made to bounce.

Toys of the moment have arisen in every generation, doubtless the favourite of the Olympian games gave his name to the charioteer or toy wrestler in ancient times, just as the little man who removes his hat with such admired politeness is M. Carnot or Mr. Chamberlain, while Kruger showed his face on puzzles four years ago, and every leaden soldier must now wear Khaki.

272

The special toy made at the time of the French Revolution, the little disc of ivory alternately rolled away and caught again, was the toy used so much by the Emigrant nobles who were driven away from Paris, that it received its name Emigrette from them ; we have spoken of this toy in our chapter on ball play.

There are tops whose shadow casts the profile portrait of Louis XVI. and Marie Antoinette, these are turned in box-wood and are indeed interesting reminiscences of toys with the impress of history ; they are illustrated in our chapter on tops. The children of the Revolution had their tiny Phrygian caps and danced the horrible carmagnoles in their play ; little models of the guillotine

TOPS WHOSE SHADOWS GIVE PROFILE PORTRAITS OF LOUIS XVI. AND MARIE ANTOINETTE.

were made to "work," and the bodies of pigs with heads of Louis XVI. were decapitated. Models of the Bastille were popular ; playing cards with figures of revolutionary heroes were made when kings, queens, and aristocratic knaves were taboo. In examples before us we see the

273

Queen of Clubs as a female figure clutching Divorce; the words beneath are "Liberté de Mariage." The King of Hearts with the cockade of liberty in his cap is labelled "Egalité de Devoirs." The Knave of Spades tramples the Noblesse underfoot; he is in the blouse of a working man and wears the cap of liberty, beneath is written "Egalité de Rangs." The Knave of Diamonds is represented by a youth in a liberty cap with wings; he is called the "Génie du Commerce." Such cards are seen in interesting variety at the house of Madame de Sevigné in Paris.

The relegation of certain toys to certain seasons is especially noticeable in the playthings which owe their origin to religious rites. At Christmas-time the toy-markets of Spain, Italy, France and all Roman Catholic countries are flooded with playthings representing the Infant Christ in the cradle; we have before us the Bambino roughly carved in one piece with the cradle, the body of the child swathed in the Italian manner, the colouring crude, but realistic. This was purchased in Rome at Christmas-time for a few sous. Miniature images of the Magi, with almost grotesquely black faces and oriental turbans, are sold in thousands. The Virgin Mary and St. Joseph, tiny stables with oxen in the stalls, toy stars, shepherds, their sheep and the angels,—all are in the hands of the little ones at Christmas-tide. The figures of saints also appear in the toy-shops and on the stalls of cheap vendors of playthings at the time of year, when their special day is celebrated. St. Nicholas and St. Christopher and others are made, we know, by thousands for use in Church, but they are also made in miniature as toys for children. In imitating the serious

Guillotine of the
nch Revolution.
8 in. high.

XVIIIth Century Toys for playing various games inspired
by religious teaching. Brass Candlesticks. 2 in. in height,
from the Germanische Museum, Nuremburg.

Ecclesiastical Dolls dressed in habits of religious orders, from the South
Kensington Museum collection. 12 in. in height.

Japanese Fête, when toys are attached to branches of trees, as on our Christmas Tree.

doings of "grown-ups," children have annexed the game of religious exercises with enthusiasm ; it is played by the hour without levity, and with all the reverence and feeling which children are so ready to lavish on the signs and symbols which are brought to their notice through observation of the doings of adults.

There is a vast industry in the preparation of toys of this nature,—tiny censers, candlesticks, altars, banners, receptacles for holy water, votive hearts, arms and legs and so forth in tinsel, composition, lead, and wood, are to be purchased in Spain and Italy at all seasons of the year ; quantities of them are made in the south of Tyrol and also in Nuremberg, where we found an interesting old collection. There is a great trade done in St. Cecilias with little musical instruments, St. Theodoras in glittering armour, St. Christophers with Infant Christs on their shoulders, St. Florians with buckets, St. Lawrences with gridirons, Madonnas crowned with stars, St. Peter with his keys, St. John with a lamb, and more saints, angels, and martyrs than we can count. In some cases these are carved in wood by the cottage workers, who also turn out their farmyard animals, trees or dolls by the thousand ; the painting and decoration is, however, done at the great warehouses as the orders for the toys come in. Frequently the makers of the large figures for Church use are also the purveyors of religious toys for children.

In Spain during Holy Week, when the crowd assembles to see the processions from the churches, the pious spectators who with bent heads are muttering Aves as the religious relics and symbols pass by, purchase for their children fac-similes of the censers, wax tapers, monstrances and pyxes in lead, wood, wax or composition from the

277

Special
Toys for
Special
Occasions
and those
suggested
by Sacred
History.

itinerant vendors, who line the streets crying their wares. On one of these we read of the toy merchant's mark, the identical stamp which is placed on a wooden horse or trumpet.

All the objects appearing in the famous nativity processions are made in miniature for the children. These spectacular processions, instituted in the Middle Ages for the instruction of the people, were got up in the most elaborate manner. Some figures of the Magi which have been used for this purpose are now in South Kensington Museum; they are twenty inches in height, modelled in terracotta; the faces and limbs have the special characteristics required for each individual; the thick-lipped negro face of one is shown off well by the turban of rich brocade. A splendid brocaded coat trimmed with rich gold lace covers the baggy oriental breeches of satin; spurs, oriental slippers, the caparisoning of the horse,—all are made with exquisite finish and accuracy; the modelling of the horse is excellent, the whole stands as a splendid specimen of one of the costly and artistic figures at one time much used, now with less frequency, but still surviving in a few of the Spanish and Italian towns and villages.

The richness of the collections of such figures and accessories at Munich is almost incredible; here examples are seen from Sicily, Naples, Padua, and all parts of Italy. The accessories are exquisitely modelled, and gold, silver, and precious stones are freely used. The swords of the military are of richly chased steel, the handles of gold, ivory, or coral, while the scabbards and dagger cases are sometimes of tooled leather or shagreen. The vessels are of silver, copper, or brass repoussée; the gifts of the three kings are frequently of gold and silver, bibelots of immense

value. Not only are the Nativity or cradle scenes represented, but other scenes from Bible history. An immense
collection at the Industrial Museum at Nuremberg shows
figures ranging from two and a half to five and a half
inches in height, in all the important events in the life of
Joseph, of Abraham, and other patriarchs in Jewish history.
The beautiful scenery which forms the background to
the complete specimens of these religious representations
in miniature, add considerably to the artistic effect ; and
though these peopled panoramas are by no means the toys
of children, we feel we must mention them cursorily as an
offshoot of the subject of religious dolls and puppets.

Amongst the toys connected with religion are the
cheap toys of Notre Dame de Lisse, a little French
village whose industry successfully competes on a small
scale with the cheap toy production of Germany and the
Black Forest. At certain times of the year the Church
dedicated to the Black Virgin is crowded with Roman
Catholic pilgrims, who love to take away with them cheap
souvenirs of the faith and devotion which has inspired
them to make the pilgrimage ; often they are accompanied
by their children, who want a paper mill, a wooden cat,
dog, or horse ; if the children are not there they must have
a toy taken to them at home. Such are some of the very
human reasons which have given rise to the flourishing
industry in cheap toys, which is a curious exotic on French
soil, for except in the poor quarters of Paris, which produce
the common tin soldiers and moving toys, fine and
expensive toys are almost exclusively made in France.

Hundreds of thousands of toys are also specially made
for decking the fir branches of the Christmas-trees of the
world, more especially of Germany and England. Light

Special
Toys for
Special
Occasions
and those
suggested
by Sacred
History. glittering articles, which reflect the tiny tapers fastened all over the tree, are the special toys prepared for this special occasion. It was early in the nineteenth century that the custom of decking a fir-tree with glittering toys, gifts, and wax lights at Christmas-time was introduced into England ; the custom was adopted with enthusiasm by Queen Victoria, amongst the other German customs beloved for the sake of her husband the Prince Consort.

In Japan, toys are tied to the branches of trees, and after being carried about, to the delight of the children, are distributed amongst them.

With regard to the origin of the gift-tree at Christmas, information is extremely difficult to obtain ; certain it was, however, that December 24, our Christmas eve, was Adam and Eve's day, so that the Christmas-tree is in all probability connected with the tree of knowledge in the Garden of Eden. An old legend of the third century tells how Adam, when dying, sent Seth to Paradise to fetch oil from the tree of mercy. In a hymn by Venantius Fortunatus, who died about 600 years after the commencement of the Christian era, the tree is described as one of—

> Mighty fruitfulness, a sweet and splendid tree,
> Thy laden bough bears fruit like no other.

It is undisputed that in the early accounts of Christmas-trees, apples always, figure largely as decoration, tied to the branches as if they were growing. In 1605 a description of a tree at Strasburg is given. A fir-tree is erected in the room on which are hung roses made of coloured paper, apples, wafers, sugar, etc. ; no lights are mentioned, nor are they spoken of in Peter Hebel's dialect poems.

Lighted Christmas-trees are spoken of by Gottfried Kissling of Zittau, teacher of law at Wittenberg in 1737. A woman prepared a small tree for each member of her family, according to their height, and decorated them with lights and presents. Stilling speaks of Christmas-trees lighted and covered with gilt nuts, sheep, dolls, dishes, fruit, confectionery and figures of the Child Christ in 1740 at Nassau : at the end of the eighteenth century the custom of setting up trees in rooms had become so general in Germany and Saxony that prohibition against cutting down the trees was necessary, and permission was granted in certain places to take poor or superfluous trees.

Comparatively recently, trees have been placed in the churches in Germany. An Advent Tree is also put up on Advent Sunday, and a fresh candle tied on to a branch each Sunday when those already there are lighted ; with every candle a fresh prophecy concerning Christ's advent is read out of the Old Testament.

In France Christmas-trees were introduced in Alsace and other districts on the frontier ; the Princess of Mecklenburg and Duchess of Orleans took them to Paris in 1840 ; they were not sufficiently general to be seen in the markets and flower-shops, however, until half a century later, and were then chiefly bought by resident Germans ; through them also they have been introduced into America.

In St. Petersburg they have been adopted as an amusement for the children by gentlefolks, but are by no means a national institution.

In Denmark, Sweden, and Norway they have been used since the eighteenth century by rich and poor alike.

The old custom of giving or receiving toy fish on

Special
Toys for
Special
Occasions
and those
suggested
by Sacred
History. April 1, much indulged in on the Continent and to a
slight extent in England, is of doubtful origin ; some
attribute it to the opening of the fishing season, which
commences about this time, but this is hardly credible,
though certainly the disappointed fisher folk are frequently
the dupes of the fishes which they pursue in vain.   A
French legend recounts how Louis XIII. took prisoner a
Prince of Lorraine, causing him to be incarcerated in the
Castle of Nancy.   The prisoner duped his guards, and
being a fine swimmer, made his escape by way of the
river Meuse ; hence the connection of the fish with the
vain and foolish errands and mocking surprises which are
the custom on all-fools'-day.   Others trace the origin still
farther back to the Passion of our Saviour, the Poisson
d'Avril having been corrupted from passion, the vain and
tedious journeyings of the great Victim from the judge
to Pilate, from Pilate to Herod, and from Herod to
Pilate, being the foundation of the mocking courses now
connected with the day.   However this may be, it is
certain that the date coincides with that of the Passion.

Certain it is also that the fish plays an important and
mysterious part throughout the Scriptures, from the
adventures of Jonah to the choosing of the fishers of
Galilee.   The connection of several of the Miracle Plays
with the fish, the finding of its form amongst the earliest
Christian signs in the Catacombs—all points to its
important and mysterious significance.   We must not
omit to mention that the zodiacal sign of the month
of April is the fish.   The boys' festival in Japan is
celebrated by the stringing of paper carp and other fishes
outside the abode of the merry-makers.

The origin of the egg gifts at Eastertide has also a

Celebration of the Boys' festival in Japan on the 5th day of the 5th month. Paper fish are hoisted like flags at the door of each house in which there is a male child.

LES ÉTRENNES.
From Parisian caricatures.

deep significance. It must not be forgotten that until the end of the sixteenth century the new year began at Eastertide ; the custom of exchanging gifts at this time has survived, though the date of the commencement of the year has been changed. That the present should take the form of an egg is not surprising, for the egg has from earliest times been the mystic symbol of generation, of origin, and fecundity, shown especially by nature in the spring-time of the year. Persian, Egyptian, and Hindu legends tell the same story. The egg is the symbol of the new life of the spring-time, the New Life emphasised in the Christian faith by the Resurrection.

Very beautiful toys are sometimes enclosed in the elaborate egg-shaped boxes which are themselves works of art. Watteau, Lancret, and other great masters have not considered such work of decoration unworthy of their efforts.

The removal of the commencement of the year to January necessitated the New Year's presents being given at that time, which coincides with the old festival of the Strena. The name Étrennes shows its derivation, but though the time of gift-giving was changed with the change of the year, the eggs of Eastertide still remained as symbols of new life. The Easter gift is usual in nearly every country in Europe, in Russia especially, when the exchange of eggs is almost universal and accompanied by some ceremony.

It was an ancient custom in Greece to celebrate the return of the swallow in the spring. Children ran about the streets in small parties (much as they used to do in England on May Day with their garlands), holding in their hands roughly carved swallows of wood, in which

**Special
Toys for
Special
Occasions
and those
suggested
by Sacred
History.**
the tail, exaggerated in size, enabled the child to turn the
toy in the air, balancing it like a kite, a piece of string
being attached.   The graceful festival still remains in the
old French song :—

> Elle arrive, elle arrive, l'hirondelle,
> Messagère du printemps.

Toys and gifts were showered upon the young Greek
from the day of his birth ; he was scarcely laid in his
cradle before the friends of the mother brought gifts for
the infant ; on the fifth day, when the grand ceremony of
the initiation of the child into the religion of the family
took place, fresh gifts were brought, and in the old wives'
custom, surviving to the present day, of taking the baby
a tour in the house, omitting the ascension of any stairs,
we probably have a relic of the Greek custom of the
ceremony of going round the foyer of the Greek house.
Birthday anniversaries were invariably fêted in Rome,
and the birthdays of the Emperors were made occasions
for public holidays and costly gifts.   Toys are always
showered upon the little ones at such times, birthday
anniversaries and Christmas-time being the most important, and in fact the only festivals in the toy calendar
of Western Europe.

In the Middle Ages, when the great fairs were held
under warrant of ancient charters, granted by Kings to
Bishops or Burgesses, they were the chief occasions of
bartering or purchasing all merchandise not made in the
immediate district, and of hiring domestic servants and
labourers.   Such days were red-letter days for the
children, for then they saw the toys and trifles which
were so important a feature in the display ; "fairings"

286

for the little ones, fairings for sweethearts and wives, toy **Fairings.**
trumpets, hobby-horses, tiny paper mills, ribbons, laces,
and geegaws—all were the more acceptable because they
had never been seen in toy-shops and stores; to the
inhabitants of country districts the booths of the annual
fair were a revelation.

At Market Drayton seven fairs were held. Derby
Fair was held six weeks before Christmas; Gorley Market
opened by the ringing of the church bell; Coventry Fair
was one of the largest in England.

Pack Monday Fair was held at Sherborne in Dorset
until quite recently. Onion Fair at Chertsey was held on
Holy Rood day. Bartholomew Fair was an important
toy exchange near London, and at Stratford-upon-Avon
was held one of the largest of the statute fairs; but they
are too many to enumerate. On the Continent they
were of equal importance in the Middle Ages, and were
also the chief means of toy-selling.

In the eighteenth century the Fair of St. Germain in
Paris was the great toy market of France—we had almost
written of the world. There is an old print which shows
the stalls drawn up in regular alleys; the place is thronged
with buyers.

Many of the fairs in France were suppressed in 1839,
but re-established by Napoleon III. in 1852 for the
purpose, says the decree, of permitting the industrious
work-people of Paris to sell their work direct to the
public, and thus to make a good profit. The light booths
and stalls are still erected and a great trade done in
toys of every description before the New Year; "useful
presents" are taboo in the eyes of the little ones, and
dolls, toy soldiers, walking monkeys, animated birds, tops,

Special
Toys for
Special
Occasions
and those
suggested
by Sacred
History.
bats, panoplies of war, and the thousand and one novelties
make their début every year at the great fair on the
Boulevards.

In the East, religious toys take an important place
amongst the playthings of the children.   In China, where
religious forms enter more fully into the everyday life
perhaps than in any other country in the world except
India, where every article of beauty or utility has its
ornament or dedication of a religious character, every
domestic object is represented or inhabited by good or
evil spirits, and nearly every action is propitiatory to a
deity or a demon, and the rules of religion dictate the
actions of the mother towards the child from the hour of
its birth.

On a kakemono, in which scenes from child life in
China in the fourteenth and fifteenth centuries are represented, we see a tiny praying-mat ; the table or altar is in
miniature ; on it is the figure of a deity a few inches high ;
two tiny vases, one with a floral offering and one holding
joss sticks, are at the side.   Three children with grave
faces and clasped hands kneel before the miniature altar,
and in the background an older girl tries to induce a
chubby baby to kneel.

The tilting toys of China, fully described in our
chapter on dolls, are founded on the tradition that Buddha
cannot fall ; its Chinese name means " rise up, little priest,"
or " struck not to fall " ; it is generally made of stiff paper
or cardboard, painted red to represent an old man holding
a fan.   In Japan this toy is made to represent the idol
Daruma, and is called by his name.

Mrs. Little, in one of her books on modern life in
China, says : " To Chinese children I always think life

288

in a Chinese city must be very pleasant. There are the great Festivals: the Chinese New Year, the Dragon Boat Festival, when each district of the city mans a boat shaped like a dragon, and all paddle about like mad, naked to the waist, and with a strange shout that must be very dear to children. There are the visits to the graves when all the family go out into the country together; and the long processions when the officials are carried through the city in open chairs and long fur gowns, hundreds of umbrellas of gay colours going before them. All the beggar children of the city have a high game then. With fancy dress of various sorts 'over their rags, they walk or are carried round the city, sometimes as living pictures, sometimes representing conquered aborigines, sometimes even Englishmen in short square coats and tight trousers. In the spring-time a procession goes to meet the Spring and sacrifice an ox in the river bed to its honour. At other times it is the image of the fire god that is carried round, to show him the buildings he is honoured to protect."

CHAPTER XIII

EDUCATIONAL TOYS AND GAMES.

Educational Toys and Games. IN their desire for knowledge, children will break their most cherished toy in order to ascertain the secret of movement or sound. Question after question will come, quickly following the train of thought as it penetrates deeper, unsatisfied, until the depths of cause and effect have been plumbed.

Well-meaning persons of all ages have utilised this instinct of inquiry for the purposes of instruction, but without much result, for as a rule the educational toy is not a great favourite, children prefer to go their own way in acquiring knowledge; to use a homely simile, they love to open the oyster with their own knife, even though they damage their little fingers by the process.

Montaigne has said that the games of children are not play to them, they must be judged as their serious actions.

It is undoubtedly true that "the time when the child has no masters is the time when he learns the most and the quickest; when we compare the amount of knowledge acquired before a child is six years old with that learnt

LE CHATEAU DE CARTES.
Engraved by J. M. Leotard, from a picture by F. Boucher.

Six Cards from Le Jeu des Reines Renoucés, designed by Della Bella, the Florentine Artist, by order of Cardinal Mazarin, to instruct the young King of France in 1644.

in after years, we are astonished at his precocity." **Toys are the First Teachers.** Their toys are their first teachers, they are the educators of the senses, par excellence, the sense of touch and sight.

Amongst educational toys, card games have perhaps been the favourite vehicle for imparting information of a useful kind : of playing-cards of the ordinary kind we shall not speak, though their history is indeed a fascinating one, for they are essentially the playthings of adults.

We would classify the toy cards or playing-cards of children as—

1. Educational instructive cards, either biographic-historical or political-historical.

2. Amusing and humorous cards.

There is a tradition that *Minchiate*, the Italian game, in which both emblematic and numeral cards were used, as in our playing-cards of the present day, was invented by Michael Angelo to teach children arithmetic ; however this may be, such games have now become associated more especially with the games of hazard of adults. That they were not always put to this use is proved by the fact that cards are not mentioned in the long list of games of a gambling character prohibited by Charles V. in 1369.

An early pack of cards, probably made at Bologna, gives instruction in heraldry and geography, while serving the ordinary purpose ; these cards of the eighteenth century measure $4\frac{7}{8}$ by $2\frac{2}{8}$ inches ; the backs are decorated with shields.

Of the seventeenth century is a pack made at Naples, which are accompanied with an explanation affording instruction in heraldry, geography, and history. The small volume which forms a guide to the game is

dedicated to the Dauphin by M. de Brianville, Abbé de
St. Benout, 1672.

The players are to range themselves round a table
covered with a map of Europe ; the cards are then dealt
and exchanged.   He who is first after the dealer then
describes the blazonry of the card he holds, forfeiting one
if he makes an error, either to the player who corrects

CARD-PLAYING BY WOMEN IN MEDIÆVAL TIMES.
From a MS.

him or to a bank if there is one.   M. Gautier devised in
1686 a new pack of heraldic cards to serve the purpose
of a kind of grammar of the science.   We should imagine
some assistance was much needed by the players with the
Naples pack, which Mr. W. H. Willshire in his erudite
description quaintly remarks was " a very sorry recreation
for the royal urchin for whose edification it was devised."

Another heraldic pack, of Naples make, affords in- struction to children in heraldry and history ; in the last quarter of the seventeenth century, in a later edition 1725, it is supplemented by a geographical discourse from Michael Angelo Petrini. We fear by this time the poor children had more pill than jam to cover it.

In the first half of the seventeenth century Jean Desmarests, a French academician, undertook, at the suggestion of Cardinal Mazarin, to prepare a series of card games for the purpose of instructing the young king. Four series of instructive cards were produced, Desmarests undertaking the general designs and arrangements, and Della Bella, the Florentine artist and engraver, the illustrations. These games were exclusively sold by Henri Le Gras in 1644.

The first was a game founded on fables, gods, demi-gods, goddesses and heroes of antiquity ; each figure card had a short history printed on the lower part of the card.

The second game gave the history of France, and was called " The Game of the Kings of France," a selection being made from Pharamond to Louis XIV.; abridged accounts of each monarch were placed beneath each portrait.

" Le jeu des Reines Renommées " was the third game, when portraits of queens, heroines, and illustrious women from remotest antiquity were used, and an account of striking incidents in their history was given.

The fourth game prepared for the young Dauphin was a geographical game, when a figure in national costume emblematic of a geographic division of the globe was represented, and beneath, the situation of the country, the climate, and other dull and tiresome facts. These sets of cards are extremely valuable, not only on account of their rarity and historic interest, but because of the two hundred fine plates prepared for them by Stefano Della Bella.

In the eighteenth-century cards for piquet, a set of thirty-two was designed, with the secondary object of teaching geography. The aces of the different suits represent respectively a place of the celestial or the terrestrial hemisphere ; the degrees of latitude and longitude were marked on the maps.

Military science was used in connection with cards for the instruction of boys. " Le jeu des Fortifications " was brought out in Paris in the seventeenth century.

A variant of this game a few years later shows a monarch investing a hero with some dignity or reward ; the upper half of each card exhibits a neatly designed and engraved representation of some military operation. The game is dedicated to Monseigneur le Duc de Bourgogne.

Mythology, history, and biography are all used as subjects for new games or the amplification of old ones. In one of the latter of the early nineteenth century the kings are Caesar, Alexander, Charlemagne and Homer ; the queens Judith, Saint Genevieve, Lucretia, and Joan of Arc ; the knaves Gullemberg, Christopher Columbus, Moses, and Napoleon I. ; other celebrities, such as Cuvier, Newton, Archimedes, Plato, and Franklin also appear, while on the aces are given the histories of Cain and Abel, the Creation, the Deluge and the Crucifixion.

Satirical cards were, we imagine, never the playthings of children ; the allusions to the dominant political party, to the King or famous men of the day, were too subtle to be appreciated by boys and girls.

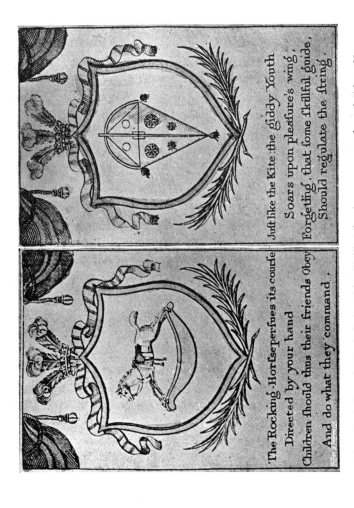

The Rocking Horse persues its course
Directed by your hand
Children should thus their friends Obey
And do what they command.

Just like the Kite the giddy Youth
Soars upon pleasure's wing,
Forgeting, that some skillful guide,
Should regulate the string.

Two Cards from the Pack designed by Wallis " for the amusement of youth " in 1788.
4 in. by 2½ in.

The Cretan Labyrinth, from a XVth Century engraving, Florentine, attributed to Baccio Baldini

The charades in action, however, the dialogues, pantomimes, quotations, and proverbs, which formed the subject of the card games of the early nineteenth century in England, France, and Germany, were essentially toy games; it is interesting to note that a wedding was the subject of a game both in London and Paris. In that published in France the description of the game is entitled "La Dot," Nouveau Jeu. Each player has twenty counters, and is supposed to represent one of the persons assisting at the ceremony.

On a series of thirty-six cards published in Paris, we find our old friend Polichenelle on no fewer than four of the cards; on one he is represented on stilts; the remaining cards show male and female figures in characteristic costumes. This game is called "Le Jeu de Polichenels Vampires."

Ninepins form the subject of another children's card game of the early nineteenth century. A large skittle is shown on a landscape background on nine cards, bowls on another nine, a running dog on three cards, and prostrate skittles on the remainder. Counters are required, and a paper of directions and rules is included with the pack.

"Jeu des Vicissitudes Humaines," or "Les Peines et les Plaisirs," include pictures of a lady smashing drawing-room chairs, and another going through the marriage ceremony, amongst the series of twenty-four; counters of blue, red, yellow, and white stained bone accompany this game.

"Le Jeu de Lotto en Cartes à rire" includes twenty-four long cards divided into twenty-seven squares differently coloured; comical designs ornament some of the cards.

Educational Toys and Games.

Though many of the early cards of the fifteenth and sixteenth centuries had animals such as lions, monkeys, peacocks, and parrots on them, we must not be misled into believing that they belonged to the toy card class prepared for children's use ; such signs were frequently used on the round Flemish cards especially of Nuremberg, Frankfurt, and Cologne, being but the signs for the numeral cards used in games of hazard, just as the Aces, Kings, Queens and Knaves are represented in the four suits of hearts, diamonds, spades, and clubs.

Columbines, violets, parroquets and roses were also used as suits, and others too various to enumerate ; such variations, however, were not enough to particularise them as children's toy cards.

Perhaps the most distressing invention of all from the children's point of view was the grammatical playing-card, "ingeniously contrived for the comprising of the general rules of Lillie's grammar," published in London in the seventeenth century.

Running it close as an instrument of mental torture is the arithmetical toy card of the eighteenth century, when " an arithmetical question is proposed and the sum worked in detail on each card. The whole is enclosed in a frame-like border. The ace of hearts illustrates the subtraction of Cloth Measure, the ace of spades the reduction of money, the ace of clubs the reduction of Cloth Measure, the knave of clubs, the last card of the series, works out Question 5 in Practice. The whole sequence is thus made to include the arithmetic of addition, subtraction, multiplication, division, reduction, the rule of three and practice."

We have found one example only in which the

300

elements of religion are used in connection with toy or educational cards ; this is a pack of fifty-two numerals, published in London in the eighteenth century.   On the upper portion of the card is the mark of the suit and the value in Roman numbers ; below, occupying more than half the card, is a whole-length figure followed by a description.   Veiled women, books of Divine law, flaming fire, serpents, and such emblematic figures are shown.

On an uncoloured series in outline of the eighteenth century the inventor's intentions are thus set forth :—

> These cards are truly well designed
> To ground all Letters in youth's minde.

> Bouth youth and age may learne hereby
> All sorts of Letters speedily.

> These cards may be a scoole to thee
> If you discern what you may learne.

"Wallis's Emblematical Cards for the Amusement of Youth" were published in London, September 15, 1788, price one shilling, neatly coloured.

In the centre of each piece on a large shield the emblematic object is represented.   Above the shield is the crest of the Prince of Wales ; a motto scroll, curtain-like drapery, palm branches, and other accessories.   On the lower part of each card is a verse of four lines referring to the emblem above.   Each card has a yellow border between engraved lines ; the emblems are twelve in number, and are many of them toys.   No. 1 has a crown, 2 a clock, 3 a ship, 4 an anchor, 5 a cannon, 6 a basket of flowers, 7 a horn, 8 a guitar, 9 a harlequin, 10 a rocking-horse, 11 a kite, 12 a boy with a whipping top.

Educational Toys and Games.

On a series of forty-five cards invented by Miss Jane Roberts, after " directions for playing the game," the inventor hopes that this simple division of the thirty-five reigns or thirty-six periods of English history between the nine centuries which have elapsed since the Conquest, will enable the players with a little practice to remember the exact line of succession to the British Throne.

Riddle questions derived from Shakespeare form the subject of one game, love-letters of another. Comic conversation cards give the following couplet :—

> Most packs are in full cry when game they're after,
> This comic pack now try whose game is laughter.

Many games were brought out early in the nineteenth century based on the play of the good old Happy Family where Master Pott and Miss Bung, Mrs. Chipp and the Tape Family have brought so much pleasure and amusement to the nursery, pure fun and amusement being unadulterated with maps or grammar, Kings and Queens or Heraldry.

The educational card game for children is well known in the East. Mr. Stewart Culin in writing of children's playing cards of China and Korea, says :—" One of the earliest writing lessons set to a Chinese child commences —' Once there was a great man.' This forms the basis of many card packs which are as a rule hand-written on smooth oiled paper."

There are also children's cards based on the lucky formula : Happiness like the Eastern sea—and such wishes for good luck.

" Flower cards " are also used which have connection

302'

with dominoes ; the Chinese have but one word for cards
and domino cards.

Occasionally these playing-cards are painted on tablets of bone.

In Japan a proverb game of cards is much played by children ; forty-eight comprise the pack, half of which bear a picture, the other half a proverb. After the cards are dealt, the picture cards are laid face upwards and the proverbs fitted to them.

Poem cards are played in the same number, the picture of the poet and quotation from his works being placed together during the game.

In Japan a game is played with fifty-two shells which much resemble a card game. We are indebted to the Viscountess Tadasu Hayashi, wife of the Japanese Ambassador to the Court of St. James, for our knowledge of this game, which she played with us. The shells resembling mussels are painted inside with elaborate landscapes ; much green and gold is used with very happy effect. They are dealt round by the players, who then try to pair ; each shell will fit one other in the set, so that the bi-valve closes firmly and the shells are passed round amongst the different players until each shell has its corresponding half, the player who first pairs all his shells being declared winner.

The riddle games, puzzles and acrostics, anagrams, and such childish amusements are to be found in the books which have come down to us from the eighteenth and nineteenth centuries.

That the labyrinth was known to the Greeks is proved by the frequent appearance of this form of puzzle on coins. Extraordinarily complicated labyrinths were made in the

Educational Toys and Games.

Middle Ages, but these were not children's games; the simpler designs can be found in children's books, and have always been an interesting and fascinating diversion

LABYRINTH PUZZLES FROM GREEK COINS.

for the quiet and studious amongst them, as well as for adults.

The Sphinx is one of the riddle and puzzle books published in London in 1820 by Nowell and Burch.

It measures five and a half inches by three; here are a few examples taken from its pages :—

> My first denotes equality,
> My second denotes ability,
> My whole's a sort of Parable.
> Answer : Parable.

Why is the letter E like London ?
> Answer : Because it is the capital of England.

This has an eighteenth-century flavour about it when improvement and education lurked in every recreation.

Why has a glass-blower more power than any other tradesman to make the letters of the alphabet run, and a barber to stop them ?
Answer : The former can make a D canter (Decanter), the latter can put 2 Ps (Toupees) in irons and tie down a Q (queue).

Frolics of the Sphinx, published at Oxford in 1812, is described as an entirely original collection of Charades, Riddles and Conundrums.

HOT SPICE GINGERBREAD, SMOKING HOT.
One of the cries of London. By Wheatley.

Game of the Zoetrope family. The card is
balanced on the handle and turned rapidly, when
the figures have the appearance of movement.
One of the toys of Queen Victoria. At Kensington
Palace.

Card puzzles and distortions. From the
Germanische Museum, Nuremburg.

Such books as these were not only used by children, **Puzzle** but also eagerly perused by adults in the days when **Cards.** pastimes such as riddles and rebuses formed the amusement at evening parties, and the lady or gentleman who could commit such stuff to memory shone as a brilliant person.

Ou est la Bergère ?

Puzzle cards, on which a hidden figure has to be found amongst the lines of a picture, have been known for many

L'embarras du Bulgaire

Il quitte sa maison avec toute sa famille, mais où est le chat !

years; their popularity wanes and increases at fairly regular intervals in our nurseries.

The printed cardboard battledore, which was supposed to combine amusement with instruction, was made in the shape of the toy used in the game of battledore and shuttlecock ; it was a successor of the hornbook, and was printed on a double fold of stiff cardboard with a third flap folding over like a pocket-book.   These "battledores" were issued by many publishers in the early nineteenth century and were illustrated ; one before us is called *My New Battledore*, published by Joseph Toller ; its original price was one penny.   A basketmaker at his work illustrates the cover, easy words and syllables for reading are inside, commencing with ab, eb, etc., and going on to a second lesson, add, bad, etc.   "Dame Trot and her cat" or the dearly loved "Mother Hubbard" and her dog are shown in the space between the first and second lesson.

Toys made of sweet stuff and gingerbread were usually sold at fairs in the eighteenth century, at the same time as gingerbread hornbooks and battledore books.   In fact, book gingerbread impressed with the alphabet at a halfpenny a slice was cried in the London streets until early in the nineteenth century, and is the subject of one of Wheatley's "Cries" ; such slices may still be bought with the alphabet upon them.   The late Mr. Andrew Tuer in his *History of the Hornbook* says :—" The wooden moulds used for stamping the gingerbread were in the form of short planks about two inches thick, on which were cut series of devices, with others on the reverse side. The long brown slabs were impressed and, after being baked, were cut up.

Some moulds of gingerbread toys used by one Stagg, a gingerbread maker of East Street, Taunton, a successor of a long line of gingerbread makers who supplied the

markets and fairs of Somerset, show very varied devices ; **Ginger-bread Toys.**
one, the *Royal George*, shows the frigate under full sail ;
its subject dates it as the end of the eighteenth century,
the wreck taking place in 1782. Another is in the
shape of an old flint-lock gun ; the fashionable shaped
clock of the period, which we now call the grandfather's
clock, was made as a gingerbread toy ; this measures
about six inches in height, while the King on horseback
with flowing wig and full-tailed coat is slightly smaller.
A row of four ladies and gentlemen dressed in the
fashion of Queen Anne must have been extremely
appetising when shining in all the glory of tinfoil. Our
expression of " taking the gilt off the gingerbread " may
be traced to these edible toys, which were sold at half-
price when broken or when the golden ornament had
peeled off.

> Sing Hey diddle, diddle,
> The cat and the Fiddle,

formed the subject of another gingerbread toy ; in fact
animals of all kind were stamped out in the spiced
mixture for the children, as they are now in sugar pigs,
mice, horses, men and women, such articles of diet being
most popular amongst the little ones at the fairs. A
cock in breeches was a favourite device of the eighteenth
century, such jokes being quite in accordance with the
fun of a fair.

Not only were these toys of sugar and gingerbread
made for sale at village festivals and at the great fairs,
they were also given by shopkeepers to good customers
as a sort of makeweight or reward. We have seen large
ginger or rose lozenges· stamped with the words, Buy
your tea at So-and-So's, as the modern development of

the gratuitous sweetmeat, and know of a large order from
Burmah being placed with a firm who sends tons of
sweets abroad ; such toys were to have mottoes printed
upon them in Burmese.

Fairs where gingerbread and toys were exclusively sold
existed.   Two gingerbread fairs were held each year in
Birmingham until well on into the nineteenth century,
the warrant having been given in the thirteenth century.
Long lines of market stalls held all sorts of gingerbread
in every imaginable shape and form ; none was sold at
any other time.

In South Germany and the Netherlands figures of
flour and honey were made and elaborately coloured.
Whole processions, the guests attending a marriage feast,
musicians, peasants and farmyard animals, — all were
cleverly modelled in the easily-moulded sticky mixture
which was afterwards coloured.   The ruffs, hooped skirts,
and voluminous coats of the seventeenth and eighteenth
centuries are elaborately shown, and the varnish-like coating
of paint outside has preserved the figures.   In India
large quantities of sweetmeat toys are made.— balls,
bats, tops, cups, goblets and pans ; all are made of sugar
and coloured ; frequently their brightness is enhanced
with pieces of gilt paper.

Of the old toys whose basis is some scientific principle,
those belonging to the Zoetrope family were perhaps the
best known.   Both the Phenakisticope and the Zoetrope
were based on the principle of the retention on the retina
of an impression for a minute length of time, until another
impression is in view.   All the objects represented are
shown in a succession of scenes, so that the movements,
being sufficiently quickly graduated, have the appearance

THE SHADOW RABBIT.

After Sir David Wilkie.

Grotesque Figures. As used in Java for Shadowgraphy. Legendary
history is taught by means of itinerant shows, which were in existence
before the introduction of Mahometanism into the island. The figures
are of leather, from 18 in. to 2 ft. high. The sticks are of horn.

of life. Whether we twirl round a Zoetrope peeping through the holes, watch the spinning of a Phenakisticope, move a card round where graduated pictures are printed, or watch the mighty effect of a modern biograph where 4000 different pictures pass before our eyes in three minutes, the principle is the same. Other scientific toys which reflect by distortion, such as convex and concave mirrors, are occasionally made use of and have been since very remote times, either as simple toys or as a principle in the construction of toys.

The Kaleidoscope was invented early in the nineteenth century by Brewster, an Englishman, and the furore which it produced in Paris has only been equalled by the popularity of the marionette shows in former times ; several patents were applied for in Paris for the improvement of the toy after 1818. These two examples, the Italian Marionettes and English Kaleidoscope, show that though Paris has produced extraordinarily popular and ingenious toys, other countries have competed successfully.

Toys which work by means of a magnetised needle have been known since the early half of the nineteenth century ; floating tortoise, fish, or duck drawn along by a magnet are amongst the most delightful forms of applied science producing white magic for the nursery. In June 1838 an article in the *Dublin University Magazine* drew attention to this form of plaything ; a Nuremberg firm exploited the idea with great success, and such toys are still most popular.

It is said that Roger Bacon discovered the possibilities of the magic lantern during his study of the nature of shadows, and so famous was his scientific toy that it did not escape the accusation of magic. The matter was

313

eventually laid before the Pope, to whom a primitive lantern was shown. Innocent IV. was so delighted with the toy and saw its nature so well, that he declared it perfectly harmless and took great pleasure in showing it to his friends.

There is an old engraving on wood of the seventeenth century which shows a box in which is placed a lamp; a small chimney above carries off the lamp-smoke, a highly polished metal reflector intensifies the light, an aperture focuses the rays which pass through a delicately painted picture and are thrown upon a blank wall. The picture, we notice, is that of an evil-doer who is expiating his crimes in most animated-looking flames; other pictures of saints, with the instruments of their martyrdom, are ready to be passed through the light.

In a dictionary published in 1719 the magic-lantern is described as "a little optical machine which enables one to see in the dark, on a white wall, many spectres and frightful monsters of a sort that those who do not know the secret believe it to be done by magic art." Itinerant magic-lantern showmen, mostly Italians, travelled all over Europe. Carle Vernet early in the nineteenth century shows one of these men in his series of *Cris de Paris*; he has his simple lantern and a box for the slides, oil, etc., strapped to his back; he is beating on a tambourine, doubtless to attract a crowd. In this same picture an organ-grinder, apparently of the same nationality, carries his instrument on his back. As early as the reign of Louis XVI. the method was known of giving animation to the figures shown on the screen by means of two different pieces of glass, one of which is fixed, the other moved by the showman.

Shadowgraphy, as it is now called, originated in China or Java. Italy and Germany were the first European countries where puppet shadows thrown on a screen were made to enact a little play; the movements are made by means of a hidden hand which manipulates the figures. A piece of linen or oiled paper was stretched in a frame for the purpose of displaying the early shadowgraphy. Seven or eight feet between the light at the back and the frame, flat figures of wood or cardboard were moved, so that their shadows cast by the light behind them fell upon the screen. Baron Grimm, writing of such an entertainment in 1770, says rather pompously : " After the opera I do not know of a more interesting spectacle for children, it lends itself to marvellous enchantments and the most terrible catastrophes." In 1773 a little theatre was opened in Paris under the name of *Theatre des recreations de la Chine* by one Ambroise, who in the following year came to London, bringing with him the simple machinery necessary for the display of his moving shadows.

Dominique Seraphin brought shadowgraphy to perfection. After touring the provincial towns during several years, he opened a permanent establishment at Versailles, and after showing his entertainment several times to the Royal Family, was in 1784 allowed to call it *Spectacle des Enfants de France*. In the same year he transported his properties to the recently built Palais Royal, where he or his descendants remained till the year 1858.

In Korea shadow pictures are made on the wall with the hand just as we see in Wilkie's picture " The Shadow on the Wall," where the father is twisting his fingers into a shape which is shadowed as a rabbit. In China shadow-

315

play nearly always represents a priest of Buddha as the central figure. Pieces of paper are used in carrying out the delusions, besides other simple accessories such as are employed in our European shadowgraphy entertainments. The priest is made to dance in imitation of the movements made in the performance of religious rites.

In Japan the game is called shadow pictures ; shadows are made with the hand, and various pieces of paper bent to the shapes required are used ; a favourite subject is that of a bird-catcher, whose implement is a long pole smeared with bird-lime.

Nowhere has the art of shadowgraphy been brought to such perfection as in the Island of Java ; the special puppets used are most elaborate and of infinite variety ; the performances consist of long and intricate histories taken from the earliest period of Javan fable down to the destruction of the Hindu empire of Majapahit. These are named according to the periods of the history which they represent. We are told in Sir Stamford Raffles' *History of Java*, " A white cloth or curtain is drawn tight over an oblong frame of ten or twelve feet long and five feet high, and, being placed in front of the spectators, is rendered transparent by means of a hanging lamp behind it.

" The figures are made in turn to appear and act their parts. Previous to the commencement of this performance the D'alang (stage manager), who is seated behind the curtain, arranges the different figures, for convenience sticking them into a long plantain stem which is laid along the floor.

" The play then commences, and as the several characters present themselves, extracts of history are repeated and the dialogue is carried on at the discretion of the stage manager. He not only puts the puppets in motion but repeats their parts." Sir Stamford Raffles enters into most interesting and minute details with regard to the subject of some of these shadow plays, and tells us how the constant exhibition of these plays in every part of the country gives the children an extraordinarily correct knowledge of the legendary history of their country.

The puppets used are about 18 inches to 2 ft. high, stamped or cut out of thick pieces of leather, generally of buffalo hide; they are painted with great care and at considerable expense, in order that some resemblance to the character represented may be obtained.

The whole figure, however, is strangely distorted and grotesque, the nose in particular being unnaturally prominent. This distortion is made purposely, in order that the amusements of the people may be in accordance with the Mahometan precept, which forbids any exhibition or dramatic representation of the human form; these figures, however, as is proved by their appearance on ancient coins, existed in their present form before the introduction of Mahometanism. The figures, for the shadowgraphy performances, are fastened upon a horn spike and have a piece of thin horn hanging from each hand, by means of which the arms, which are jointed at the elbow and shoulder, can be moved at the discretion of the showman. On the Hindu island of Bali these figures, though not so much distorted, also exist.

On the night of the festival of Diwali in India children carry lanterns and occasionally men exhibit a large cylindrical paper lantern, over the sides of which a number of shadow-figures pass in succession. This effect of

317

Educational Toys and Games. shadowgraphy is obtained by means of a light frame set with paper figures; this revolves round the central lamp. The lamp has long been known in the East, and is alluded to in the quatrain in FitzGerald's version of Omar Khayam :—

> We are no other than a moving row,
> Of magic shadow shapes that come and go
> Round with the sun illumined lantern held
> In midnight by the master of the show.

CHAPTER XIV

TOPS, TEETOTUMS, HOOPS, BOARD-GAMES, COUNTERS.

AN enthusiast has declared that "if more attention were **Scientific** paid to the intelligent examination of the behaviour of **Top-** tops, there would be greater advances in mechanical **spinning.** engineering and kindred industries. There would be a better general knowledge of astronomy, geologists would not make mistakes by millions of years, and our knowledge of light, radiant heat, and other electro-magnetic phenomena would extend much more rapidly than it does."

Though we speak here of top-spinning and hoop-trundling as the pastimes of childhood only, do not let us forget that some of the most interesting and beautiful of Nature's laws are "played with" in the handling of these most fascinating of toys.

It is in Japan that top-spinning has, for centuries, been elevated to a mathematical science ; not only is the top the most popular toy in the whole of the country, but its pre-eminence, in the favour of the children, extends through India, China, and Persia, where not only children, but grown people spend hours in this fascinating pastime,

319

**Tops,
Teeto-
tums,
Hoops,
Board-
Games,
Counters.**

and professional top-spinning is a recognised form of entertainment; all the more enjoyed, because probably nearly every onlooker is himself proficient, if not an expert in the art.

In England there are many puzzling problems for the boy who gets out his whip-top or spinning-top and string. There are tops which nobody seems able to spin, and there are others that behave well under the most tryingly unscientific treatment. How treasured are these latter, only the owner of a really good spinning-top knows; so highly prized, that no "swop," however temptingly baited, can be entertained; and yet nobody, not even the makers, seem to know why one top "goes" well and another badly, even in the hands whose touch and handling have a knowingness in them which is not to be despised.

How many children have given up such a problem as hopeless of solution until, perhaps in after years, they see the play of an expert spinner, when the old desire comes back to them to understand the mysteries that surround them.

"Such a desire." says Professor John Perry, "may be seen in the eyes of the excited crowd who stand by the hour, under the drooping cherry blossoms beside the red-pillared temple of Asakusa in the Eastern capital of Japan, watching the *tedzu-mashi* directing the evolutions of his heavily rimmed *Koma*. First he throws away from him his great top obliquely into the air and catches it, spinning, on the end of a stick, or point of a sword, or any other convenient implement; he now sends it about quite carelessly, catching it as it comes back to him from all sorts of directions; he makes it run up the hand-rail of a staircase, into a house by the door, and out again by the window; he makes it travel up like a cork-

High Play with Human Spools.

The Duet.

Diabolo in 1812.

A Domestic Scene.

screw. Now he seizes it in his hands, and with a few **Chinese** dexterous twists gives it a new stock of spinning energy ; **Top-play.** he makes it travel along a stretched string or the edge of a sword ; he does all sorts of other curious things with his tops, and suddenly sinks from his masterful position to beg for a few coppers at the end of his performance. . . ."

Perhaps it is only in Japan that such an exhibition is possible ; the land where the waving bamboo, and the circling hawk, and the undulating summer sea, and every beautiful motion of Nature are looked upon with tenderness ; and perhaps it is from Japan that we shall learn the development of our childish enthusiasm.

In China, Japan, and Korea the number and variety of tops is very large, whereas in Western countries there may be a dozen distinct kinds, half of which would be known to a European boy : in these Eastern countries there are hundreds, each having its special use, mode of spinning or whipping, or season for use.

In China, top-play is described under two terms— " solitary pleasure," and " conch-shell play " ; for the latter the shells are ground, so that the heads are flat and the tips pointed ; sometimes these tips are weighted with lead. A special game is played with this variety of top. Several are required, a cord is wound round the top to get the impetus required, and three tops spin together on a slanting mat. We have the picture of such a game before us ; the player sits watching the progress of the game, his string in his hand. The shell that is knocked off the mat first loses the game. When they collide or go " out " together, the game is " drawn."

The " priest top," so called on account of the

**Tops,
Teeto-
tums,
Hoops,
Board-
Games,
Counters.**

resemblance of its rounded head to the shaven head of a priest, is also played with a string.

Special tops are used for whipping on the ice ; they are shod with iron and are rather heavy.

Since the end of the seventeenth century a very wide-spreading top with long point has been popular ; the long pointed spindle is made of iron, and it is round this that the cord is wound. This top is frequently spun on a wooden bat like the Japanese battledore, used to strike up the wooden-headed Japanese shuttlecock ; the top is the size of a man's fist.

The pinching top is somewhat similar in shape, but the long spindle is on the head instead of the foot ; on this elongated head is strung a small piece of india-rubber tubing, which is seized when the top is lifted up.

The catching top is of wood with an iron spindle round which the cord is wound ; it has a broad wheel-shaped head, and is thrown sideways and caught up frequently in the hand, as we see practised by Europeans.

Fighting tops used by boys in a top-fighting game are heavily shod with iron ; this variety is also set in motion with a cord.

The hand tops or twirling tops, set in motion with a twist of the fingers, are very numerous. Sometimes they are acorn-shaped, and occasionally children make them themselves with an acorn and a spindle of split bamboo. Sometimes the twirling tops have a body of wood with incised rings. There is another variety which is named after a flat cake, which it somewhat resembles.

Other Eastern varieties of tops are the thunder or humming tops of Japan. Such tops, made of bamboo, are also used in Java ; they are frequently made with a section of bamboo, which has sealed ends dividing each growth; **Whist-** a bamboo spindle is used; these tops are occasionally to **ling Tops.** be found highly ornamented.   Whistling tops are made by fastening a whistle to the head of the spindle, or cutting a small hole in the body of the top through which the air hums or whistles as it passes; lantern tops, by fixing a gaily painted tiny paper lantern in the head of the top.   Another uncommon variety which we have never seen in England releases smaller tops from its girth as it spins.

Our modern game Diabolo, which was played with such enthusiasm for a short time in 1907, originally came from China, where it has been played for centuries under the name of Koen Gen.   This game partakes somewhat of the nature of top-spinning in its more complicated manifestations; the spool or Devil having been whipped up or driven with a cord to a certain velocity, is tossed up by the player, caught again on the cord, and made to perform other evolutions.   This pastime was much enjoyed in Napoleon's time, and there is an interesting print showing the little corporal and his generals enjoying the game.   Other prints of the early nineteenth century show that caricaturists of the day did not fail to apply the craze to their own purposes, and human spools are being spun and tossed.

In the Musée Carnavalet in Paris many varieties of spool can be identified in an old print called " The Devil Omnipotent." ˙Some are almost like balls with a nearly invisible groove for the string, others elongated and of the shape of the old hour-glasses; others again have holes pierced in the sides so that as the air hums through them, a buzzing sound is emitted.   It is said that such pierced

Tops,
Teeto-
tums,
Hoops,
Board-
Games,
Counters. Devils of large size are still used in China by street
hawkers, the humming noise being associated with the
sale of special wares. To many middle-aged people the
Diabolo craze of last year did but renew their pleasure in
an old game, and old-fashioned sticks and spools were
unearthed from store cupboards where they had long lain
neglected.

In Japanese and Chinese pictures of the thirteenth and
fourteenth centuries, children are shown both spinning

WHIPPING THE TOWN TOP.
From an old MS.

and whipping tops. We know of no Egyptian tops,
though their hoop-bowling and spinning games were far
more elaborate than those in vogue at the present day.

A marginal drawing in a manuscript at the British
Museum, of the fourteenth century, gives an excellent
picture of a man and a boy whipping an enormous top
in a quite impossible position on the side of a small
mound ; doubtless artistic licence necessitated that the
central object should be raised at the side of a hill, so
that it should be sufficiently seen. We notice that the
whips used have several lashes with knobs at the end.

In a sixteenth century engraving by Selliman the boy
whipping a top has two lashes on his whip ; in this case
again the top is enormous, quite as big as the child's
head.   Whether this is due to artistic licence or was the
real size of the top of the period, we do not know.
Large tops were undoubtedly used.   In a print of the
eighteenth century in Brand's *Antiquities*, entitled " Town-
top," we see three men, with single lashes to their whips,
whipping a top the size of a small bucket and of the
same shape.   There is no spindle or point of any kind
apparent, so we fear that accuracy was not the forte of the
engraver.   " This ' Town-top ' was the top formerly kept
in every village," says Brand, " to be whipt in frosty
weather, that the peasants might be kept warm by
exercise, and out of mischief while they could not work."
In *Poor Robin's Almanack* for 1677 tops are mentioned
in the " Fanatick's Chronology."

These large tops, whipped by several people alternately,
are made use of by several artists in caricature.   George
Cruikshank, in one entitled " The Corsican Whipping-Top
in Full Spin," places Napoleon's head as the top; his
limbs have each been whipped away by one of the
European Powers, who are represented as boys handling
huge lashed whips.   Holland is hugging his prize, an arm
of Napoleon, on which is written the United Netherlands,
and so on.   The spoil of the mighty conqueror is being
shared by the crowned heads of Europe.

That tops were well known to antiquity, many
allusions by contemporary writers prove ; Perseus in his
third Satire says—we quote from Dryden's translation—

> The whirling top they whip
> And drive her giddy till she falls asleep.

Tops, Teeto- tums, Hoops, Board- Games, Counters.

From Virgil's Seventh Æneid, Dryden gives us—

As young striplings whip the top for sport
On the smooth pavement of an empty court,
The wooden engine whirls and flies about,
Admired with clamours of the beardless rout,
They lash aloud, each other they provoke,
And lend their little souls at every stroke.

Tops are found as toys in all parts of the world. In Borneo a very large wooden variety, with a spindle 7 inches long, is used. In Florida Island, one of the Solomon group, tops are made of large hard nuts; a spindle of bamboo wood is run through the pierced nut. In Polynesia a game of forfeits is played with several spinning-tops; this is also known in the Hawaiian group.

Though scarcely a top, we must classify the spinning dice, or teetotums, with the tops, which are more essentially children's toys. The teetotum is sometimes used by the little ones as the sole instrument in a game, the numbers marked on the side of the circular top-like toy, which falls over on successive spinning, being added together, the highest total being declared winner; more often the teetotum is used in conjunction with any of the numerous board-games, such as backgammon, the many variants of the race game, and others which require the men or pieces to be moved by the throw of dice or spinning of a teetotum. In Japan, China, India, Ceylon, and the Malay Peninsula teetotums are found in wood, ivory, metal, lacquer, and are sometimes very beautifully and artistically ornamented. We have before us a very fine teetotum of black lacquer, measuring $4\frac{1}{2}$ inches from the point to point of the spindle, and $2\frac{1}{4}$ inches across the dice. The numerals are in gold paint, and red also figures in the decoration. A very fine collection of **Teeto-** teetotums of every period and style was at one time in **tums.** the possession of Mr. FitzHenry ; they have since been dispersed.

A fine engraving by Chardin called " Le Toton " shows a quaintly grave and old-fashioned little boy of about seven years of age ; he is dressed in the full-skirted coat and long vest of the eighteenth century, his hair bagged and tied up with a black silk bow, in front it is rolled off the high forehead like a wig ; the child is gravely watching the spinning of a teetotum during an interval evidently between more serious studies, for pens, ink, books, and a folio of paper are scattered on the table.

The wooden die . used in the Chinese game of " Dignitaries " is a block 4 or 5 inches long, having five sides which slope from the middle to the ends. Its longitudinal edges are notched with from one to five notches ; the men in the game are moved according to the number which comes uppermost. This game is permitted in schools, where dice games are prohibited, and it is likely this special kind of teetotum was suggested to avoid the use of dice in children's games.

A similar die was used in England, in playing a game called Lang Larence, once popular at Christmastide. This name of Lawrence was probably suggested by the marks or bars on the die resembling those of a gridiron, the instrument of St. Lawrence's martyrdom. Such dice were also used by the Greeks and Romans, and specimens remain in glass, ivory, and bronze.

Very beautiful also are some of the old counters used in games played with or without teetotums. Finest specimens of antique ivory carving are on old counters,

**Tops,
Teeto-
tums,
Hoops,
Board-
Games,
Counters.** dominoes, and chessmen. At the Ashmolean Museum
at Oxford, pieces of the thirteenth century are in excellent
preservation ; there is still sharpness of outline, and in
some cases traces of colouring. A thirteenth century
draughtsman carved in walrus ivory shows St. Martin
dividing his cloak with the beggar ; behind is the head
of an ass ; the picture is framed with a bead-like ornament
which is often seen on such pieces.

Some counters dated 1587 are elaborately painted
with the crest and arms of English peers ; there is a
covering of talc on each side, so that the handling of the
counters has not dimmed the elaborate and brilliant
heraldic blazon.

Counter boxes are sometimes made as round metal
cylinders, which hold the pieces exactly piled on each
other ; a silver box of such a kind holds sixpences of
the time of Queen Elizabeth. Coins were frequently used
as counters. Very elaborate and beautiful work has been
lavished on the boxes. An ivory box of 1700, 2 inches
by $3\frac{1}{2}$, has the death of Abel carved upon it.

A box made in commemoration of the birth of Prince
Charles Stuart, the Young Pretender, is dated 1720.

An interesting historical box was given by the first
Duchess of Marlborough to Queen Anne. It has the
royal arms inlaid in ivory on the large outside box and
on each of the four small boxes which fit into it. This
box was eventually given by Queen Anne to Mrs.
Masham, the rival favourite.

An ivory counter box made in Paris has revolving
discs fitting into the lids of the small boxes ; such discs
were used as markers. This box was made by Mareaval
le Jeune in the eighteenth century.

Maucala Board, with cowrie shell counters. Made
in the form of the Sisoo Fish.

English Chessmen of the XIIIth Century. Bishop, King, and Castle, in carved Ivory. $2\frac{1}{2}$ in.

Indian Chessmen.   Rook, King, and Knight.

Though the games of chess, draughts, backgammon, **Japanese**
magic squares, and other varieties requiring boards and **Board-games.**
men can hardly be looked upon as the play of children,
yet a book on toys of youth would hardly be complete
without a brief notice of them, chiefly because so many
simple games, which are really children's games, have been
founded on these more abstruse and intricate varieties.

We have before us a charming Japanese print of tiny
children playing sugoroku, which is the Japanese form of
backgammon; this game is most usual at the New Year.
Double sixes and Korean backgammon is played according to the throws of the dice or the spinning of the
teetotum; the wooden pins, or men, are called horses,
fifteen are employed on each side, a colour distinguishing
those belonging to the two players. In this game many
of the terms are identical with those of domino play.

Backgammon, as played in China, has been described
by Dr. Hyde. The board is divided into eight equal
parts by transverse lines, and the pieces number sixteen
on each side; they are moved according to the throw of
the dice. The first player who gets all his pieces to the
opposite side, wins the game. Backgammon is played by
children in Siam and in the Malay Peninsula in a manner
very similar to the European method.

Mancala, a board-game played chiefly by women and
children in the East, consists of the removal of counters
(cowries being generally used for this purpose) from one
hole in the board to another, according to the spinning
of a teetotum; the board is often made in the form of
the Sisoo fish, and it is sometimes inlaid with ivory or
pearl; occasionally it is made in a large size, and has
legs beneath, so that no table is required.

**Tops,
Teeto-
tums,
Hoops
Board-
Games,
Counters.** " Chess, draughts, and backgammon," says Mr. Falkener
in his learned work, *Games Ancient and Oriental*, " or
games resembling them, have been played in all civilised
countries and at all times. In some instances there is
little or no variation of the same game in different
countries ; in others the difference is such as to con-
stitute a new game. . . . We have not as yet found them
in Nineveh or Babylon, though we are convinced they
were played there ; but we see them depicted on the
walls of Egypt ; and the most ancient of all the games
of chess, the details of which are known to us, comes from
India."

In the British Museum may be seen fragments of the
draught-board of Queen Hatasu, who lived about 1600
B.C.; and 3000 years before she lived, the game was well
known. When the Egyptians depicted the enjoyment
of the future state, dancing, song, and the playing of
various games were invariably shown. Draughts was
played in the Egyptian Elysium according to the seventeenth chapter of the " Ritual of the Dead." In a papyrus
of the comparatively recent date of Trajan one may see
in the British Museum that a lion is seated on a stool
playing chess with a goat ; on the board between them
are eight pieces, four with pointed heads, four on the
lion's side with flat heads.

There were two other Egyptian board-games ; one
resembling draughts is still played under the name of
Seega ; it is the Indus Labriancularum of the Romans.
The other is Jan, the game of robbers, which, like the
Labroves or Thewis of the Romans and Greeks, is some-
times called the Sacred Way.

Chaturanga, the Indian progenitor of all chess games,

is put down by Sir William Jones as going back to a
period of 3900 years; it is said to have been invented by
the wife of Ravana, King of Ceylon, when his capital was
besieged by Rama; it was a game of war in which the
King and his allies went to wreck a hostile king and his
allies, each having horsemen, ships, elephants, and allies
on foot.

Chinese chess is dated at 200 B.C., and was supposed
to have been invented by the general Han Sing to amuse

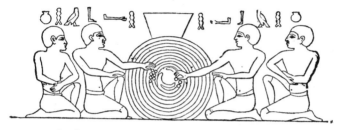

AN EGYPTIAN BOARD-GAME LIKE PIGS IN CLOVER.
From a fresco.

his soldiers on the approach of winter, when besieging a
town.

Japanese chess differs from other variants of the game,
in having all the men of one colour, so that the pieces
serve either for the player or his adversary. Chess
tournaments appear to have originated in the East;
"once every year on the 17th day of the 11th month the
masters of the game met at Yedo and fought a grand
tourney within the precincts of the Palace."

Burmese chess is common to the regions between India
and China, namely, Tibet, Burmah, Siam, and Cochin
China. The board, which is one of eight cells, is made
of a height suitable for players seated on the ground.

Tops,
Teeto-
tums,
Hoops,
Board-
Games,
Counters. The Turks have a board of cloth embroidered to form the cells ; such a cloth can easily be rolled up or unfolded on a carpet or divan.

In a Persian MS. a vision is described in which Mahomet presents the writer with a bag of chessmen, by using which he was ever afterwards victorious ; the variety of the game indulged in by the fortunate player is called Tamerlane's chess.

The Chinese game of " Enclosing " is of great antiquity, dating back to 2300 B.C. ; it is a game played on a board of eighteen squares each way.

Pachisi is the national game of India, and was played by Akbar, who had enormous courts made at all his palaces ; traces of these are to be seen at Agra and Allahabad ; the game was played by him with live figures, which moved according to the throw of the dice ; the board is generally made of cloth and divided into squares by embroidery.

How interesting to see the great Akbar, not as the mighty conqueror, but in the hours of relaxation, his toys being on the same mighty scale as all other matters connected with him. Professor Chamberlain in *The Child a Study in the Evolution of Man* says : " Play more than anything else reveals national and racial character, the touch of the people is upon them (the games), and ' by their plays shalt thou know them.' "

The hoop, that spinning toy which has always exercised such a fascination over children, was well known to the Greeks and Romans. It was the iron hoop beloved of our boys, but in these days for some mysterious reason taboo for girls, which was used by the Greeks ; the hoops were of large size, and driven and guided by a small

336

baton as they are now ; there was another game played **Rod and**
with a small hoop, the players using rods which were **Hoop**
Games.
grasped in both hands.

In an old book of children's games *Les Graces* is
described.   Two 3-feet wands were used, and a small

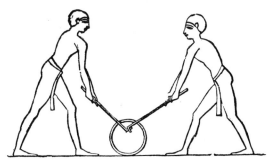

EGYPTIAN ROD AND HOOP GAME.
From a fresco.

leather-bound hoop about ten inches in diameter ; the
hoop was threaded on the crossed wands and then shot
off them to as great a distance as possible.   Great
dexterity was acquired by the players in guiding the
hoop to the desired goal ; an opponent sometimes caught
the hoop in its flight.   This game still survives.

CHAPTER XV

KITES, AIR-BALLS, SHUTTLECOCKS, FIREWORKS.

Kites, Air-Balls, Shuttle-cocks, Fire-works.

IT is in the Eastern hemisphere that we must look, not only for the origin of that delightful toy, the kite, but also for its most ingenious and varied development. There it is not only the plaything of childhood, but also, like so many of the other toys whose home is in the East, such as the top, it is the serious pursuit of grown men. We venture to assert that what horse-racing is to England, kite-flying is to the Chinese, the Indian, and the native of Japan ; it is in fact the national sport, and fortunes are lost and won on the chances of the game.

Various legends obscure the origin of the kite ; in Korea its invention is attributed to a general who fought in the war with Japan 400 years ago. His soldiers were discouraged by reverses, and attributed their misfortunes to the appearance of falling stars. Their leader made a kite, attached a small lantern to it, and declared the newly-risen star to be an auspicious omen. This story is, however, of much too recent date to account for the origin of the kite, for it was known in India and China long before the sixteenth century ; the general may have

known of them, and ingeniously made one to serve his **Origin of the Kite.**
purpose.

Another military hero is said to have bridged an impassable river by first passing a rope across by means of a kite, which was guided so that it became entangled and fixed firmly in a tree ; the rope was the means of a bridge being built over, on which the army crossed in safety.

Yet another legend of much more ancient origin, dating from 196 B.C., tells us that it was a Chinese general who used the first kite to measure the distance required for a tunnel, which was to reach the centre of the stronghold of a beleaguered city ; through it soldiers passed, surprised the besieged, and opened the gates to the besiegers.

We leave our readers to choose the myth which most directly appeals to them. In one point only do all the stories agree—on the profession of arms for the inventor, and his invention being for the purpose of circumventing the enemy.

The deeper significance of the kite as the " over soul " of the Egyptians and the scapegoat of the Koreans may have been attributed later. " On the 14th day of the first month," we are told in Stewart Culin's book on Korea, " it is customary to write on kites in Korean characters a wish to the effect that the year's misfortunes may be carried away with the kite. Mothers write this for their children, and add the date of birth. The letters are placed along the bamboo frames, so that they may not be seen by any one who might be tempted to pick up the kite when it eventually reaches the ground again."

Boys and girls who know only the kites of Western

**Kites,
Air-Balls,
Shuttle-
cocks,
Fire-
works.**

Europe would be astonished at the variety in shape,
colouring, and mode of flying, according to the use of
the kite, in some of the complicated aerial games.

There are rectangular kites made on bamboo frames
covered with stout paper, having a circular hole in the
centre ; a triangular piece of paper, called a " crow's foot,"
is pasted at each corner.

There are gaily - coloured kites in China which are
either made of bands of vari-coloured papers or have such
pasted upon the body of
the kite ; these are called
the " woman's robe kites."

KITE OR LIVE INSECT WITH STRING
ATTACHED.

From a mediæval MS.

The Korean kites
shown in the Museum of
Archæology of the Uni-
versity of Pennsylvania,
were obtained through the
courtesy of His Majesty's
Commissioner at the
Colombian Exhibition ;
they are uniform in size,
17 inches by 22 inches ;
they have a hole in the
centre 8 inches in diameter, and are variously coloured.
In Korea, boys and girls, men and women, from the king
downwards, fly kites during the first half of the first
month ; after this time any one who attempted to take
part in the sport would be laughed at. Why there
should be this " close time " for kites in Korea, we have
not been able to discover.

The names of some of the Japanese kites will give
an idea of their infinite variety of form. One variety is

340

Girls playing with the Highly Decorated Battledores used in Japan.
From a drawing by Hokusai.

THE PARACHUTE.

From an XVIIIth Century Engraving. Wm. Hamilton, R.A.

popularly known as *ako*, octopus, or *ika*, cuttle-fish. Varieties
Such kites have long tails made of lengths of white paper **of the**
about 12 inches long ; the frame is made of two strips of **Kite.**
bamboo placed at right angles.

A favourite emblem for the decoration of a kite is a
stork or a tortoise ; such devices are usually in white
paint on a richly-coloured ground.   Often the kite is in
the form of a bird ; a fan is also a popular shape.   A devil
kite is used for fighting, and a servant kite is to be found
in Japan.

The Chinese kites are somewhat different from those
of Japan ; they are even more varied in form.   Birds,
centipedes, crabs, and representations of men are much
favoured.   The size is estimated by the number of sheets
of paper used in its construction, such as a six-sheet kite.

A humming kite is one of the ordinary shape with a
large bow of bamboo, on which a cord of raw hide is
attached ; the air passing over makes a loud humming
sound ; the kite must be a large one or it will not bear
the extra strain.   Though children sometimes make their
own kites they are usually constructed by professionals.
The kite itself is cheap, but the string, which must be of
excellent quality, is very expensive.   In Korea it is
wound round specially constructed reels, which are made
on the principle of the old-fashioned silk-winder and
considerably facilitate the winding and unwinding
processes.   In China and Japan, however, a short length
of bamboo is used, on to which the string is wound simply
or in elaborate designs.

Kite-fighting is a regular sport, and specially prepared
strings and kites are necessary.   The line, which is
usually of closely woven silk, is dipped in fine glue or

**Kites,
Air-Balls,
Shuttle-
cocks,
Fire-
works.**

rice paste, which does not impede the flying by its weight nor render the string less flexible. On to this glue powdered glass or porcelain is sprinkled, so that its surface is like sand- or glass-paper. The art in flying a fighting-kite lies in the guiding, so that the line crosses that of another kite and cuts it. Directly the lines are crossed, skilful flyers let out line, as immediately it becomes taut the rubbing of the prepared line of the adversary cuts it.

When a fine fighting-kite is cut, hundreds of boys follow it till it drops, for there is said to be no proprietorship in an escaped kite. All the string attached to it, which is sometimes a valuable haul, is forfeit to the finder. Kite-string, whether of cotton or silk, is sold by weight. A game similar to kite-fighting is played by boys with short pieces of the specially prepared string. They attach a weight to a yard length of string and whirl the weight, so that it crosses and cuts that of an

Toy Windmill.

From a miniature painting on
an old manuscript.

adversary in the same way as the kite-strings cut each other in the air.

Another toy dependent on the wind for its working is the toy mill. These are frequently represented in old prints, and were made in every kind of material, from the cheap little paper-mill, sold in the streets for a penny, to the most costly models in precious metals, fit gifts for royal children.

In 1390 a toy windmill of gold, studded with pearls, was prepared for Isabel of Bavaria, and appears in the household accounts. Mills are sometimes made of empty

344

shells, which are fastened on to a wooden stick, and on **Paper**
being filled with air revolve, as do the lighter paper-mills. **Toys.**

Parasols in paper also form windmills. These mills are
sometimes elaborate,
having primitive-
looking structures
roofed with flags on
the top, the sails
being attached to
the side, as with the
windmills for prac-
tical purposes in the
country.

Other cheap toys
into which paper
enters largely as a
material, such as
Jack-in-the-boxes or
surprise box toys,
were known as early
as the sixteenth
century. This is
proved by their
having been men-
tioned by a writer

THE WINDMILL SELLER.
From an engraving by Poisson, 1774.

of that epoch. . . . Rousseau's allusion to the toy as a
means of removing the groundless fears of a child will be
remembered.

Air-balls or balloons were invented, runs the legend,
by a man of science, who, on the point of starvation
through the failure of his great ideas, suddenly bethought
him of placing some red colouring matter inside a

345

**Kites,
Air-Balls,
Shuttle-
cocks,
Fire-
works.**

bladder, and distending it with air. So successful was
the toy that he became sufficiently affluent to carry out
his other schemes. The idea has been very considerably
exploited, and the toy has become much more popular
since the introduction of india-rubber films, which allow
of much more lightness and uniformity. Miniature
Montgolfières, as will be seen from our print of the
eighteenth century, and parachutes, date back to the
time when Montgolfier made his celebrated ascent.

In Japan the battledore and shuttlecock is associated
entirely with the play of girls. According to *The
Japanese Book of Months*, it was customary to send, in
the month of December, a battledore and shuttlecock to
the house where a baby girl had arrived during the year ;
if the baby were of the male sex, a bow and arrow were
sent. The battledore has the same name, and is of the
same shape as the paddle used by women for washing
clothes. It is generally made of kiri wood, or, in very
cheap toys, of cedar. The inevitable decoration is much
in evidence on its flat surface, and one frequently sees
pictures of famous actors and actresses depicted on
battledores.

Occasionally the decoration is most elaborately executed
in relief, whole landscapes with elaborately dressed figures
being given. The padded dresses of damask and satin
are skilfully arranged on the flat surface, the hair of the
women is dressed, the weapons of the men glued, upon
the back of the battledore, until a beautiful little
picture in semi-relief is made. We have seen one belonging to Vicomte Tasada Hayashi, the Japanese
Ambassador in London, measuring 23 inches in length,
the handle being only $2\frac{1}{2}$ inches, the whole of the

346

Native shop in Japan for the sale of Battledores and Shuttlecocks.

LE GOUVERNANTE.

Painted by Chardin.   Published 1739.

rest of the surface being occupied by the battledore. So light was this beautiful implement that its superior size and lavish decoration did not limit its practicability.

Nor was the shuttlecock any less beautiful. The arrangement of the feathers, stuck into the berry which forms the head, was made to resemble a flower, and a dozen of the shuttlecocks, placed in a cleft of thin bamboo for safe carriage from their distant country looked like the flowering branch of one of the lovely Japanese fruit trees.

The Japanese shuttlecock is made of the seed of the soap berry, into which several small feathers are fastened— a curious connection again with the feminine industry of washing, though we do not know that the soap berry is ever used for washing purposes, though children blow bubbles with water in which the skin of the soap berry has been soaked.

In the collection of toys which amused the late Queen Victoria in her childhood, there are no fewer than four battledores of the ordinary parchment-covered, wooden-frame variety.

The Chinese and Korean shuttlecock is a much more substantial toy than those we have been describing. This is necessitated by the fact that in these countries the shuttlecock is kicked up in the air, instead of being struck with a bat; it is extraordinary with what skill the little Chinese boys kick the toy, keeping it up in the air for quite a long time, just as the Japanese children and we of the West keep it up by striking time after time with a battledore. The Chinese shuttlecock is made of several layers of snake skin, and is called " Chicken feather swallow." It is weighted as heavily as required

349

Kites,
Air-Balls,
Shuttle-
cocks,
Fire-
works.

with Chinese cash placed between the layers of skin; several large feathers are stuck in the head thus made. The whole measures about five and a half inches in height.

That this game was played as early, if not earlier than the fourteenth century in China, is proved by the fact that in the "Roll of the Hundred Children," a silk painted record of the games of children in the Ming dynasty, two boys are shown playing at kicking the shuttlecock, as vigorously as they may be now seen at Hongkong or Shanghai. They are chubby, round-headed little Chinese boys kicking their shuttlecocks, whilst two companions watch the fun; one can imagine that a merry contest is going on, and those waiting will presently prove their dexterity and beat the previous performance. Chinese children may be seen for hours playing the game and practising the strokes, for it is by no means easy to give a backward kick so as to lift the shuttlecock with the sole of the foot, and yet keep the balance. The bound feet of the girls and women would, one would have thought, preclude all possibility of playing the game, but that they do so to some small extent we read in Mrs. Little's *Intimate China*, in which she says :—"The ladies (native Chinese) announced they were coming. Their special delight was our battledore and shuttlecock. They had been accustomed to use the heels of their crippled feet for battledore, and were not easily tired of playing in our pleasanter fashion."

When the game of battledore and shuttlecock came westward we do not know; mercifully the Japanese, rather than the Chinese or Korean form of the game reached Europe, and we have the hand-bat or battledores of parchment strained over wooden frames, and the string bats. In an old print of the sixteenth century two boys are playing the game just as we do now ; close to them two others are in precisely the same attitudes, but their battledores are made of crossed and knotted strings, and they are in the act of striking a ball instead of the feather-weight shuttlecock. In another engraving of the same century a man and woman are playing with wooden or leather - covered battledores, and with the feather - tipped shuttlecock. In 1761 battledores and shuttlecocks are advertised for sale in Boston, and several

BATTLEDORE AND SHUTTLECOCK IN THE
FOURTEENTH CENTURY.

From a Harleian MS.

portraits of colonial children have been painted with these toys in their hands, that of Thomas Aston Coffin being one of them.

The swing, as a toy in which suspension in the air plays a part, may be mentioned here. It dates from remotest antiquity, and is always a favourite game with children. Possibly the first was made when a mother, wishing to place her babe out of harm's way, fastened the cradle to the branch of a tree. The pleasant rocking motion would soothe the child, so that the delight of the swing to an infant would be utilised still further. In Athens swings were much used by children. There are obscure allusions to a special fête of swings, but it is not known in what way it was celebrated. There was a

351

**Kites,
Air-Balls,
Shuttle-
cocks,
Fire-
works.**

chant sung by those who swung, and, as with so many of
the Greek games which we now associate exclusively
with children, people of mature age also indulged in the
pastime.

Swinging has more than once been represented on
vases. In one picture a girl has just pushed forward
her companion, who is seated in a chair-like swing

CHAIR SWING RESEMBLING A NURSERY SWING.
From a painting on a Greek vase.

suspended by ropes; a similar picture is to be seen on a
vase at the Louvre. In another representation a swing
of the kind which we now call a nursery swing is being
used by a child, the guarding bars being necessary on
account of his youth. Two men are also to be seen
swinging a child on a medal struck at Rome.

Though fireworks are not essentially the toys of
children, we must not omit to mention them as some of

352

THE SWING.
From an XVIIIth Century Engraving.

The Firework, painted on silk in 1400 by one of the Kano School of
Japanese Artists, who used only Chinese subjects.

the most popular playthings of boys of all ages, not only **Fifteenth-Century Fire-works for Children.** in Europe, but also in those Eastern countries where fire-work displays are of very much more frequent occurrence than in our own country, and also date from very much more remote times.

The earliest pictorial record of a firework used as the plaything of a child that we have been able to find, is that given in a finely painted kakemono, where, on the silk surface, an artist, of the Ming dynasty, has painted a charming group of children anticipating the much-dreaded but much-loved report of a squib which is about to go off. It is probable this scene was painted about 1400 A.D. A little fête or festival is being celebrated amongst the children ; women are watching their games through a screen ; at the right of the picture in the foreground some little ones are looking into a basket filled with good things ; game, fruit, and parcels of sweetmeats are piled up. It is in the firework group, however, that we are chiefly interested. The squib stands upright on the ground ; a chubby lad of about six years old holds a lighted taper at arm's length, and is lighting the twisted paper at the top, leaning away from it. Four other children are running away, holding their hands over their ears to shut out the expected bang, and one is trying to climb up a pillar in order to get a better view of the proceedings. This picture is of the Kano school of Japanese painters. who always chose Chinese subjects.

Fireworks undoubtedly reached Europe from the East ; they are mentioned in Chinese and Indian writings of the highest antiquity. There is a firework festival in China, In India there is a special caste of makers and assistants in the firework trade. The manufacturer of fireworks,

Kites,
Air-Balls,
Shuttle-
cocks,
Fire-
works.

called in India Gonri, is a most important trader ; hundreds of thousands of these ephemeral toys are let off every year, not only at special festival times and at the great entertainments given by the native princes, but also on birthdays and other minor family occasions, when humbler demonstrations of joy are desired. We in Europe who, on the rarest occasions, invest a few sovereigns in fireworks for the children's amusement, would be astonished to see the frequency of the pyro-technical displays in India, China, and Japan.

In making the Indian fireworks, a grindstone is used for powdering the various ingredients ; there is a ramrod of iron and a ramrod of wood, for, as we know, the greatest care must be exercised in ramming, lest a spark should be engendered. A wooden roller is used in making the cases for the Roman candles and such special forms. A flat heavy knife, a file, and wooden platter—such are the principal amongst the primitive implements used in the construction of the elaborate and complicated fire-works of India.

Hand Catherine-wheels are made as well as those to be fixed on a pole, bombs of many kinds containing coloured stars, fire-balloons, rockets, Roman candles, maroons, set pieces, such as miniature forts and bastions.

In the different provinces different names are given to the pieces, such as the pipes in which the explosive powder is placed, the case for the axle, the axle itself, the spokes, the rim of the wheels, and other important details in the building up of the firework.

Aquatic fireworks are also made, when those portions of the device which come in contact with the water have to be protected by grease or oil. Water-devils are much favoured in China, floating Chinese trees, gerbs, Roman candles for aquatic displays, water-mines, and fire-fountains are known and skilfully made by means of the simple hand-tools of the Orientals. **Fire-works on Buddha's Birthday.**

The special firework night in Japan is the eighth day of the fourth month, which is celebrated as Buddha's birthday: in Korea this same day is the occasion of cracker-firing and illuminations, possibly in connection of the Buddha festival, borrowed from Japan, associated with an earlier religious celebration connected with the Vernal Equinox. Toys are sold in abundance during the day; these generally take the form of images of birds and beasts, and towards the evening hundreds and thousands of lanterns specially made, " image lanterns " as they are called, are brought out. Each person has a lantern, which he tends during the night; it is believed that, if its flame burns clearly and steadily, the watcher will have a long and happy life. There are firework displays on a grand scale throughout the country, and each individual buys his quota of crackers or squibs which he lets off promiscuously.

It is likely that the native fire-brigades have rather a busy time during the night of this festival, which takes place in towns where the houses are largely built of straw and paper and furnished with straw matting and bamboo. Japanese firemen are most agile with their light ladders of bamboo, and sometimes give acrobatic performances, when the long fire-hooks are used for steadying the ladders and the firemen mount them, keeping them in an upright position by balance. We have not heard that there is much time for such performances on the night of Buddha's birthday.

357

**Kites,
Air-Balls,
Shuttle-
cocks,
Fire-
works.**

The celebration by the Hindus of the festival of Diwali, when the goddess Lakshmi, who presides over the good and evil luck of merchants, is fêted, is always an occasion for elaborate firework displays. Line after line of fire flashes into existence until every large building is outlined in colour, for illumination is much used. Then the firework display takes place, while the delighted crowd let off squibs, crackers, and other minor pieces. A strange effect is seen on such occasions amongst the hosts of pigeons, birds held sacred in Amritsar and many other cities ; they increase enormously in numbers ; it would be dangerous for any one to kill a pigeon near the Golden Temple of that town. The fireworks create a panic amongst the sacred birds, and they wheel round in the air while the noise and light continues, fluttering and alarmed.

Fireworks are not spoken of as a pastime in Europe before the sixteenth century. In England at the time of the gorgeous show and jousts during the reign of Elizabeth they are frequently mentioned ; previous to that time we read in Strutt that when " Ann Bullen was conveyed upon the water from Greenwich to London, previous to her coronation in 1533, there went before the Lord Mayor's barge a small galley or vessel full of ordnance, in which vessel was a great red dragon, continually moving and casting forth wild-fire, and round about the said vessel stood terrible, monstrous and wilde men, of fire making a hideous noise."

This vessel, with the fireworks, was usually exhibited when the Lord Mayor went upon the water at night, especially when he had been to Westminster on Lord Mayor's day.

When Queen Elizabeth went to Kenilworth Castle there were several displays of fireworks, mostly of the aquatic kind, which are less frequently used now. In Nichols's *Progresses of Elizabeth* they are thus described: —"On the Sunday night after a warning piece or two, was a blaze of burning darts flying to and fro, beams of stars coruscant, streams and hail of fire sparks, lightenings of wild-fire on the water; and on the land flight and shot of thunderbolts, all with such continuance, terror, and vehemence the heavens thundered, the waters surged, and the earth shook." Gasgoyne speaks of diving fireworks; we are not aware that such things are still made. "On the Sunday were fireworks showered upon the water, passing under the water a long space, and when all men thought they had been quenched, they would rise and mount out of the water again and burne furiously until they were utterlie consumed."

On the Thursday following, "there was at night a show of very strange and sundry kinds of fireworks compelled, by cunning, to fly to and fro, and to mount very high into the air upward, and also to burn unquenchable in the water beneath."

Sixteen years afterwards, when Elizabeth was entertained by the Earl of Hertford in Hampshire, after supper there was a grand display of fireworks, which show them to have been most elaborately made at this early period. The commencement of the display was indicated by the firing of small cannon; this custom seems to have long been continued.

We read: "There was a castle of fireworks of all sorts which played in the fort; answerable to that, there was at the Snail Mount, a globe of all manner of fireworks as

359

Kites,
Air-Balls,
Shuttle-
cocks,
Fire-
works.

big as a barrel. When these were spent there were many running rockets upon lines which passed between the Snail Mount and the castle in the fort. On either side were many fire wheels, pikes of pleasure and balles of wildfire which burned in the water."

The old prints of firework displays are extremely interesting; we are indebted to Mr. S. Holliday for facilities for examining some rare early specimens in his possession; those engraved by Hollar are probably unique.

In the time of James I. there were "abiding in the city of London men very skilful in the art of pyro-technic or of fireworks"; these appear to have consisted chiefly of squibs, crackers, wheels, fire-trees borrowed from the Chinese, and rockets.

At this time a display did not take place as a firework show only. Now, the lighters are concealed as much as possible, and the figures are of fire only, without the assistance of any visible human forms. In the early days men fantastically dressed formed quite an important part of the show; these fought each other with poles or clubs charged with squibs or crackers, or they stormed castles full of fireworks, while pasteboard dragons, running upon lines, vomited fire, "like verie furies."

In the *Seven Champions of Christendom*, printed in 1638, are the lines:—"Have you any squibs, any green men, in your shows, and whizzes on lines, Jack pudding upon the rope or resin fireworks?"

In a charming line engraving of the eighteenth century five children are playing at soldiers: one urchin is holding a cracker which he is just lighting with a smouldering piece of resinous rope; the captain of the band is all unconscious of the close proximity of this realistic toy war-engine.

In the reign of George II. a firework display was ruined by the timbers belonging to one of the set pieces taking fire, through the explosion of one of the gunpowder

GREENMAN FLOURISHING HIS FIRE-CLUB.
From Bate's treatise on fireworks issued in 1634.

trains, which communicated from one part to another through wooden channels.

From the earliest years of the nineteenth century it was customary for one of the Artillery regiments to give a grand display of fireworks on Tower Hill on the evening of the King's birthday. This was eventually discontinued by the desire of the inhabitants in the neighbourhood.

**Kites,
Air-Balls,
Shuttle-
cocks,
Fire-
works.**

At Marylebone Gardens fireworks were used with acting, special pieces being arranged : one of these was " The Forge of Vulcan," another the " Descent of Orpheus to Hell in search of his wife Eurydice." A French actor named Farre was employed ; he it was who arranged the performances, when wheels, fixed stars, figure pieces, "and other curious devices" were introduced into the pantomimical spectacles. Fireworks were used at Ranelagh Gardens, at Vauxhall and Bermondsey Spa in the eighteenth century.

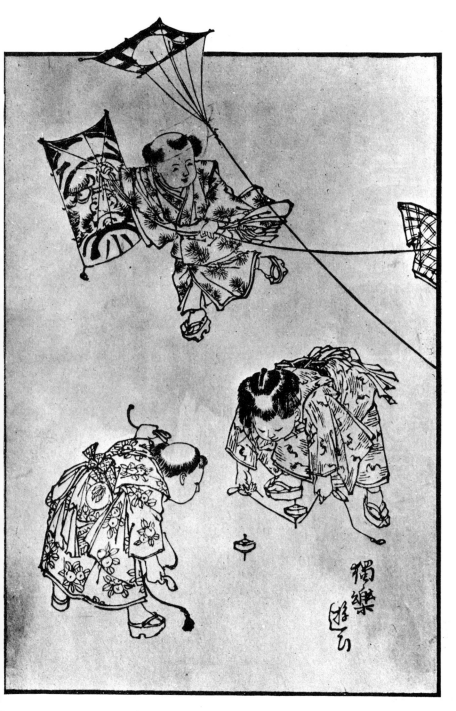

Top Spinning and Kite Flying in Japan.   From a drawing by Hokusai.

Egyptian Bread Kneader, with movable arms.   7 in. long.

Egyptian Toy Animal, with movable jaws manipulated by a string.   8 in. long.

CHAPTER XVI

AUTOMATIC AND MECHANICAL TOYS.

Mechani-
cal
Figures
of the
Middle
Ages.

MECHANICAL toys are no new thing. In ancient Greece, where moving statuary astonished or amused both rich and poor, there was scarcely an Athenian house which did not possess its mechanical toy. A contemporary of Hadrian gives an account of a wooden dove which flew: explanations are given as to the movement being caused by filling the body with air, which, gradually escaping, the bird could by no means be made to fly again until refilled, nor could it fly longer than a certain time.

Such simple motive power used in making toys was also applied to the figures of madonnas and saints by the Church all over Europe in the Middle Ages; but while the Church employed mechanical devices in the conducting of her services where the figures of saints were exposed, she was extremely severe with makers of scientific toys so cleverly constructed as to be incomprehensible, except when explained by the employment of magic. In 1086, when the Abbé Hugnes went to the Abbey of Clugny, the benediction was refused to one of the candidates for the noviciate, on account of his being a

Automatic and Mechanical Toys. mechanician or micromancer : this accusation was constantly being brought forward against the clever students of mathematics and physics of that day.

The speaking heads of brass or wood, which figure in the writings of the Middle Ages, were dangerous toys for the makers. One made by Albert-le-Grand possessed limbs which were articulated as well as the body ; each limb had, it was said, been under the influence of certain constellations : this figure was eventually smashed to pieces by that shining light in the Church, Thomas Aquinas, who, fearing and detesting it, made an end of it and proved its fallibility at the same time.

The construction of the marionettes whose movements depended on simple strings, which could be examined and handled, was, on the whole, a safer trade than the making of abstruse mechanical contrivances, which not infrequently landed their designers in serious difficulties. Sometimes the two systems of hidden mechanical appliances and outside wires and strings were combined, especially in the construction of monstrosities, which were used in processions on the feast-days of certain brave chevaliers or saints, those especially who were famous as having delivered their countries from the power of monsters. At Amiens, Metz, Orleans, Poictiers, and Constance, such creatures were paraded in solemn procession up to almost the end of the eighteenth century ; they were called papoires. An effigy of the Grand Dragon of Paris, killed by St. Marcel, was paraded round the cloisters of Notre Dame, while the children shrieked and offered it cakes and fruit, the movable jaws working in an alarming manner.

In Venice, in the sixteenth century, an enormous

female figure, working with hidden mechanical contrivances, was paraded during eight days to celebrate the abduction and eventual restoration, many centuries before, of twelve virgins who were attacked by pirates of Trieste ; this festival, which was called the festa of the Marias, suggested the name marionettes for the moving figures.

Monsters were frequently used in the miracle plays of the Middle Ages, and later in the survivals at Chester, Coventry, and other places, when gigantic figures of Samson, Goliath, Saint Christopher, the dragon of Saint George, the whale which swallowed Jonah, and other natural and unnatural objects were represented by basket-work or pasteboard frames in the shape required, within which a man or boy was placed to make the movements, with the help of simple machinery ; the jaws snapped, wings or limbs moved, or eyes were rolled by ingenious concealed devices. Long after the suppression of miracle plays such things were used in civic processions, May-day celebrations, Royal pageants, and in the organised games at Christmas, which have long ceased to exist.

When Queen Elizabeth stayed at Kenilworth in 1575, "there were by the castle gate six gigantic figures with trumpets, real trumpeters being stationed behind them," says a small pamphlet called *Princely Pleasures at Kenilworth Castle* ; again, later, there was a hunting in the afternoon, and on the Queen's return she was entertained with another show upon the water, in which appeared a person, in the character of Arion, riding upon a dolphin 24 feet in length ; he sang an admirable song, accompanied with music performed by six musicians concealed inside the fish.

Such pageants and spectacles were continued until the

time of the Commonwealth, when most of the giants and monstrosities, which had so often scared and delighted the children and amused their elders, were destroyed. At the Restoration of Charles II. some attempt was made to restore them in popular favour, but the palmy days of pageants and processions in England were over ; no longer did the lions roar, the dolphins discourse sweet music, nor the dragons snap their jaws. The sole relic which remains to us now of such gorgeousness is our Civic Show of the Lord Mayor, which, shorn of its old-time pageantry and splendour, its castles, elephants, and cupids, still passes annually through the streets of the capital.

In the sixteenth century Bernardino Baldi, a mathematician, made great strides in the perfecting of mechanical appliances in human figures. Automata, worked on hydraulic principles, were produced in a most ingenious manner ; these were much used in the aquatic dramas which are mentioned by Montayne in describing his journeyings in Italy. Some of these figures made music or gestures, sometimes both, by means of a current of water passing through them.

Baldi speaks with great admiration of the simpler marionettes worked by means of strings, such as are described in our chapter on marionettes. Another extraordinary mechanical toy of which he speaks is the eagle, which was constructed under the direction of the great mechanic Torriani, surnamed Gianello, for the Spanish King Charles Quint, who was so devoted to mechanical toys of every description that many of the most subtle of the German mathematicians, and the most ingenious of the Italians, were attracted to his court. This eagle, which Baldi speaks of as a notable and undoubted fact, and one

Mechanical toy of Queen Victoria. A Doll moves
along a grooved roadway between the pagodas.

Mechanical toy. From the Germanische Museum, Nuremburg.

Chinese mechanical toy.
The jaws open and the
chop-sticks move towards
the mouth.

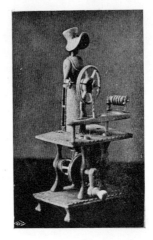

Carved Ivory toy, wound
with strings concealed in the
body. 6 in.

Tight-rope dancer. Wor
by 'counter balance. Ea
XIXth Century.

of great credit to the mechanical genius of its maker, was said to have flown a considerable distance when sent up at Nuremberg (is it here that we have the first flying machine ?) ; other writers treat the whole matter with contempt as a fable.   Torriani also made an extraordinary clock, and, during the retirement of Charles Quint in the monastery of Saint Just, was with him continually for two years, devising the mechanical toys which relieved the monotony of the King's existence.   Little figures of horses and armed men were made to play upon the King's table : they advanced against each other, and fought with lances ; other figures beat drums or blew trumpets.   In the picture of the lonely King, whose only pleasure and delight was in such toys at the great monastic retreat, there is a note of pathos.

Another quaint device of Torriani, was the sending up, in the King's chamber, of a number of little birds, which flew about (more flying machines).   " With such marvellous artifice were they made," continues the narrative with much naïveté, " that the Superior of the Convent happening one day to be present when the flight of the birds took place was alarmed lest magic should have been employed."

Besides these childish and interesting toys, the King and his clever mechanic discussed schemes of greater utility, one being for the raising of a supply of river-water to the heights of Tolido : this was carried out with success by Torriani after the death of the King.   It was owing to the Italian mathematician that the play of the Spanish marionettes, which had hitherto been only the sport of Kings and their children, were made so popular that the people could enjoy also the fun and pleasantries of the " little wooden men."

371

At the time of Louis XIII. of France, sand toys were made. In the *Memoires of Heroard* one is mentioned amongst the toys of the child Louis XIII.; it is described as "an instrument made at Nuremberg" in the form of a cupboard, where a number of persons made movements by means of sand instead of water.

Another such toy was a little ship, on which the men who formed the crew were made to use the action of rowers by means of shifting sand.

The splendid automatic toys of the time of Louis XIV. are worthy of the amusements of a grand monarch Imagine the King seated at a large table, where a diminutive coach with eight horses in miniature, magnificently harnessed, every detail complete to a buckle, is wheeling rapidly round; opposite to the King the coach stops, a lacquey descends from his place behind, opens the carriage door, lets down a step; a court lady, sumptuously attired, descends from the interior, curtseys to the King, presents a petition, takes her place again in the carriage, the door is closed, the lacquey springs to his place, and the little marvel of ingenuity drives away round the table, to be rewound, that the King may once more enjoy the clever effect of the clockwork.

A certain Père Trucket constructed another toy for the same King, which consisted of a theatre; a piece of five acts was given, the scenes changed, and the curtain raised and drawn down simply by a single touch upon a knob in the side of the little proscenium. The movements of the actors and actresses were considered most lifelike.

The speaking heads, of which frequent mention is made since the time of Albert le Grand, were most elaborate mechanical toys. One was made for the amusement of Catherine of Sweden by one Valentine Merbiz; it was claimed by its inventor to answer questions in Hebrew, Greek, Latin, and French.

Speaking heads were made by the Abbé Mical in the latter half of the eighteenth century, and presented by him to the Academy of Siena: these heads spoke certain words to each other, question and answer, concerning the King, wars and his glory being given successively; but the conversation was, to say the least, extremely limited.

The speaking head of Wolfang de Kempeleu, a Hungarian, also belongs to this epoch, and the rage for speaking heads came to a climax in 1783, when an announcement was made of the arrival in Paris of a more clever and extraordinary toy than all the others; questions were answered by it, the head apparently hanging in mid-air; long dissertations were given by it. A ventriloquist had ingeniously utilised the craze for speaking heads for his own purpose.

Jacques Vaucanson, who was born at Grenoble, in 1709, was engaged during the whole of his long life (he lived till 1782) in making mechanical toys: these, had he lived at an earlier date, would have cost him his life, through the belief that magic was the agency employed in achieving anything not clearly understood by the general public. It is said that, when a small boy, Vaucanson examined a clock without touching it or taking it to pieces; and such was his genius for nice construction that he made a similar one of wood, for he had no metal nor tools for working metal, and "the clock kept fairly good time." Besides automatic angels who flapped their wings, and such figures constructed for the churches, he made a wonderful toy flute-player, which made music ; a tambourine-player, which was hardly less celebrated ; and a chess-player, which was the marvel of the age.

Animals also were made by him ; a duck paddled along in the water seeking grain and swallowing it in such a fashion that it underwent a chemical change in the animal's body resembling digestion. We quote from Larousse's *French Encyclopædia* ; this was in 1741. The duck on being placed in the water swam about, plumed its feathers, eat crumbs of food, which were swallowed, the muscles of the neck showing their course into the body of the machine. Vaucanson also invented a machine for assisting the silk-weavers of Lyons in their work : this brought him much unpopularity from the weavers who, like the stocking-weavers and loom-workers of Lancashire at a later date, thought that machines would ruin the handworkers. According to the biography of this cleverest of all automatic toy-makers, Vaucanson died in 1782, bequeathing his collections to the Queen Marie Antoinette, who, not appreciating the legacy, contemplated presenting it to the Academy of Science ; unfortunately the precious collection was eventually dispersed.

François Camus was a mechanical genius of rather earlier date, having been born at the end of the seventeenth century. He also constructed many ingenious automatic toys, and wrote *Traité des forces mouvantes*, a rare and curious book published in 1722.

Elaborate toys, worked by counterbalance, were also made in the reign of Louis XVI. An acrobat, performing on a horizontal bar, went through his antics on the touch of a finger on certain knobs; the richness and beauty of **The Appearance of Cheap Mechanical Toys.** the decoration of this toy sufficiently indicates its date.

Another method of working a toy was by means of a stream of mercury, which, passing through a cavity, displaced the centre of gravity sufficiently to make a figure run up and down stairs. The same principle, worked with a stream of sand, was used in making many mechanical toys at the end of the eighteenth century, notably by the brothers Droz.

Mechanical toys have always appealed strongly to semi-barbarous people, especially those of Eastern origin. In the treasure-vaults of the Sultan, figures of gold, silver, and precious stones lie in abundance; mechanical contrivances and jewel-studded knick-knacks made to " work " have been sent to Constantinople from Paris, Nuremberg, and Birmingham at the cost of many thousands of pounds, and now moulder in useless profusion. In the harems of Egypt, of Arabia, and in the secluded houses of the rich women of India, costly mechanical toys serve to enliven the monotony of the lives of the inmates; dolls dance in spangled skirts, acrobats climb and juggle, and toy birds sing in gilded cages, to provoke the laughter of these children of a larger growth.

It was Cruchet, a sailor who fought at Trafalgar, who was the first to make cheap and simple mechanical toys, the forerunners of the gentlemen of tin who doff their hats, or the little carts whose wheels set in motion the arms and legs of the driver. M. Cruchet simplified the musical toys of Vaucanson, and rendered it possible for those of moderate means to possess less intricate automata. A trade-book of the first Empire period exists, in which numbers of such cheap mechanical toys are shown.

Automatic and Mechanical Toys. We obtain a curious glimpse into the intimate life and extravagance in the personal expenditure of Josephine, through the mechanical toys of the Napoleonic times. In Masson's *Joséphine Impératrice et Reine* the Salon des Marchands is described, that veritable bazaar, in the Eastern sense of the word, where was piled up, for Josephine's daily inspection, a selection of all the costliest and most beautiful merchandise in Paris. Here the great jewellers, mercers, milliners, musical-instrument makers, painters, sculptors, booksellers, picture-dealers, cabinetmakers, and traders in fine porcelain, who hoped for big orders, left their goods. It was in the expensive toys that the Empress chiefly delighted ; a mechanical masterpiece was brought by the maker or inventor who, winding it up, set it going, and left it for the Empress's approval. Probably the costly toy so delighted Josephine that she showed it to all her visitors, and had it taken to her private apartments ; then, when a child visitor admired it, perhaps one of the nieces, perhaps a child of one of the great officers of the State, Josephine gave it away. Sometimes petitioners for grants, pensions, or alms brought their children with them to claim the pity of Josephine ; then, as likely as not, they would be sent away with a dressed-up monkey playing a fiddle, a tree full of mechanical singing-birds, or an artificial orange-tree—a poor substitute for a grant or a pension.

On account of their extreme fragility there are few specimens of early mechanical toys. Occasionally costly jewelled ones are to be found in museums. The silver ships described in our chapter on silver toys are sometimes supplied with elaborate clockwork contrivances ; such, however, are rather the toys of adults than of children.

At Munich there is a coach with six horses; at Nuremberg, a canal-boat towed along by horses—the driver smokes a huge German pipe, two other figures manage the steering gear. These are really children's toys. An elaborate six-horse coach with attendant servants is also at Nuremberg; the horses' heads are ornamented with feathers, the servants wear the three-cornered hat of the period; one of them precedes the coach on foot, ringing a large bell; in this specimen the wheels of the coach are movable, the horses' feet do not touch the ground.

We know of an interesting little carved ivory toy of late eighteenth-century workmanship; it stands about 6 inches in height; the figure of a woman is seated at a spinning-wheel; the wheels and feet can be set in motion by a device in connection with strings, which are hidden in the body of the toy; the head also moves from side to side.

There are several mechanical toys amongst those preserved in Kensington Palace in the room which was once the nursery of Queen Victoria; one of these is a hand-loom about 22 inches in length, on which jute is being woven into a coarse cloth, the other is a miniature tree-planted roadway, on which a $2\frac{1}{2}$-inch figure of a little wooden doll moves along grooved lines; two of these run parallel; a small pagoda-shaped building at either end partly conceals the action of the puppet as it turns into the path parallel with the one just traversed.

Another mechanical toy which was a great favourite with the Queen, consisted of a miniature stage about 8 inches long and 3 wide; on this, three figures, brilliantly dressed in silks and satins, dance and pirouette in a

Automatic and Mechanical Toys. most animated and laughable manner to the strains of a little musical-box concealed beneath the stage ; the whole is enclosed in a neat little rosewood box in the shape of an upright piano, and there is a leather strap for suspension round the neck of the little royal owner when "playing at being showman."

The Germans, as makers of automatic toys, have always excelled in their work. The mechanical toys of Nuremberg were world-famous when, in the seventeenth and eighteenth centuries, all moving toys were wonderfully intricate. Paris is now the centre of the industry.

Music frequently accompanied the movements of an automatic toy. Molière presented before the King a manikin figure, who played any airs demanded of him when set to a spinet. At the end of the performance the figure was opened, when a living musician of minute stature was found to be concealed within. The taste for automatic musicians still continues, and we have to-day a toy Paderewski, who moves his hands and tow-coloured head while a musical-box tinkles beneath him. Cats and dogs beat drums as they are wheeled along ; rabbits clash cymbals. Musical-boxes are now produced which give the latest operatic airs, with full orchestral accompaniment.

In the cheaper mechanical toys, strings or elastic tightly twisted cause the movement to be made as they unwind, and the tension is relaxed. Sometimes a handle has to be turned, cessation from the turning causing the toy to relapse into immobility. Counterpoise, which was the principle of movement in the old mercury and sand toys, is still used in the construction of mechanical toys. It is this force which causes the active miller of to-day to run up a ladder, detach a sack, and descend with it on his

378

head. Some toys are worked on hydraulic principles; these are always favourites, for children dearly love the mess which invariably accompanies a water-toy, whatever precautions may be taken.

Clockwork toys are undoubtedly the most complicated of all playthings; they give surprise and pleasure to their little owners, but they do not inspire love and devotion as do the dolls of our girls, nor do they stimulate activity or originality like the tops, kites, cricket bats, and penknives of our boys. "I don't like toys that play with me, I like to play with them," is the feeling in the child's mind, says Mr. Cooper, with perfect appreciation of the matter, in his *Twentieth Century Child*.

Steam and electrical toys such as locomotives, miniature gas-engines, and batteries we do not describe, as they came after the first quarter of the nineteenth century, where our tale ends.